MASTERING THE
Georgia 7th Grade CRCT
in
Reading

Zuzana Urbanek
Margaret Dupree
Sara Hinton
Kristie White

Project Director: Dr. Frank J. Pintozzi

American Book Company
PO Box 2638
Woodstock, GA 30188-1383
Toll Free: 1 (888) 264-5877   Phone: (770) 928-2834
Fax: (770) 928-7483   Toll Free Fax: 1 (866) 827-3240
www.americanbookcompany.com

ACKNOWLEDGEMENTS

The authors would like to gratefully acknowledge the editing and technical contributions of Marsha Torrens.

We also appreciate the formatting assistance of Yvonne Benson as well as the writing assistance of Bethany White and Kim Hill.

This product/publication includes images from CorelDRAW 9 and 11 which are protected by the copyright laws of the United States, Canada, and elsewhere. Used under license.

Chapter 4

Georgia 7th Grade CRCT in Reading
Preface

Mastering the Georgia 7th Grade CRCT in Reading will help students who are learning or reviewing standards for the **Georgia 7th Grade CRCT in Reading**. The materials in this book are based on the GPS-based CRCT standards as published by the Georgia Department of Education.

This book contains several sections:

    1) General information about the book itself

    2) A diagnostic test

    3) An evaluation chart

    4) Ten chapters that teach the concepts and skills needed for test readiness

    5) Two practice tests

Standards are posted at the beginning of each chapter, in the diagnostic and practice tests, as well as in a chart included in the answer manual.

We welcome comments and suggestions about this book. Please contact us at

American Book Company
PO Box 2638
Woodstock, GA 30188-1383

Call Toll Free: (888) 264-5877
Phone: (770) 928-2834
Toll Free Fax: 1 (866) 827-3240
Visit us online at
www.americanbookcompany.com

Preface

About the Authors:

Margaret DuPree has a B.A. in English from the University of Georgia and is completing her M.A. She has tutored college students in literature and composition as well as children with learning disabilities to improve their reading and comprehension skills.

Sara Hinton has a B.A. from Columbia University and an M.A. in The Teaching of English from Teachers College, Columbia University. She taught middle school language arts and college courses in writing, grammar, and literature for several years.

Kristie White is a language arts teacher in the Georgia Public School System. Since 2000, she has taught a variety of language arts and English courses ranging from the middle grades through the college level. Her Ed.S. degree is from Mercer University.

About the Project Coordinator:

Zuzana Urbanek serves as ELA Curriculum Coordinator for American Book Company. She is a professional writer with 25 years of experience in education, business, and publishing. She has taught a variety of English courses since 1990 at the college level and also taught English as a foreign language abroad. Her master's degree is from Arizona State University.

About the Project Director:

Dr. Frank J. Pintozzi is a former Professor of Education at Kennesaw (GA) State University. For over 28 years, he has taught English and reading at the high school and college levels as well as in teacher preparation courses in language arts and social studies. In addition to writing and editing state standard-specific texts for high school exit and end of course exams, he has edited and written numerous college textbooks.

Georgia 7th Grade CRCT Reading Diagnostic Test

The purpose of this diagnostic test is to measure your knowledge in reading comprehension. This diagnostic test is based on the GPS-based CRCT standards for Reading and adheres to the sample question format provided by the Georgia Department of Education.

General Directions:

1. Read all directions carefully.

2. Read each question or sample. Then choose the best answer.

3. Choose only one answer for each question. If you change an answer, be sure to erase your original answer completely.

4. After taking the test, you or your instructor should score it using the evaluation chart following the test. This will enable you to determine your strengths and weaknesses. Then, study chapters in this book corresponding to topics that you need to review.

1

Let Love Go On

Carl Sandburg

Let it go on; let the love of this hour be poured out till the answers are made, the last dollar spent and the last blood gone.

Time runs with an ax and a hammer, time slides down the hallways with a pass-key and a master-key, and time gets by, time wins.

5   Let the love of this hour go on; let all the oaths and children and people of this love be clean as a washed stone under a waterfall in the sun.

Time is a young man with ballplayer legs, time runs a winning race against life and the clocks, time tickles with rust and spots.

Let love go on; the heartbeats are measured out with a measuring glass, so
10 many apiece to gamble with, to use and spend and <u>reckon</u>; let love go on.

1. The author uses personification in   R1-G
which of the following lines from the
poem?

   A.   "let all the oaths and children and
people of this love be clean as a
washed stone under a waterfall in the
sun"

   B.   "let the love of this hour be poured
out till the answers are made"

   C.   "Time runs with an ax and a hammer, time slides down the hallways
with a pass-key and a master-key"

   D.   "the heartbeats are measured out
with a measuring glass"

2. Which of the following is MOST   R1-D
likely a theme of this poem?

   A.   Time is like a baseball player.

   B.   We cannot stop time from passing.

   C.   Heartbeats are in short supply.

   D.   People are easily discouraged.

3. What is the meaning of the word   R2-D
<u>reckon</u> in line 10 of the poem?

   A.   heartbeat   C.   count

   B.   wreck   D.   ignore

4. The author repeats the phrase "let   R1-D
love go on" throughout the poem to
emphasize that

   A.   love causes too many problems.

   B.   love may change but it always
exists.

   C.   time does not always move faster
than love.

   D.   love is easily replaced by something
else.

5. The line, "time is a young man with   R1-G
ballplayer legs" is an example of
which
literary device?

   A.   alliteration   C.   hyperbole

   B.   simile   D.   metaphor

Read the following lines from the poem.

> …time runs a winning race
>
> against life and the clocks, time tickles with rust and spots.

6. Which of the following literary devices is used? R1-G

   A.   onomatopoeia

   B.   internal rhyme

   C.   alliteration

   D.   consonance

7. What is the tone of this poem? R1-H

   A.   confused

   B.   angry

   C.   melancholy

   D.   humorous

1   Do elephants cry? Can whales fall in love? Recent evidence suggests that, like humans, animals may experience a variety of emotions ranging from fear and aggression to love, sadness, and joy. In fact, animals and humans also share a similar brain anatomy and chemistry.

2   For many years, scientists believed animals displayed only instincts, such as the impulse to flee from predators or the urge to attack intruders. Scientists called these instincts primary emotions because they required no conscious thought. Most scientists believed animals were incapable of experiencing higher emotions such as happiness, sadness, or jealousy. One notable exception was the scientist, Charles Darwin. He insisted that humans and animals share common emotional links. At that time, few scientists accepted his idea.

3   The basis of early data on animal behavior was experiments using caged animals. Today, scientists frequently watch animals in their natural settings. They conduct field studies which involve careful observations over long periods of time. Researchers take detailed notes on what they see and hear. They photograph and videotape a wide variety of animal behaviors. Then, the scientists complete the scientific process by <u>drawing</u> conclusions based on their observations.

4   As a result of field studies, researchers now know animals display an array of emotions. Elephants do show classic instinctual emotions. They will charge when they sense danger. They will use their massive size and sharp tusks to protect themselves. But, do elephants cry? It appears so. Or at least they mourn, especially when an old elephant dies. The herd stands quietly beside their loved one for days. They form a circle around the remains and touch it with their trunks. They will even form a funeral procession. The herd will carry the bones and tusks of their dead comrade for many miles over many days.

5   A great deal of field research takes place on boats. Whales are the most interesting sea creatures to observe. Based on a recent sighting in the South Atlantic Ocean, scientists believe some whales might be capable of falling in love. The <u>scientists aren't trying to beat around the bush</u>; they want to do more research before making a more definite statement. A researcher observed two whales embracing and rubbing each other with their flippers after they had mated. When they finally swam away, they continued to touch each other.

6   Even dying of a broken heart is possible in the animal world. Primatologist Jane Goodall tells the story of a 50-year-old female chimpanzee who died of old age. Holding her hand and nudging her occasionally, her eight-year-old son refused to leave her lifeless body. Whimpering and moaning, he gradually stopped eating and withdrew from the troop. After mourning more than three weeks, he also died. Gooodall concludes that he died of grief.

7   Animals show joy and pleasure in their daily lives too. A happy dog wags its tail and jumps for joy at the sight of its master. Cats purr when they're content. After a long absence from each other, even elephants greet their friends by flapping their ears, spinning in circles, and rumbling and roaring in trumpet-like sounds.

8   New research on the brain provides more evidence that humans and animals share similar emotions. Neuroscientists discovered humans and animals share a common brain part called the amygdala. Stimulating this part of the brain creates intense fear. Rats and humans lose their sense of fear after damaging their amygdala. This fact suggests similar wiring in humans and rats

9   Modern medical research and animal field studies have shown Charles Darwin may have been right all along. Animals, like humans, may be capable of both instinctual and higher levels of emotion.

8. As it is used in paragraph 3, the word <u>drawing</u> means   RC3-A

    A.   lottery.

B. sketching.

C. process of deciding something.

D. pulling or sucking something in.

9. What are primary emotions?   RC4-C
                                RC3-A

   A. instincts and impulses

   B. higher level emotions

   C. monkey-like behavior

   D. family based emotions

10. Which of the following is a feature   RC2-F
    which makes this a nonfiction
    passage?

   A. The passage has a clear plot and
       setting.

   B. The passage has interesting
       characters.

   C. The passage has multiple themes.

   D. The passage is based on facts.

11. The phrase "scientists aren't trying   R2-C
    to beat around the bush" in para-
    graph 5 means

   A. scientists are playing hide-and-go-
       seek.

   B. the scientists are not evading the
       issue.

   C. scientists enjoy looking at whales.

   D. whale behavior is hard to under-
       stand.

12. Based on the passage, readers can   RC2-A
    conclude

A. observing animals is an important
    part of the study of animal behavior
    and emotions.

B. scientists feel all animals have the
    same brain.

C. elephants have stronger emotions
    than other animals.

D. research is based on guessing to
    form ideas about animal behavior
    and emotions.

13. What is the author's main reason   RC2-E
    for writing "Animal Emotions"?

   A. To persuade readers to get involved
       in research on animal behavior.

   B. To entertain readers with stories
       about animals.

   C. To inform readers about ongoing
       research into animal emotions.

   D. To describe to readers how chimpan-
       zees and elephants behave when a
       family member dies.

14. This passage MOSTLY uses which   R1-C
    type of organizational structure?

   A. persuasive

   B. comparison and contrast

   C. cause and effect

   D. chronological

15. Which of the following is the topic   R1-A
    sentence of the passage?

A. "Do elephants cry?"

B. "Recent evidence suggests that, like humans, animals may experience a variety of emotions ranging from fear and aggression to love, sadness, and joy."

C. "The basis of early data on animal behavior was experiments using caged animals."

D. "Researchers take detailed notes on what they see and hear."

16. Which sentence supports the author's claim that elephants feel sadness?   R1-E

A. "They will charge when they sense danger."

B. "Elephants do show classic instinctual emotions."

C. "They will use their massive size and sharp tusks to protect themselves."

D. "They form a circle around the remains and touch it with their trunks."

17. Based on the context clues in paragraph 8, who are *neuroscientists* and what do they study?   RC3-C

A. Neuroscientists are doctors who study the brain.

B. Neuroscientists are scientists who study rats.

C. Neuroscientists are doctors who study whales.

D. Neuroscientists are scientists who study emotions in elephants.

Read the following two passages and then answer the questions that follow

The First Moccasins

A Native American Story

There was once a great Chief of the Plains who had very tender feet. Other mighty chiefs laughed at him; little chiefs only smiled as he hobbled past; and though they did not dare to smile, the people of the tribe also enjoyed the big chief's discomfort. All of them were in the same canoe, having no horses and only bare feet, but luckily very few of them had tender feet. The unhappy medicine man who was advisor to the Chief-of-the-Tender-Feet was afraid and troubled. Each time he was called before the chief he was asked, "What are you going to do about it?" The "it" meant the chief's tender feet.

Forced by fear, the medicine man at last hit upon a plan. Though he knew that it was not the real answer to the chief's foot problem, nevertheless it was a good makeshift. The medicine man had some women of the tribe weave a long, narrow mat of reeds, and when the big chief had to go anywhere, four braves unrolled the mat in front of him so that he walked in comfort. One day, the braves were worn out from seeing that the chief's feet were not worn out. They carelessly unrolled the mat over a place where flint arrowheads had been chipped. The arrowheads had long ago taken flight, but the needle-sharp chips remained. When the big chief's tender feet were wounded by these chips, he uttered a series of whoops which made the nearby aspen tree leaves quiver so hard that they have been trembling ever since.

That night the poor medicine man was given an impossible task by the angry chief: "Cover the whole earth with mats so thick that my feet will not suffer. If you fail, you will die when the moon is round."

The frightened maker of magic crept back to his lodge. He did not wish to be put to death on the night of the full moon, but he could think of no way to avoid it. Suddenly he saw the hide of an elk which he had killed pegged to the ground, with two women busily scraping the hair from the hide, and an idea flashed into his groping mind. He sent out many hunters; many women were busy for many days; many braves with hunting knives cut, and women sewed with bone needles and rawhide sinews.

On the day before the moon was round, the medicine man went to the chief and told him that he had covered as much of the earth as was possible in so short a time. When the chief looked from the door of his lodge, he saw many paths of skin stretching as far as he could see. Long strips which could be moved from place to place connected the main leather paths. Even the chief thought that this time the magic of the medicine man had solved tenderfoot transportation for all time—but this was not to be!

One day, as the big chief was walking along one of his smooth, tough leather paths, he saw a pretty maiden of the tribe gliding ahead of him, walking on the hard earth on one side of the chief's pathway. She glanced back when she heard the pitter patter of his feet on the elkhide pathway and seemed to smile. The chief set off on the run to catch up with her, his eyes fixed on the back of She-Who-Smiled, and so his feet strayed from the narrow path and landed in a bunch of needle-sharp thorns! The girl ran for her life when she heard the hideous howls of the chief, and Indians in the distant village thought that they were being attacked by wildcats.

Two suns later, when the chief was calm enough to speak again, he had his medicine man brought before him and told the unhappy man that next day, when the sun was high, he would be sent with all speed to the land of shadows.

That night, the medicine man climbed to the top of a high hill in search of advice from friendly spirits on how to cover the entire earth with leather. He slept, and in a dream vision he was shown the answer to his problem. Amid vivid flashes of lightning, he tore down the steep hillside, howling louder than the big chief at times, as jagged rocks wounded his bare feet and legs. He did not stop until he was safely inside his lodge. He worked all night and until the warriors who were to send him on the shadow trail came for him, just before noon the next day. He was surrounded by the warclub armed guards. He was clutching close to his heart something tightly rolled in a piece of deerskin. His cheerful smile surprised those who saw him pass. "Wah, he is brave!" said the men of the tribe. "He is very brave!" said the women of the tribe.

The big chief was waiting just outside his lodge. He gave the guards swift, stern orders. Before the maker of magic could be led away, he asked leave to say a few words to the chief. "Speak!" said the chief, sorry to lose a clever medicine man who was very good at most kinds of magic. Even the chief knew that covering the entire earth with leather was an impossible task.

The medicine man quickly knelt beside the chief, unrolled the two objects which he took from his bundle and slipped one of them on each foot of the chief. The chief seemed to be wearing a pair of bear's hairless feet, instead of bare feet, and he was puzzled at first as he looked at the elkhide handcraft of his medicine man. "Big chief," the medicine man exclaimed joyfully, "I have found the way to cover the earth with leather! For you, O chief, from now on the earth will always be covered with leather." And so it was.

The following passage is one version of the myth of Pandora's Box, from Greek mythology.

According to the Ancient Greeks, Pandora (meaning "all-gifted") was the first woman on Earth. She was created from water and earth by Hephaestus, the blacksmith of the gods. Hephaestus gave Pandora wonderful gifts and talents. These included beauty, musical ability, charm, and many others.

Pandora was also given a box by the gods. At all times, Pandora carried this box with her. The gods told her never to open it. Pandora was naturally curious, and one day she could not take it any longer. She opened the box, causing evil—such as greed, anger, and suffering—to escape and spread over the Earth. Pandora tried to shut the lid, but its contents had already escaped and could not be put back. However, one thing had not escaped: hope. It remained in the jar for a long time, because Pandora was afraid to go near the box again. One day, Pandora decided to open it, and hope fluttered out. This helped people comfort themselves whenever the evils of the Earth caused problems in their lives.

The Greeks used this story to explain why there was suffering and sadness in the world. At the same time, they used the story to explain how people use the spirit of hope to help them get through times of misfortune. In modern times, we say that someone is "opening a Pandora's box" if they are doing something potentially harmful and irreversible.

Questions 18 and 19 are related to both passages.

18. How are "The First Moccasins" and "Pandora's Box" similar? R1-I

    A. They both explain how shoes were made.

    B. They both explain how something came to exist.

    C. They both come from the same culture.

    D. They both explain why people experience misfortune.

19. Which of the following does NOT explain how these stories are different? R1-I

    A. One is about an actual object; the other is about things you can't see or touch.

    B. The main characters in the two stories are not of the same gender.

    C. The stories come from two very different cultures.

    D. Neither main character makes any mistakes.

The following questions are related ONLY to "The First Moccasins."

20. What is the main conflict in "The First Moccasins"? R1-A

    A. chief vs. self

    B. chief vs. tribe

    C. chief vs. nature

    D. medicine man vs. chief

Read the following quote from the story:

> *"Two suns later, when the chief was calm enough to speak again..."*

21. Based on context clues, what does two suns mean? R2-A

    A. two years

    B. two days

    C. two decades

    D. two months

22. What is the theme of this passage? R1-A

    A. Medicine men are clever and brave.

    B. Some people are weaker than others.

    C. Persistence and patience are the best problem solvers.

    D. Do not run from your problems or your feet will get hurt.

23. Based on the events in the passage, which of the following MOST likely happened to the medicine man? R1-E

    A. The chief hated the moccasins and killed the medicine man.

    B. The moccasins did not fit the chief, and he imprisoned the medicine man.

    C. The chief loved the moccasins and rewarded the medicine man.

    D. The chief liked the moccasins but punished the medicine man anyway.

24. When the medicine man faces death at noon, which plot component does it represent? R1-E

    A. the introduction

    B. the climax

    C. the resolution

    D. falling action

25. The author describes the chief as   R1-F

   A.   severe and impatient.

   B.   intelligent and wise.

   C.   compassionate and thoughtful.

   D.   foolish and naïve.

26. In the beginning of the story, why   R1-B
    were the people afraid to smile at the
    hobbling, tender-footed chief?

   A.   because they were angry at the chief

   B.   because they blamed the chief for
        their tender feet

   C.   because they did not want to anger
        the big chief

   D.   because the little chiefs would be
        angry with them

27. What caused the chief to stray from   R1-E
    the leather path and hurt his feet on
    the sharp thorns?

   A.   He wanted to go elk hunting.

   B.   He was trying to avoid the arrow-
        heads that were under the path.

   C.   He was trying to catch up with a
        pretty maiden.

   D.   He was angry at the medicine man
        and started to chase him.

Wildlife Trade

1   Elephants are killed for their tusks. Other wild animals are hunted for other parts of their bodies. Have you ever seen a rug made of zebra skin, or a piece of jewelry made of a lion's tooth? These are some of the thousands of wild animal body parts that are traded throughout the world every year.

2   Many international agencies try to have some control over the trade in wildlife. One of these agencies is the Convention on International Trade in Endangered Species (CITES). The CITES Animals Committee meets regularly. At each meeting, the committee receives reports about the trading of different wild animals. Following this passage is a chart from one of these reports. This chart was part of a report submitted to the CITES Animals Committee meeting that took place in South Africa in 2004.

3   The chart shows the trade activity in narwhals over a period of ten years. Narwhals are a species of whale that lives in the Arctic Ocean. Like elephants, narwhals also produce ivory. They each have a single tusk that can be as long as eight feet. Narwhals are also hunted and traded for their bones, teeth, skin, and meat.

4   The chart is followed by a comment, which is part of the report to the committee. The comment tells the committee whether or not the scientists who prepared the report are concerned about the featured animal. If they are concerned, then they recommend a closer review by the committee. If, however, they find that the trade is within legal limits or if the animal is not endangered, then they do not recommend a closer review.

Narwhal Whale

Look carefully at the chart about trade in narwhals, read the comment and then answer the questions that follow.

	Exporter	Term	1993	1994	1995	1996	1997	1998	1999	2000	2001	2002

Gross Exports of Monodon Monoceros (Narwhals)

	Exporter	Term	1993	1994	1995	1996	1997	1998	1999	2000	2001	2002
1	Canada	Bodies	0	0	0	0	10	0	0	0	3	0
2	Canada	Ivory Carvings	0	0	0	5	0	0	0	0	0	0
3	Canada	Ivory pieces	0	0	0	0	0	0	0	0	4	0
4	Canada	Live	0	0	0	0	0	0	0	0	6	0
5	Canada	Meat (kg)	0	0	0	0	0	0	0	0	30	0
6	Canada	Skull	0	0	0	0	3	1	5	0	0	0
7	Canada	Teeth	4	0	0	0	0	0	4	0	4	0
8	Canada	Tusks	45	35	75	76	123	78	77	37	162	94
9	Denmark	Live	0	0	1	0	0	0	0	0	0	0
10	Georgia	Carvings	10	0	0	0	0	0	0	0	0	0
11	Georgia	Teeth	42	0	0	0	0	0	0	0	0	0
12	Georgia	Tusks	8	0	0	0	0	0	0	0	0	0
13	Germany	Ivory Carvings	0	0	1	0	0	0	0	0	0	0
14	Greenland	Bones	168	166	1	5	8	6	3	1	0	0
15	Greenland	Carvings	572	499	740	740	544	248	748	34	21	193
16	Greenland	Ivory Carvings	0	0	0	0	0	3	0	0	0	0
17	Greenland	Ivory pieces/scraps	5	6	18	16	10	9	41	0	0	0
18	Greenland	Meat (kg)	0	353	387	1023	618	2558	0	0	0	636
19	Greenland	Skin pieces	158	208	0	0	0	0	0	0	0	0
20	Greenland	Teeth	208	85	99	54	28	25	767	675	9	30
21	Greenland	Tusks	267	258	208	240	211	116	106	68	25	45
22	Norway	Tusks	0	0	0	0	0	0	0	0	0	1
23	United Kingdom	Bone Carvings	0	0	1	0	0	0	0	0	0	0
24	United Kingdom	Tusks	0	0	0	2	0	0	0	0	2	1
25	United States	Skin	0	0	0	61	0	0	0	0	0	0

Comment: Levels of trade from Canada and Greenland appear to be stable. However, despite the Animals Committee's recommendation in 1995, a <u>comprehensive</u> survey has still not been done, and the impact of current levels of trade on populations is uncertain. It is therefore recommended that this species should be reviewed.

28. According to the chart, in what year was Greenland's gross export of meat the highest? R1-B

A. 1994   C. 1998

B. 1996   D. 2002

29. You decide to write a poem based on the subject of this passage. RC2-C
Which of the themes below would relate the BEST to the messages of the passage?

A. the importance of conservation

B. the importance of hunting animals

C. the similarities between animals and objects

D. the similarities between people and objects

30. What is the author's purpose for writing this passage?   RC2-E

  A. to persuade
  B. to inform
  C. to entertain
  D. to motivate

31. According to the information in the chart, what was Canada's main export between 1994 and 1997?   R1-B

  A. carvings   C. tusks
  B. meat   D. teeth

Read the passage below. Then answer the questions that follow.

---

excerpt from The Awakening, by Kate Chopin

Mr. Pontellier finally lit a cigar and began to smoke, letting the paper drag idly from his hand. He fixed his gaze from the beach. He could see it plainly between the gaunt trunks of the water-oaks and across the stretch of yellow camomile. The gulf looked far away, melting hazily into the blue of the horizon. The sunshade continued to approach slowly. Beneath its pink-lined shelter were his wife, Mrs. Pontellier, and young Robert Lebrun. When they reached the cottage, the two seated themselves with some appearance of fatigue upon the upper step of the porch, facing each other, each leaning against a supporting post.

"What folly! to bathe at such an hour in such heat!" exclaimed Mr. Pontellier. He himself had taken a plunge at daylight. That was why the morning seemed long to him.

"You are burnt beyond recognition," he added, looking at his wife as one looks at a valuable piece of personal property which has suffered some damage. She held up her hands, strong, shapely hands, and surveyed them critically, drawing up her lawn sleeves above the wrists. Looking at them reminded her of her rings, which she had given to her husband before leaving for the beach. She silently reached out to him, and he, understanding, took the rings from his vest pocket and dropped them into her open palm. She slipped them upon her fingers; then clasping her knees, she looked across at Robert and began to laugh. The rings sparkled upon her fingers. He sent back an answering smile.

"What is it?" asked Pontellier, looking lazily and amused from one to the other. It was some utter nonsense; some adventure out there in the water, and they both tried to relate it at once. It did not seem half so amusing when told. They realized this, and so did Mr. Pontellier. He yawned and stretched himself. Then he got up, saying he had half a mind to go over to Klein's hotel and play a game of billiards.

"Come go along, Lebrun," he proposed to Robert. But Robert admitted quite frankly that he preferred to stay where he was and talk to Mrs. Pontellier.

"Well, send him about his business when he bores you, Edna," instructed her husband as he prepared to leave.

"Here, take the umbrella," she exclaimed, holding it out to him. He accepted the sunshade, and lifting it over his head descended the steps and walked away.

"Coming back to dinner?" his wife called after him. He halted a moment and shrugged his shoulders. He felt in his vest pocket; there was a ten-dollar bill there. He did not know; perhaps he would return for the early dinner and perhaps he would not. It all depended upon the company which he found over at Klein's and the size of "the game." He did not say this, but she understood it, and laughed, nodding good-by to him.

Both children wanted to follow their father when they saw him starting out. He kissed them and promised to bring them back bonbons and peanuts.

32. The author MOSTLY portrays Mr. Pontellier as   R1-B

    A.   playful.   C.   indifferent.

    B.   frustrated.   D.   affectionate.

33. The tone of the first paragraph is   R1-H

    A.   lethargic.   C.   carefree.

    B.   hostile.   D.   hopeful.

"You are burnt beyond recognition," he added, looking at his wife as one looks at a valuable piece of personal property which has suffered some damage.

34. What does this statement from the   R1-F passage suggest about the relationship between Mr. and Mrs. Pontellier?

    A.   Mr. Pontellier is worried about Mrs. Pontellier's well-being.

    B.   Mr. Pontellier mostly sees Mrs. Pontellier as an object he possesses.

    C.   Mrs. Pontellier is valued by Mr. Pontellier because of her personality.

    D.   They both see each other as possessions to be taken care of.

35. Based on the text, you can tell that   R1-C the setting of the passage is

    A.   in a warm coastal area.

    B.   in the middle of a large city.

    C.   in a wooded area.

    D.   in a cold climate.

The Arctic Fox

The arctic fox, as its name indicates, lives in the Arctic region of the Northern Hemisphere. In order to protect itself from the bitter cold of the tundra, the arctic fox wears a thick, white coat in the winter. The white coat also provides excellent camouflage for its snowy surroundings. Sometimes its coat has a blue-gray hue to it. Blending into its surroundings helps the arctic fox catch its prey, while avoiding hungry polar bears at the same time. When temperatures rise in the summer, the rocks and plants of the tundra are exposed. To maintain its camouflage, the arctic fox's coat turns a brown or gray color.

The arctic fox finds food in a variety of ways and will eat almost anything. It will even eat vegetables! The fox typically feeds on small mammals, but when food is scarce, it will also eat a polar bear's leftovers. Foxes that live near the coast will also feed on small birds, such as puffins. When it finds itself with an abundance of food, the fox will bury some of it in the snow and eat it later. To catch small prey such as lemmings and voles, the arctic fox listens for the sound of scurrying rodents. Then, it jumps up and down on the snow to break through it and catch the rodent with its paws.

In order to survive the Arctic temperatures, the fox's body has adapted to its frigid environment. The ears, nose, and legs are all small and thus have a small surface area. This reduces heat loss because there is less skin for heat to escape from. The thick fur on its paws protects the fox's feet from the snow and keeps frost out. Its long, bushy tail helps maintain balance and also provides extra cover to help keep it warm in cold weather. The fur on its body is the warmest of any mammal. The physical features and behavioral characteristics of the arctic fox are a striking example of how all animals adapt in order to survive in their surroundings.

36. According to the passage, which of the following is NOT an average food source for the arctic fox?   R1-A

   A. reptiles
   B. a polar bear's leftovers
   C. puffins
   D. lemmings

37. The author of this passage would probably agree with which of the following statements?   RC2-A

   A. The arctic fox is not good at finding food.
   B. The arctic fox does not have to hide from polar bears.
   C. The arctic fox is well adapted to its environment
   D. The arctic fox does not know how to store food.

38. How is this passage organized? R1-C

    A.   logical order

    B.   chronological order

    C.   comparison and contrast

    D.   narrative order

39. The coat of the arctic fox is gray or R1-A
brown when

    A.   it is scared.

    B.   it is hungry.

    C.   winter begins.

    D.   it is summer.

You do not need to refer to the passages to answer questions 40 and 41.

40. Which word contains a prefix that R2-B
means two?

    A.   reverse   C.   bilingual

    B.   redo   D.   restore

41. A text that contains concrete, fact- RC2-F
based evidence is written in which
genre?

    A.   fable

    B.   myth

    C.   poetry

    D.   nonfiction

A Healthy Choice

Thai food is the healthiest food you can eat. It contains much less fat than typical American food and numerous herbs and spices that help digestion. Block Medical Center recently conducted a study on patients with high cholesterol. Patients substituted lower fat foods five times a week for their typical meals. The study found that the majority of the patients lowered their cholesterol twenty percent or more.

Part of the reason why Thai food is so healthy is because of the way it is prepared. Thai food is often grilled, boiled, or stewed. These methods lower fat and maintain vitamins and nutrients in the food. American food is often deep fried or pan fried in grease or oil.

Another reason Thai food is so healthy are the ingredients. Lemon grass, ginger, garlic, basil, and lime are all used in Thai cooking and are very good for you. Many believe these ingredients can cure a headache, relieve pain, and even cure the flu or the common cold.

Thai food really is the healthiest food you can eat. No other food comes close to providing a balanced, nutritious diet.

---

42. What is the author's argument in this passage? `7R1-D`

    A. Healthy food helps lower cholesterol.

    B. Thai food tastes delicious.

    C. Thai food is the healthiest food to eat.

    D. American food is better tasting than Thai food.

43. What evidence does the author give to support the argument? `7R1-E`

    A. The author uses a medical study to support her argument.

    B. The author discusses the healthy ingredients in Thai food to support her argument.

    C. The author discusses the healthy preparation of Thai food to support her argument.

    D. The author uses all of the above to support her argument.

44. Which sentence should be added to the first paragraph to strengthen the author's argument? `7R1-D`

    A. Block Medical Center conducts many different studies.

    B. The lower fat foods fed to the patients in the study came from a Thai restaurant.

    C. American restaurants outnumber Thai restaurants twenty to one.

    D. My cousin and her family love Thai food and eat it every night for dinner.

The following graphic is the home page for a Thai restaurant's Web site. Use the graphic to answer questions 45 and 46.

45. Consider the message of the passage. Which of the following would be the BEST addition to the Web site? LSV2-A

   A. nutritional information about menu items

   B. a brief history of Thailand

   C. links to other Thai restaurants in the area

   D. information about other types of healthy food

46. Which of the following suggestions for an additional image would be LEAST appropriate for this Web site? LSV2-A

   A. a picture of a healthy Thai dish

   B. a photograph of the restaurant

   C. a drawing of Thailand

   D. a picture of a plate of fried food

The Fearful Traveller in the Haunted Castle

by George Moses Horton

Oft do I hear those windows open
And shut with dread surprise,
And spirits murmur as they grope,
But break not on the eyes.

Still fancy spies the winding sheet,
The phantom and the shroud,
And bids the pulse of horror beat
Throughout my ears aloud.

Some unknown finger thumps the door,
From one of faltering voice,
Till some one seems to walk the floor
With an alarming noise.

The drum of horror holds her sound,
Which will not let me sleep,
When ghastly breezes float around,
And hidden goblins creep.

Methinks I hear some constant groan,
The din of all the dead,
While trembling thus I lie alone,
Upon this restless bed.

At length the blaze of morning broke
On my impatient view,
And truth or fancy told the joke,
And bade the night adieu.

Twas but the noise of prowling rats,
Which ran with all their speed,
Pursued in haste by hungry cats,
Which on the vermin feed.

The cat growl'd as she held her prey,
Which shriek'd with all its might,
And drove the balm of sleep away
Throughout the live-long night.

Those creatures crumbling off the cheese
Which on the table lay;
Some cats, too quick the rogues to seize,
With rumbling lost their prey.

Thus man is often his own elf,
Who makes the night his ghost,
And shrinks with horror from himself,
Which is to fear the most.

47. Using the theme of this poem as inspiration, you are asked to complete a research project for your science class. Which of the following would be the BEST topic? RC2-C

    A.   a report on the most popular breeds of cats in America

    B.   a report on haunted castles from around the world

    C.   a report on the health risks of rat infestations in city buildings

    D.   a report on the most common fears and phobias people have

48. What is the setting of this poem?

    A.   the woods   R1-C

    B.   the kitchen

    C.   a castle

    D.   an abandoned house

Many cell phones have a "ringtone composer" that lets you input a new ringtone simply by pressing a series of keys in order to get a melody. The following list of instructions explains how to use the ringtone composer. Read the instructions. Then answer the questions that follow.

> 1. Go to your phone's ringtone composer. This is found in "settings" or "tone settings."
>
> 2. Press "new tone" or "my melodies." Then "edit," to edit the current melody.
>
> 3. Each number on your keypad plays a different note. Press different numbers in different sequences to create a melody. When finished, press the "ok" or "done" key in your ringtone composer and follow the instructions.
>
> 4. Your ringtone composer should let you name, listen to, and save your new ringtone. Your ringtone composer will even let you adjust the tempo. Your new melody will be listed with your other ringtones.
>
> 5. If you want to try creating a different melody, you can! To delete a previously entered ringtone, edit the ringtone in your ringtone composer and replace the notes with a new melody.

49. According to the instructions, what should you do after you press "new tone"? R1-F

    A.   Type the number sequence.

    B.   Press "settings."

    C.   Press "edit."

    D.   Press "ok" or "done."

50. If you don't like the ringtone you made, how do you create a new one? R1-F

    A.   The phone does not allow this.

    B.   Go to "edit" and replace the old melody.

    C.   Go to "settings" and type the melody you want.

    D.   Go to "new tone" and type the melody you want.

EVALUATION CHART FOR 7TH GRADE GEORGIA READING DIAGNOSTIC TEST

Directions: On the following chart, circle the question numbers that you answered incorrectly, and evaluate the results. These questions are based on the *Georgia Standards for 7th Grade Reading*. Then turn to the appropriate chapters, read the explanations, and complete the exercises. Review other chapters as needed. Finally, complete the practice test(s) to assess your progress and further prepare you for the **Georgia 7th Grade CRCT in Reading**.

Note: Some question numbers will appear under multiple chapters because those questions require demonstration of multiple skills.

Chapter	Diagnostic Test Question(s)
Chapter 1: Vocabulary	3, 8, 9, 11, 12, 17, 21, 29, 37, 40, 47
Chapter 2: Understanding Organizational Patterns in Texts	14, 38
Chapter 3: Analyzing Features of Informational Texts	15, 36, 39
Chapter 4: Analyzing the Author's Argument	13, 16, 30, 42, 43, 44, 45, 46
Chapter 5: Understanding Common Graphic Features and Following Directions	10, 14, 28, 31, 38, 41, 45, 46, 49, 50
Chapter 6: Understanding Literature	2, 4, 20, 22, 23, 24, 25, 26, 27, 32, 34, 35, 48
Chapter 7: Figurative Language, Tone, and Mood	1, 5, 6, 7, 33
Chapter 8: Literature Across Cultures	18, 19
Chapter 9: Reading Across Subject Areas	12, 20, 22, 26, 29, 32, 37, 47
Chapter 10: Extending Meaning	9

Chapter 1
Vocabulary

This chapter covers the following Georgia standards.

ELA7R2	Understand and acquire new vocabulary and use it correctly in reading and writing.
ELA7RC3	Acquire new vocabulary in each content area and use it correctly.

Reading is a lifelong journey of learning, discovery, and adventure. Learning new vocabulary is necessary to develop and increase your reading, writing, and speech levels. Encountering unfamiliar words can create a variety of challenges. There are many tools available to aid in determining the use and meaning of an unfamiliar word. These tools will provide the knowledge for using new vocabulary words correctly in reading and writing. You will learn to use the following concepts. Each concept will provide you with strategies to read with ease and confidence.

- Context Clues through Restatement
- Synonyms in Context
- Antonyms in Context
- Cause and Effect
- Root Words
- Prefixes
- Suffixes
- Idioms
- Analogies
- Dictionary Skills

All of these tools will help you in your reading adventure. Once you learn how to use and apply these tools; your journey will take you to exciting places!

CONTEXT CLUES

Context clues are one of the most useful tools in determining the meaning of a word. Context is the words and ideas that surround the unfamiliar word. These words and ideas can give clues to the meaning of the unfamiliar word. Context clues provide a strategy for decoding the meaning of the new vocabulary in the text. Assessment tests often ask for the meaning of a word in context. Context clues redefine or restate the meaning of a word in the same sentence or the next sentence, as in the example provided:

Example: The little girl was an *introvert. Her shy and solitary ways kept her from making friends.*

The *second* sentence restates the meaning in simpler terms.

Many writers take into consideration that the reader may not be familiar with more challenging vocabulary. In order to help the reader; the writer provides clues. Restatement may state the word in simpler terms or even provide a definition within the next sentence.

Practice 1: Word Meanings from Context Restatement

The following sentences contain clues to the meaning of the words in bold print. Circle the correct corresponding letter choice for the meaning of the word as used in the sentence. The first one is done for you. The answer choice is highlighted in bold print.

It was a sad and haunting **strain** that met our ears as we entered the old theater. There was a beauty in the voice that we would never forget. This would be a special concert.

1. What does "strain" mean in the context of the selection?

   A. effort   B. injury   **C. melody**   D. filter

I want you to **weigh** his words carefully. He seems sincere and presents his arguments well. There is, however, something that does not quite ring true about the candidate.

2. What does "weigh" mean in the context of the selection?

   A. to measure the mass   C. to think about

   B. to put pressure on a scale   D. to be important

Michael is an **ardent** supporter of his presidential candidate. That became obvious to me when I found out how much time he has donated to the campaign. Perhaps Michael knows what he is doing.

3. What does "ardent" mean in the context of the selection?

   A. old   B. intelligent   C. foolish   D. very strong

Mary, of course you didn't pass the test. You read too many comics. Even worse, you studied **infrequently**.

4. What does "infrequently" mean?
   - A. all the time
   - B. at the library
   - C. while listening to music
   - D. not often

It is important to **scour** the tub after frequent use; this will cleanse stubborn dirt.

5. What does "scour" mean?
   - A. to frown
   - B. to yell
   - C. scrub well
   - D. lightly touch

SYNONYMS IN CONTEXT

Synonyms are often present in text and used as context clues to determine the meaning of a word. A synonym is a word that has the exact same meaning or similar meaning as another word. Synonyms are often present in text to give further meaning. It is very helpful to have another word that means the same as the challenging word. The following example sentence shows the use of a synonym as a context clue:

The rider rode at a **brisk** pace so the horse could enjoy a nice *quick* run before returning to the barn.

The word *quick* has the same meaning as *brisk* and gives the reader a clear picture as to the meaning of the unfamiliar word.

Practice 2: Word Meanings From Context – Synonyms

Each highlighted word in the selection should be replaced by its synonym. Use the context to help you decide which word should be used and underline the correct synonym. The first one has been done for you.

Rene was **1. seldom** (commonly, <u>rarely</u>) hungry when she woke up in the morning. It took at least an hour for her to even want to think about food. She had only been awake for a few minutes when her father called, "Rene," what do you **2. desire** (want, reject) for breakfast?" "**3. None** (Nothing, Everything) that I can imagine!" Rene **4. replied** (responded, asked) as she bounded down the stairs. "Food is the last thing on my mind, Dad. I'm on my way to meet Ingrid so we won't be **5. late** to school (tardy, early)." "Have you **6. told** (informed, concealed) your bus driver that you won't be here?" Mr. Renaldo **7. asked** (announced, inquired). "I'm **8. sure** (certain, doubtful) that I mentioned it to her yesterday. The only question is whether or not she'll remember," Rene answered as she **9. left** (exited, entered) her house. She smiled as the early summer sunlight **10. heated** (cooled, warmed) her face.

ANTONYMS IN CONTEXT

Synonyms use words that are alike to make a comparison. **Antonyms** use words that are opposite in meaning to make a comparison. An antonym is a word that is the exact opposite of another word. The opposite meaning will give the reader a clue to the meaning of the challenging word. The opposite word or phrase will be familiar so that it is easy to discover a similar word or meaning for the new vocabulary.

> The child was taught to **suppress** her laughter rather than have loud ***outbursts***.

The word *outburst* is the opposite of *suppress*. *Outburst* is an uncontrollable response whereas *suppress* means to control.

Practice 3:   Word Meanings in Context – Antonyms

Somewhere in each selection you will find a pair of words in parenthesis. These words will be antonyms or opposites. Underline the word that makes sense in the context. Use a dictionary if you're not sure of the meanings of both antonyms. The first one has been done for you.

1. Mr. Sheffield was a very good teacher. Everyone agreed that kids learned a lot when they spent a year in his class. Some kids did wish that he would be a little **(lenient, strict)** about the rules. If anyone so much as whispered during study time or happened to forget a home-work assignment, he or she was in big trouble.

2. Jennifer was very **(gullible, skeptical)**. We found it all too easy to convince her that a mummy was roaming around in her cellar. As we added more and more crazy details to our story, she grew more frightened. Finally, we decided it was best to confess that it was just a hoax.

3. Sometimes Mike can be very **(insensitive, sensitive)** to others' feelings. Do you remember the time that Jules told us she was taking a beauty course? Mike said that it must be a miracle course. He was trying to be funny, but her feelings were really hurt. He didn't mean what he said. The problem is that he didn't think about how Julie would take the comment.

4. All the trees and all the flowers,
   Sunlit clouds that **(gloom, illuminate)** the sky,
   All the gentle April showers,
   They have worth; we can't deny.

5. All the man-made **(golden, leaden)** treasures,
   They have value. They have style.
   I've found more than all their measure
   In the beauty of your smile.

CAUSE AND EFFECT

Cause and effect is also a very helpful tool in understanding words and/or phrases. **Cause and effect** is the relationship between two things when one thing makes something else happen. In literature, there will be an event or action, and the reader can often guess the result of this action. The reader may come across unfamiliar words or phrases, but there is a general understanding because of the nature of **cause and effect**. In literature as in life, for every action there is another action. A student who never studies is one action; therefore, the student receiving poor grades is the result of the first action.

The student who never studies = **cause**

Receiving poor grades = **effect**

Here are some common conjunctions that can be used to express cause and effect:

since	as a result	because of + noun phrase
because	therefore	due to + noun phrase
consequently	for this reason	so

Practice 4: Determining Cause and Effect

Place the correct letter for the word below that will complete the sentence on the line provided following each sentence. Use the cause and effect strategy to determine the correct word to complete the sentence. The first one is done for you. Use the dictionary if necessary.

a. concentration	**c.** aggression	**e.** corroded	**g.** dehydration
b. treacherous	**d.** stamina	**f.** drenched	**h.** warped

1. The young lady went out without a raincoat, and, therefore, was **f. (drenched).**

2. She left her CDs outside in the blazing sun, and, as a result, they became _____.

3. There was an ice storm and, consequently, the roads are slippery and _____.

4. The runner ran a quarter of a mile more each week so she would increase her _____.

5. Because the batteries were left in the rain for several days, they became _____.

6. The dog bit the postman and had to be sent to animal control due to its _____.

7. The extremely hot, dry weather and lack of ample water caused _____.

8. Students must focus in order to increase their level of _____.

ROOT WORDS

Examining **roots** and **affixes** will help a reader figure out the meaning of a new vocabulary word. The root word is the base word. Most root words come from the Greek or Latin languages. Familiarity with a root word can aid in the process of **decoding** or figuring out the pronunciation and meaning of an unfamiliar word. A **root word** is a word that has nothing added at the beginning or the end, and it has a meaning. New words can be made from root words by adding beginnings (**prefixes**) and endings (**suffixes**).

Most words used in the English language today were not originally English. These words were borrowed (taken) from other languages. The majority of English words come from the Latin or Greek languages. It is helpful to know some of these origins or "roots" of English vocabulary. It may be possible to guess the meaning of an unknown word when one knows the meaning of its root. Knowing prefixes and suffixes can also assist in the process. An English word can consist of three parts: the **root**, a **prefix,** and a **suffix**. The root is the part of the word that contains the basic **meaning** (definition) of the word. The root is the base element of the word.

For example, *agree* is a root word that can mean one of these three definitions. They are all related in meaning.

> *agree:* to go along with, to take one's side, or approve
>
> *agree*able: easy to get along with
>
> dis*agree:* to go against, to not takes one's side

All of these words have **grown** from their **root word**. They share parts of the same spelling, and they are linked in terms of meaning. They are known as a **word family**.

In a word family, all the words share parts of the same spelling and have linked meaning.

Root words are helpful because:

- You can use a root word to help you with other spellings.
- If you recognize the root of a word when you are reading, it can help you to work out what the word is and what it means.

Here are some more examples of root words and the word families that grow from them:

use	**use**less, **us**able, **us**ed, **us**ing, **us**er, mis**use**
employ	**employ**ment, un**employ**ment, **employ**er, **employ**ee, **employ**ing
manage	**manage**r, **manag**ing, **manage**s, **manage**able, un**manage**able
beauty	**beaut**iful, **beaut**ifully, **beaut**ician
faith	**faith**ful, **faith**fully, un**faith**ful, un**faith**fully

Some Common Roots

Root	Meaning	Example
arch	to rule	monarch
belli	war, warlike	belligerent
bene	good	benevolent
chron	time	chronology
dic	to say	dictation
fac	to make, to do	artifact
graph	writing	telegraph
mort	to die	mortician
port	to carry	deport
vid, vis	to see	invisible

Practice 5: Matching Roots

Match the root word to its meaning by writing the letter of the answer choice on the line provided. Use the dictionary if necessary. The first one has been done for you.

__F__ 1. graph, as in autograph   A.   good

_____ 2. tele, as in telephone   B.   year

_____ 3. bene, as in benefit   C.   distance

_____ 4. ject, as in inject   D.   to carry

_____ 5. ann, an in annual   E.   time

_____ 6. path, as in pathetic   F.   writing

_____ 7. chron, as in chronology   G.   to speak

_____ 8. dic, as in dictate   H.   to throw

_____ 9. aud, as in audible   I.   feeling

____ 10. port, as in portable   J.   hear

AFFIXES

Affixes consist of **prefixes** and **suffixes**. A **prefix** is a word added to the beginning of a base word, and a **suffix** is added to the end of a word. A **prefix** is a word element that is placed in front of a root. A prefix changes the word's meaning or makes a new word. A **suffix** is a word element that is placed after the root. The suffix changes the word's meaning as well as its function (use). Prefixes and suffixes are called *affixes* because they are affixed (attached) to a root.

SOME COMMON PREFIXES

Prefix	Meaning	Example
pre-	before	precede
de-	away, from	deter
hypo-	under, too little	hypoglycemic
hyper-	over, too much	hyperactive
mal-	bad	malfunction
retro-	backward	retroactive
poly-	many	polyclinic
bi-	two	bicycle
un-	not	unneeded
semi-	half, partly	semicircle
equi-	equal, equally	equivalent
omni-	all, everywhere	omniscient
anti-	against	antibacterial
pro-	forward	propel
inter-	between	interstate
ob-	against	objection
mono-	one, alone	monopoly
epi-	upon	epitaph
mis-	wrong	mistake
sub-	under	submarine
trans-	across, beyond	transcend
over-	above	overbearing
ad-	to, toward	advance
non-	not	nondairy
com-	together, with	composite
re-	back, again	regress
ex-	out of	expel
in-	not	insufficient

Practice 6: Matching Prefixes

Match the prefix to its meaning by writing the letter of the answer choice on the line provided. Use the dictionary if necessary. The first one has been done for you.

__J__ 1. pre, as in prehistoric

_____ 2. bi, as in bicentennial

_____ 3. mis, as in misunderstood

_____ 4. un, as in unmistakable

_____ 5. ex, as in exhale

_____ 6. pro, as in produce

_____ 7. de, as in determine

_____ 8. ad, as in advertise

_____ 9. semi, as in semi-annual

_____ 10. anti, as in antisocial

A. away, from

B. in front of

C. forward

D. against

E. out of

F. wrong

G. two

H. half, partly

I. not

J. before

SOME COMMON SUFFIXES

Suffix	Meaning	Example
-able, -ible	able to	usable
-er, or	one who does	competitor
-ism	the practice of	rationalism
-ist	one who is occupied with	racist
-less	without, lacking	worthless
-ship	the art of skill of	leadership
-fy	to make	dignify
-ness	the quality of	kindness
-tude	the state of	rectitude
-logue	a particular kind of speaking or writing	monologue

Practice 7: Matching Suffixes

Match the suffix to its meaning by writing the letter of the answer choice on the line provided. Use the dictionary if necessary. The first one has been done for you.

__F__ 1. able, ible as in capable   A.   having the quality of

_____ 2. fy, as in justify   B.   the art or skill of

_____ 3. er, or, as in actor   C.   study of

_____ 4. ive, as in active   D.   full of

_____ 5. logy, as in biology   E.   related to

_____ 6. less, as in penniless   F.   able to

_____ 7. age, as in message   G.   having the nature of

_____ 8. ish, as in foolish   H.   to make

_____ 9. ship, as in partnership   I.   one who does

_____ 10. ness, as in selfishness   J.   without

ROOT WORD TREE

Write a root at the base of the tree. On the branches, write six or more words that use that root.

Root Word

Add prefixes and suffixes to the root words provided and place on the tree branches. See how many new words you can make.

1. port

2. clear

3. able

4. tract

5. use

6. age

ANALOGIES

In creative writing such as prose or poetry, **figurative language** is used to make the text more imaginative. **Analogies** are an example of this figurative language. An analogy is an **extended comparison** in which two things or ideas that are different are related in some way. The comparison gives the reader a new way to understand an idea. Look at this example:

I was shut up in a tiny glass-enclosed room with no visible outlet for air; an apparent bug in a jar with no holes in the top for air. I was small and helpless, trapped in a tidal wave of despair and misery, drowning in the suffocation of captivity.

The writer makes an extended comparison between two situations that have similarities. The person in the glass-enclosed room feels as a bug would feel in a jar with no escape and no visible outlet to allow in air. The writer uses the images of a tidal wave, drowning, and suffocation to draw a vivid picture of helplessness.

When you read, take time to interpret the meaning of language used in special ways. Analogies help you experience familiar things in new and surprising ways.

Practice 8:   Making Analogies

The words below complete the sentences with a comparison. Write the letter of the answer choice that completes the sentence. The first one is done for you.

A.   butterfly floating and flitting through the air.
B.   An avalanche overcame me
C.   impenetrable black hole
D.   Fire and flames tormented
E.   The fire was a raging lion on patrol
F.   A giant hand shook and tossed
G.   villain meant to strangle and choke progress.
H.   gone up in a cloud of smoke.

1.   **F. (A giant hand shook and tossed)** our boat, and then the storm subsided.

2.   _____, and I could not see an end to my homework.

3.   Her hopes and dreams had _____.

4.   _____ to devour all that stood in its path.

5.   The dancer was a _____.

6.   Fear is a _____.

7.   _____ my feet after the running competition.

8.   Boredom is an _____.

FUN WITH IDIOMS

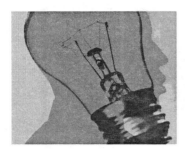

Idioms are common expressions that are used in everyday language. An **idiom** is not meant to be taken literally or at face value. Most idioms in the English language are taken for granted as to their meaning. An idiom's meaning can pose challenges, as the phrases do not always follow a clear rule but rely on drawing a picture in the mind of the reader. Most idioms are so familiar that we do not even think about their literal meaning; for example:

as easy as pie: very easy

> **Example:** "I thought you said this was a difficult problem. It isn't. In fact, it's **as easy as pie.**"

be all ears: be eager to hear what someone has to say

> **Example:** "I just got an e-mail message from our old friend Sally."

> **Example:** "Tell me what she said. **I'm all ears!**"

couch potato: someone who spends too much time watching TV

> **Example:** "You're a real **couch potato,** Jay. You need to get more exercise!"

drag one's feet: delay; take longer than necessary to do something

> **Example:** "Joe should have finished his project a week ago. Why is he **dragging his feet?**"

an eager beaver: a person who is always willing to volunteer to do extra work

> **Example:** "Jan is certainly **an eager beaver.** Any time there's work to be done, she's the first to say she'll help."

Practice 9: Fun with Idioms

Choose the correct letter choice for the meaning of the idioms in bold print. How many have you heard before? The first one is done for you.

1. Choose the idiom similar in meaning to **sleep or nap**.
   - A. odds and ends
   - B. over the hill
   - C. copycat
   - D. **take forty winks**

2. Choose the idiom similar in meaning to **great, wonderful**.
   - A. in the same boat
   - B. out of this world
   - C. shot in the dark
   - D. silver lining

3. Choose the idiom similar in meaning to **go to sleep**.

    A.   hit the sack   C.   walk on air
    B.   let one's hair down   D.   go fly a kite

4. Choose the idiom similar in meaning to **neat and clean.**

    A.   nest egg   C.   face value
    B.   spic and span   D.   the last straw

5. Choose the idiom similar in meaning to **die**.

    A.   spill the beans   C.   kick the bucket
    B.   watch one's step   D.   rain check

6. Choose the idiom similar in meaning to **hurry up**.
    A.   bend over backwards   C.   turn one's back
    B.   go bananas   D.   shake a leg

7. Choose the idiom similar in meaning **to the very best**.

    A.   heart to heart   C.   sweet tooth
    B.   cream of the crop   D.   ringleader

8. Choose the idiom similar in meaning to **small, insignificant amount**.

    A.   long shot   C.   hit or miss
    B.   far cry   D.   drop in the bucket

DICTIONARY SKILLS

The most comprehensive tool for determining a word meaning is using a **dictionary** or **thesaurus**. The **dictionary** provides pronunciation, synonyms, antonyms, parts of speech, and the various definitions for the word. The dictionary provides many resources for acquiring full knowledge of an unfamiliar word. The dictionary is a best friend that provides instant answers. A dictionary gives the correct spelling of the word and its special plural form. In the entry on the next page, you have the main entry word broken into syllables on the first line. The second line gives you a key as to the correct pronunciation for the word. The third line tells you the part of speech for the word, and the fourth line gives you the correct plural form. The

remaining lines are dedicated to the various definitions for the word. The dictionary will also give sample sentences. The dictionary is alphabetized with guide words across the top of the page to show which word is the beginning entry on the page and which word is the last entry on the page.

> Main Entry: **ef·fi·cien·cy**
> Pronunciation: i-**fish**-*uhn*-see
> Function: *noun*
> Inflected form(s): *plural* **-cies**
> **1 :** the quality or degree of being efficient
> **2 :** efficient operation
> **3 :** the ratio of the useful energy delivered by a machine to the energy supplied to it

Practice 10: Find the Meaning

The circus is a wildly imaginative place that can provide hours of **enchantment**. In the circus world, everything is a feast for the senses. The bright lights grab your attention while the music keeps you bouncing in your seat. The costumes are creative and **whimsical.** The clowns make for laugh-out-loud **merriment**. The laughter is still stuck in your throat and then quickly replaced with an exhale of **awe** at the death-defying **antics** of the trapeze artists. These angels of flight **defy** the laws of gravity. Tromping in on **cue** are those amazing animals. The lion's **ferocity** is tamed by the fearless lion tamer, and the elephants lumber in and then amaze

us with their grace and **dexterity.** The circus is not through with it's audience yet. The daredevil makes his thrilling entrance revving his motorcycle in preparation for the death-defying loop, which he executes with remarkable **precision**. The circus has something for everyone in the family and promises the audience a night to remember.

Use the dictionary to help define the word given from the passage and then choose the letter of the correct multiple choice answer given as a synonym. The first one is done for you.

1. enchantment
    A. distraction   B.   clueless   **C.   fascination**   D.   boring

2. whimsical
    A. ugly   B.   large   C.   boring   D.   amusing

3. merriment
    A. work   B.   boredom   C.   happiness   D.   enjoyment

4. awe
   A.   amazement   B.   horror   C.   worship   D.   disrespect

5. antics
   A.   fighting   B.   risks   C.   pranks   D.   misbehavior

6. defy
   A.   skip   B.   assure   C.   obey   D.   dare

7. cue
   A.   wind   B.   key   C.   signal   D.   total

8. ferocity
   A.   timidity   B.   shyness   C.   strangeness   D.   fierceness

9. dexterity
   A.   contact   B.   skillfulness   C.   clumsiness   D.   awkwardness

10. precision
   A.   haze   B.   uncertainty   C.   laziness   D.   accuracy

Practice 11:   Test Your Defining Skills

Study the bolded word in each sentence. Write the meaning in the first line. Then look up the word in a dictionary. Was your meaning close to the real definition?

1.   Her public speaking methods were **archaic** and ineffective.

Meaning _____

Definition _____

2.   His long essay was **fraught** with mistakes.

Meaning _____

Definition _____

3.   It was a **fortuitous** partnership, as the two participants won a trophy.

Meaning _____

Definition _____

4. The smell was beginning to **permeate** every inch of the room.

Meaning _____

Definition _____

5. The young woman who interviewed for the position had a very **congenial** personality.

Meaning _____

Definition _____

CHAPTER 1 SUMMARY

- **Context clues** use restatement of an unfamiliar word through familiar word or phrases. **Synonyms** and **antonyms** give context clues by making comparison of words or phrases that are alike as well as different.

- **Cause and effect** shows the relationship of one action to another action. When an event or action happens, that causes another event or action to occur.

- **Roots**, **prefixes**, and **suffixes** are all parts of words. The root word is the base word. A prefix added to the beginning of a base word will slightly change its meaning. A suffix added to the end of a base word will also change the meaning of the word. Knowing the definition of each of these word parts will help a reader to determine the meaning of an unfamiliar word.

- **Analogies** and **idioms** are used in creative writing such as prose or poetry. An analogy makes a comparison of things that are alike or things that are different. An idiom is a common expression that draws a picture in the mind of the reader.

- The **dictionary** is a tool that can help a reader in many ways. The dictionary can help a reader with spelling, using the correct plural form, identifying the part of speech, and with the various meanings of the word.

CHAPTER 1 REVIEW

Context Clues

Finish the sentence with the correct letter of the answer.

1. Sometimes when reading, words are defined within the sentence where they are found. This is referred to as
   - A. context clues.
   - B. reference.
   - C. helping verb.
   - D. main idea.

2. A word that has the same meaning as another word is a(n)
   - A. antonym.
   - B. prefix.
   - C. suffix.
   - D. synonym.

3. Context clues can be found
   - A. in the dictionary.
   - B. on a chart.
   - C. on the next page.
   - D. in the surrounding text.

4. Words with contrasting or opposite meaning signal a(n)
   - A. synonym.
   - B. antonym.
   - C. noun.
   - D. verb.

5. Context clues help a reader to
   - A. spell.
   - B. see a word.
   - C. pronounce words.
   - D. learn new vocabulary.

Cause and Effect

Choose the effect of each cause provided.

6. The brakes on the car became inoperable, and the car
   - A. drove as normal.
   - B. became a safety hazard.

7. The student lost control and threw a tantrum during class. The teacher
   - A. gave her detention.
   - B. gave her a reward.

8. The parent never disciplined her daughter, and she became
   - A. a joy to everyone.
   - B. uncontrollable.

9. She loves sugary deserts and candy, which is why
   - A. she developed diabetes.
   - B. she has perfect health.

10. The little boy often invented lies for no apparent reason, and soon he was considered

    A.   very reliable.   B.   very unreliable

Roots, Prefixes, and Suffixes

Choose the correct letter choice for each bolded word part. The first one is done for you..

Affix	**Definition**	**Word**
11. ad	to	addict

    A.   root
    B.   prefix
    C.   suffix

12. bio   life   biology

    A.   root
    B.   prefix
    C.   suffix

13. tion   quality, state   preservation

    A.   root
    B.   prefix
    C.   suffix

14. graph   write   graphic

    A.   root
    B.   prefix
    C.   suffix

15. ic   relating to   poetic

    A.   root
    B.   prefix
    C.   suffix

16. bi   two   bicycle

    A.   root
    B.   prefix
    C.   suffix

Idioms and Analogies

Choose the correct letter choice to identify between idiom or analogy.

17. The snaky limbs of the branches rubbed me with their coarse touch.

    A.   idiom   B.   analogy

18. Sally is as silly as a goose.
    A.   idiom   B.   analogy

19. Her coarse nature was equal to bristles on a porcupine.
    A.   idiom   B.   analogy

20. We drank our hot chocolate quick as a wink.
    A.   idiom   B.   analogy

21. My cousin was an annoying fly that buzzed around me all day.
    A.   idiom   B.   analogy

22. When it comes to tying his shoes, he is all thumbs—he just can't get that knot right.
    A.   idiom   B.   analogy

Dictionary Skills

Use your dictionary to choose the correct letter of the answer that means the same as the word in bold print.

23. Her handwriting was **illegible.**
    A.   neat   B.   cute   C.   artistic   D.   unreadable

24. The spoiled child was **incorrigible.**
    A.   hopeless   B.   pleasant   C.   funny   D.   playful

25. I **dread** the thought of the test tomorrow.
    A.   adore   B.   fear   C.   anticipate   D.   welcome

26. She **humiliated** me in front of all my friends.
    A.   glorified   B.   uplifted   C.   praised   D.   embarrassed

27. Her progress was **stilted** due to her lack of concentration.
    A.   good   B.   speedy   C.   hindered   D.   funny

Chapter 2
Understanding Organizational Patterns in Texts

This chapter covers the following Georgia standard.

ELA7R1	Apply knowledge of common organizational structures and patterns (i.e., logical order, cause and effect relationships, comparison and contrast, and transitions).

In our everyday world, we are bombarded with information that we must sort through and make sense of. Who is the best choice for homeroom representative? Why did we lose the football game? Should you choose soccer or guitar for an after-school activity? By organizing the information we know, we can start to see relationships in that information. This, in turn, helps us draw conclusions and make decisions.

LOGICAL ORDER

You are the first of your friends to see the latest movie on everyone's list. When you show up at school the next morning, everyone wants to know: How did it start out? What happened next? How did it turn out at the end?

Movies, recipes, biographies, and historical events follow a **logical order**. **Logical order** is the order in which events happen. It is a sensible way to describe what happened.

Items that are out of order can be confusing. Imagine that you are pet-sitting for a neighbor who asks you to give her dog a bath. She gives you a list of instructions that looks like this:

Rinse the soap off the dog's fur.

First, gather all of the things you will need for the job.

Rub the dog dry with the towels.

Wet the dog with the hose.

Lather soap into the dog's fur.

Presenting information in the proper order is important. It would not make sense to follow these steps in the order they are given, nor would it accomplish your task of ending up with a clean dog!

Practice 1: Logical Order

Read the following historical account about the Titanic. Write the letters on the lines so the account is in a logical order.

A. The disaster prompted changes in regulations for ships, such as having enough lifeboats for all passengers.

B. It was intended to be a luxurious way to travel across the Atlantic Ocean.

C. More than 1,000 people died.

D. The Titanic was a famous passenger ship.

E. It also made shipbuilders re-evaluate the design of large passenger crafts.

F. Though nearly 100 years have passed since it sank, the story of the Titanic continues to interest people around the world.

G. On its first voyage in 1912, the Titanic struck an iceberg and sank.

1. _____   2. _____   3. _____   4. _____   5. _____   6. _____   7. _____

CAUSE AND EFFECT

Why did we win the game? What will happen now that we've made it to the playoffs? What can we do to help us win the championship?

Cause and effect explores the relationships between ideas and events. Cause and effect looks at why things happen (the cause) and what happens as a result (the effect). Cause and effect is a tool often used to organize and discuss ideas and to solve problems.

USING GRAPHIC ORGANIZERS WITH CAUSE AND EFFECT

Events can have several causes and effects. It can be helpful to see relationships by asking questions and recording the answers in a graphic organizer.

To Determine Causes and Effects:

1. **Begin with a statement.**

Write this at the center.

2. **Ask "Why did this happen?**

Put these answers in the "causes" section.

3. **Ask "What happened because of this?"**

Put these answers in the "effects" section.

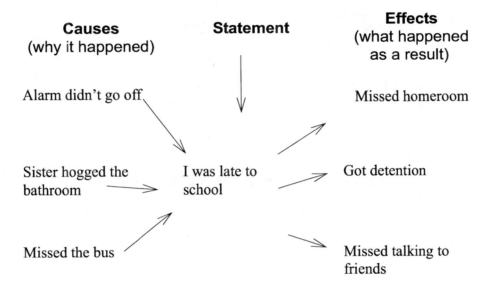

Once you see the relationships between events, you can use this knowledge to work on solving the problem. Possible solutions might include buying a reliable alarm clock or working out a bathroom schedule with your sister.

Practice 2: Using a Graphic Organizer with Causes and Effects

Choose one of the following events. Ask the questions in the box above to determine what the causes and effects are. Write your results into a graphic organizer like the one used in the example. Or create your own event.

Events:

The cat got out.

I fell asleep at dinner.

We won the football game.

I was given a surprise party.

IDENTIFYING CAUSE AND EFFECT

Writers may use cause and effect to explain a sequence of events or to try to convince others to see things from their point of view. Being able to identify cause and effect when you read is important because it allows you to see relationships between the information the author is presenting. Maybe the author is trying to explain why it is important to protect rainforests. Maybe he is discussing what caused the pilgrims to come to America.

There are certain signal words and phrases that show cause and effect is coming. Some common ones are:

Cause	Effect
because	therefore
as a result of	consequently
since	for this reason
due to	thus

Practice 3: Identifying Cause and Effect

Read the following letter from a class officer to the other students in her school. Then answer the questions that follow.

March 15, 2007

Dear Fellow Students,

I am writing to encourage everyone to use the new trash cans in the hallways. You may have noticed the piles of trash that have been littering our halls and piling up in corners. As a result of all of this mess, our custodians were spending a lot of time sweeping when they could have been doing their other jobs. Due to the litter on the floors and the extra work for the custodians, the school has installed several trash cans in each hallway. Please do your part and put trash where it belongs.

I'd like to thank the 7th graders for putting the trash cans in their hall to good use already. When I walked down the 7th grade hall with the principal this morning, we saw three full trash cans and only two papers on the floor. Consequently, our principal is giving an ice cream party for the entire 7th grade. Keep up the good work!

Sincerely,

Brenda Thompson

Milton Middle School Class Officer

1. What does Brenda say is the **cause** of the custodians spending a lot of time sweeping?

    A. There are not enough custodians.

    B. There is trash on the floors.

    C. The new trash cans don't work.

    D. Seventh graders are messy.

2. What **caused** the school to install the new trash cans?

    A. There was litter on the floors.

    B. The custodians were always sweeping.

    C. Both A and B.

    D. None of the above.

3. What was the **effect** of the seventh graders putting trash in the new trash cans?

    A. They got an ice cream party.

    B. They helped sweep the halls.

    C. They must clean all of the other halls as well.

    D. The school will put more trash cans in the other halls.

4. Which signal words and phrases identify **effects** in the letter?

    A. "as a result," "consequently," and "due to"

    B. "encourage" and "please do your part"

    C. "when," "in," and "for"

    D. "to use," "have noticed," and "were spending"

COMPARISON AND CONTRAST

Comparison and contrast means deciding how things are alike and how they are different. It is a way to organize and talk about information by looking for similarities and differences.

When you **compare** items, look for ways in which they are the same.

When you **contrast** items, look for ways in which they are different.

For instance, if you were to compare and contrast cars and trucks, you might create this chart:

Cars and Trucks	
Compare (similarities)	**Contrast (differences)**
Both are vehicles.	Trucks can carry more cargo.
Both have wheels.	Cars can have more passenger space.
Both use gas.	Cars have a trunk.

When choosing items to compare and contrast, make sure the things you are evaluating make sense together. It makes sense to compare and contrast similar things like bagels and cereal when you are choosing breakfast. It does not make sense to compare taking a ski vacation to tying your shoes. Items must have similarities.

Practice 4: Compare and contrast

Read the paragraph below. Then answer the questions that follow.

Popsicles and Ice Cream

Ice cream and popsicles are both frozen desserts. Both must be kept in the freezer. Both must be eaten quickly to avoid drips. Both make a good snack on a hot summer day. Popsicles tend to be harder than ice cream. Ice cream must be eaten with a spoon or licked from a cone, while a popsicle can be held by its stick. Popsicles are usually low in fat while ice cream is not.

1. What items are being compared and contrasted in the paragraph?
    A. all frozen desserts
    B. desserts that are good for hot weather
    C. popsicles and ice cream
    D. popsicles and all other frozen desserts

2. What is one way that popsicles and ice cream are the same?
    A. They both have sticks.
    B. Both have a lot of fat.
    C. Both must be kept frozen.
    D. Both are unhealthy.

3. What is one of the ways that ice cream and popsicles differ?
    A. Popsicles must be eaten quickly, but ice cream must not.
    B. Popsicles are harder than ice cream.
    C. Both come in wrappers.
    D. Neither can be eaten for dessert.

4. Which of these is the main way that popsicles and ice cream are similar?
    A. Both must be eaten quickly.
    B. Both make your mouth water.
    C. Both must be eaten with a spoon.
    D. Both are frozen desserts.

USING COMPARISON AND CONTRAST

The main reasons to use comparison and contrast are **to explain** and **to evaluate**.

To explain

For instance, your social studies teacher asks you to compare and contrast democracy and communism. Your response would discuss the ways these two types of government are the same and the ways they are different.

To evaluate

For instance, your parents are deciding what kind of car to buy next. As they make their decision, they will consider things like price, how many passengers the car must be able to carry, and gas mileage.

When comparing and contrasting, it can be helpful to use a graphic organizer like the one below. A graphic organizer gives a clear picture of which items you are comparing and contrasting and how they are alike and different.

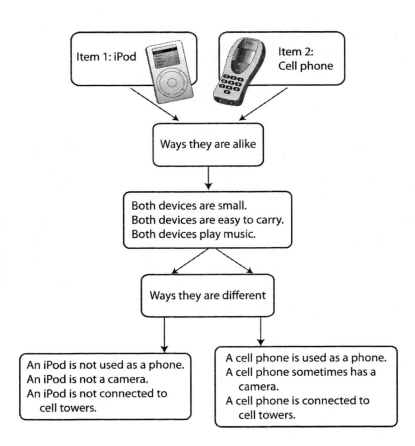

Practice 5:   Using a graphic organizer to compare and contrast

Imagine that your family has decided to get a new pet. You get to decide what kind of pet it will be. You have considered all of the options and have narrowed your list down to two finalists. Either one would be great, but which would be best?

1.   Look at the list of pet suggestions below (or think of your own).

Choose two pets to compare and contrast.

On a separate paper, create your own graphic organizer like the one on page 49. Use it to compare the two pets you have chosen.

bird	lizard
hamster	dog
cat	fish

2.   Looking at your completed graphic organizer, which pet would you choose? Why? Explain your answer in 2–3 sentences.

3.   Looking at your completed graphic organizer, would either pet be a good choice for a family with young children? Why or why not? Explain your answer in 2–3 sentences.

4.   Looking at your completed graphic organizer, would either pet be a good choice for an elderly person? Why or why not? Explain your answer in 2–3 sentences.

TRANSITIONS

Transitions are words and phrases in a text that indicate a change from one idea to the next. Transitions are ways to show connections between ideas. A good transition is one in which the text moves smoothly and logically from one idea to the next. Transitions are important because they keep an idea clear and relevant from one sentence or paragraph to the next.

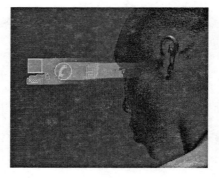

Notice how the author makes the transition from talking about cell phone cameras to talking about regular cameras in the following sentences.

The camera feature available on many cell phones is a convenient way to take pictures. A cell phone is something many people carry with them everywhere. **However**, the picture quality is inferior to that of traditional cameras.

The use of the transition word "however" signals the reader that a change in ideas is coming. By using this transition word, the writer lets the reader know that she will now move from talking about cell phone cameras to talking about regular cameras.

There are many words and phrases that can signal a transition. Some common words and phrases are listed in the box below.

also, both, like	for example, in conclusion
same, too, whereas	because, next, but
though, but, however	while, first of all, finally
instead, unlike, yet	in addition, in any case

Transition words are used to show the connection between what is written before the transition word and what is written after it. Read the two paragraphs below. The first paragraph does not use transitions; the second does use transitions.

Growing Flowers

Many people enjoy looking at flowers. Fewer people attempt to grow them. Some types of flowers are easier to grow than others. Roses are beautiful. Some people find them difficult to grow. They need fertilizer, pruning, and just the right soil. Daffodils are easy to grow. Daffodils are bulbs that can be planted in the fall and forgotten until spring, when their green tips push up through the earth. Orchids are much more difficult to grow than roses or daffodils. Roses and daffodils can live outdoors. Orchids must be kept indoors. They are sensitive and need just the right combination of sun, water, food, and temperature.

Growing Flowers

Many people enjoy looking at flowers, **though** fewer people attempt to grow them. Some types of flowers are easier to grow than others. **For instance**, roses are beautiful, **but** some people find them difficult to grow. They need fertilizer, pruning, and just the right soil. **Unlike** roses, daffodils are easy to grow. Daffodils are bulbs that can be planted in the fall and forgotten until spring, when their green tips push up through the earth. Orchids, **however**, are much more difficult to grow than either roses or daffodils. **Whereas** roses and daffodils can live outdoors, orchids generally must be kept indoors. Orchids are sensitive plants; **therefore,** they require just the right combination of sun, water, food, and temperature.

Notice how the addition of transition words makes the paragraph flow better. Transition words link the ideas in the paragraph, showing the connections between the different kinds of flowers.

Practice 6: Transitions

Read the student's composition below. Then answer the questions that follow.

Should Schools Continue to Offer P.E.?

1. Some people are starting to question whether or not schools should continue to offer physical education (P.E.). **2.** These people say that more time should be spent working on subjects like math and English to bring up test scores. **3.** They say that our P.E. time should be used for the main school subjects instead. . **4.** However, there are reasons that P.E. is important to students.

5. I feel strongly that P.E. should continue to be offered in all schools. **6.** While I agree that math and English are a priority, P.E. provides important benefits to students. **7.** First of all, P.E. provides a welcome break from all of the sitting still we must do in school. **8.** P.E. also provides some kids with the only exercise they get. **9.** In P.E., we learn sports skills, which have inspired some of us to join after school teams. **10.** Both of these reasons should be enough with all that we hear about combating childhood obesity. **11.** In addition, P.E. teaches sportsmanship skills. **12.** _____, P.E. gives some kids who are better at sports than at math and English a chance to succeed.

13. School subjects are important, but PE provides benefits that math and English cannot. **14.** Let's keep P.E. in our schools.

1. Which of the following is a transition word found in sentence 6?
   A. priority   B. also   C. while   D. P.E.

2. In sentence 11, what reason does the writer give for supporting P.E.?
   A. It provides exercise.   C. It is a break from sitting still.
   B. It teaches sportsmanship skills.   D. It is just as important as academics.

3. Which of the following would be the best choice of transition words to fill in the blank in sentence 12?
   A. Finally   B. For example   C. However   D. Although

4. Which statement would the writer most likely agree with?
   A. Time spent in P.E. could be better used doing academics.
   B. P.E. is a valuable part of the school day.
   C. Test scores will go up if more time is spent doing P.E.
   D. Academics suffer because of P.E.

5. In the first paragraph, where is a transition word used?
   A. sentence 2
   B. sentence 3
   C. sentence 4
   D. There is no transition word.

6. What transition phrase is used in sentence 7?
   A. First of all
   B. from all
   C. must do
   D. There is no transition phrase.

CHAPTER 2 SUMMARY

Understanding how to organize information helps us to make sense of the world around us. When we organize information, we can find out things like why events happened, how events are related, how things are alike and different, and the relationships between things and ideas. Knowing this information helps us to see connections, analyze information, and understand what we are reading.

Review the following concepts covered in this chapter:

- **Logical order:** the order in which events happen or a sensible way to describe what happened
- **Cause and effect:** exploring why things happen and what happens as a result
- **Comparison and contrast:** examining how two things are alike and different
- **Transitions:** the words or phrases that indicate a change from one idea to the next

CHAPTER 2 REVIEW

Read the following account of the life cycle of a frog. Then answer the questions that follow.

The Life Cycle of a Frog

A frog undergoes amazing changes as it develops from an egg to an adult frog. Frogs begin as eggs. Eggs are generally laid in the water by female frogs in batches of thousands. In about a week, the eggs hatch and continue life as tadpoles. Tadpoles live underwater, breathe with gills, and swim with the help of their tails. At the end of this phase, the tadpoles undergo metamorphosis as they transition to the form of adult frogs. In this transition, they develop four legs, they lose their gills, and they develop lungs. At the final part of the tadpole stage, they lose their tails. The final result is an adult frog.

1. How does a frog begin life?

    A.   as a tadpole   C.   as a full-grown frog
    B.   as an egg   D.   by using metamorphosis

2. What is the second stage in the frog's development?
    A.   The female frog lays eggs.   C.   The frog develops lungs.
    B.   The tadpole's tail disappears.   D.   The egg becomes a tadpole.

3. What happens at the final stage of the tadpole phase?
    A.   The tadpole turns back into an egg.   C.   The tadpole swims about with two legs.
    B.   The tadpole loses its tail.   D.   The eggs are eaten by predators.

4. What is the proper order of the four stages of development for a frog?
    A.   tadpole, frog, egg   C.   egg, frog, tadpole
    B.   frog, tadpole, egg   D.   egg, tadpole, frog

Read the following account of the Exxon Valdez oil spill. Then answer the questions that follow.

The Exxon Valdez Oil Spill

The Exxon Valdez oil spill was one of the worst oil spills in history. On March 24, 1989, the oil tanker Exxon Valdez struck a reef near Alaska, spilling millions of gallons of oil into the sea. The captain had changed the ship's course slightly because of some icebergs in the ship's path. He gave his third mate instructions about getting back on course and then went to bed. When the third mate turned the ship back on course after the icebergs, he did not turn sharply enough and, as a result, the ship struck the reef.

When the oil spilled into the ocean, it killed thousands of sea animals such as birds and seals immediately. Billions of salmon and herring eggs were destroyed. In the years that followed, animals continued to die as they ate contaminated prey. Consequently, the populations of these animals were reduced.

While billions of dollars and great efforts were spent cleaning up the area, the disaster impacted the environment for years afterward.

5. What caused the captain to change the ship's course?
    A. He was trying to avoid a storm
    B. He was tired and wanted to go to bed.
    C. He wanted to keep the ship from hitting the icebergs.
    D. He wanted to give the third mate practice steering

6. What caused animals to continue dying in the years after the oil spill?
    A. They ate contaminated prey.   C. The animals began to live in the oil.
    B. There was another oil spill.   D. The oil was never cleaned up.

7. What was the effect of the oil destroying billions of salmon and herring eggs?
    A. The population of both animals was reduced.
    B. The oil was soaked up in the destroyed eggs.
    C. The fish born from the eggs were smaller than normal.
    D. The cleanup of the spilled oil was more difficult.

8. What was the effect of the third mate not steering the ship properly back on course?
    A. The ship struck a reef.
    B. The third mate turned the ship too little.
    C. The captain was tired.
    D. The herring population is now back to normal.

Read the paragraph below. Then answer the questions that follow.

Is Venus Really Earth's Twin?

Venus, second planet from the sun and Earth's next-door neighbor, is often called Earth's twin. But how alike are these two planets really? To begin with, the planets are similar in size. They also have similar gravity and composition. Both also have volcanic activity. However, this is where similarities end. While both planets have clouds, Venus is covered with such a thick blanket of clouds that it is much hotter than Earth. As a result of the clouds, Venus has much higher levels of carbon dioxide than Earth. In addition, Earth has one moon and Venus has none. Though Venus may be more like Earth than the other planets, the two planets are actually quite different.

9. What are two ways Venus and Earth are similar?
    A. their clouds and their temperatures
    B. their sizes and their gravity
    C. their moons and their volcanoes
    D. their position in space and their moons

10. What are two ways Venus and Earth are different?
    A. their size and the number of moons they have
    B. their volcanoes and their gravity
    C. their moons and their levels of carbon dioxide
    D. their shape and clouds

11. What best describes the main point about the two planets?
    A. They are more alike than different.   C. They are equally alike and different.
    B. They are more different than alike.   D. The writer does not make a point.

12. What transition words appear in this paragraph?
    A. Venus, Earth, clouds, volcanoes   C. moons, planets, however, different
    B. but, however, in addition, though   D. alike, however, higher, clouds

13. Create a comparison and contrast graphic organizer using the information in the paragraph about Venus and Earth. When you are done, evaluate the graphic organizer and decide whether or not you agree with the writer. Explain your answer in 1–2 sentences.

14. On the Internet, find an article on Wikipedia, Microsoft Encarta, or World Book on one of the following topics:

    a famous person   beach erosion

    hummingbirds   snow

    Okefenokee Swamp   air pollution

    Atlanta Braves   MySpace

Then answer these questions:

    A. Give two reasons why you enjoyed reading the article.
    B. List two effects on you of reading the article.

15. You are making a movie about one of the following:
    A. the time you lost and then found something
    B. your best birthday party
    C. your first roller coaster ride
    D. a scary night

Think about and then list the events in the movie. Using logical order, write them in 1–2 paragraphs. Then film your movie and show it to the class. If you cannot make a film, draw out the story on paper and share it in class.

Chapter 3
Analyzing Features of Informational Texts

This chapter covers the following Georgia standard.

ELA7R1	Analyze common textual features to obtain information (including paragraphs, topic sentences, concluding sentences, introduction, conclusion, footnotes, index, bibliography).

What caused dodo birds to become extinct? Is there a solution to urban sprawl? Is animal testing ever worthwhile?

What do all of these ideas have in common? All of them are topics for the presentation of informational texts. One of the most effective ways of presenting information is to explain the results of research on a particular topic. A **research paper** is a formal paper in which an author presents research findings along with his own ideas. An author writing a research paper begins with his own thoughts on a topic. He then gathers and interprets data from a variety of sources. Next, an author develops and organizes his ideas. Finally, he presents his conclusions and cites his sources. The resulting paper

Dodo Bird

is a unique document in which the author uses facts and explanations to support his ideas.

Research papers follow a standard structure. The first section of a research paper is the **introduction**. The body of the paper follows, which consists of **paragraphs** (each with a **topic sentence, supporting sentences**, and a **concluding sentence**). **Footnotes** are also used in this section. The last section of the paper is the **conclusion**. In a separate section at the end of the paper is a **bibliography**.

INTRODUCTION

The **introduction** is the first section of a research paper. In the introduction, the author first gives some background on the topic. He might do this by providing history on his topic or by tracing the beginnings of the debate he will focus on.

Next, the author states the main point he will make in his paper. This is called the **thesis**. The thesis statement is one of the most important sentences in the research paper. The thesis statement is like a road map for the paper. It tells the reader what to expect from the rest of the research paper.

In some research papers, the author's goal is to persuade the reader to agree with him on an issue. Perhaps he is arguing that stem cell research is unethical. In this kind of paper, the thesis statement is the author's opinion on an issue.

In other papers, the author is seeking to answer why something happened or informing the reader about a topic. Perhaps he is discussing the effects pioneers had on the seasonal movements of Native Americans. In this kind of paper, the thesis statement is the main idea the author will discuss in his paper.

In both kinds of papers, the author spends the remainder of his paper developing his ideas and supporting his thesis. He does this by providing examples that show the logic of his ideas.

Here is an example of Henry's introductory paragraph about cell phones.

 Since consumers began using cell phones in the late 1980s, millions of Americans have adopted cell phones as a convenient way to keep in touch. While most Americans agree that cell phones are convenient, there is much debate about the use of cell phones while driving. It should be against the law to use a cell phone while driving. Drivers talking on cell phones pay more attention to their conversations than to their driving, which creates an unsafe environment for all motorists.

The author begins with background information:

"Since consumers began using cell phones in the late 1980s, millions of Americans have adopted cell phones as a convenient way to keep in touch."

Then he introduces the issue:

"While most Americans agree that cell phones are convenient, there is much debate about the use of cell phones while driving."

Next, he states his thesis:

"It should be against the law to use a cell phone while driving."

Finally, he gives a brief idea of how he will prove his thesis:

"Drivers talking on cell phones pay more attention to their conversations than to their driving, which creates an unsafe environment for all motorists."

Practice 1: Analyzing an Introduction

Read the introduction below. Then answer the questions that follow.

 Rising consumer awareness has led to increased attention about the safety and quality of the foods we eat. People have begun to question the amounts of pesticides that make their way into conventional foods and the effects these pesticides have on our health. They are also questioning the health implications of genetically modified food. As a result of these concerns, more and more Americans are turning to organic foods. People like organic foods because they perceive "organic" to mean safer and healthier.

1. Which of these sentences does the author use to provide background information?

    A.   As a result of these concerns, more and more Americans are turning to organic foods.

    B.   Rising consumer awareness has led to increased attention about the safety and quality of the foods we eat.

    C.   People like organic foods because they perceive "organic" to mean safer and healthier.

    D.   They are also questioning the health implications of genetically modified food.

2. What is the author's thesis statement?

    A.   As a result of these concerns, more and more Americans are turning to organic foods.

    B.   People have begun to question the amounts of pesticides that make their way into conventional foods and the effects these pesticides have on our health.

    C.   Rising consumer awareness has led to increased attention about the safety and quality of the foods we eat.

    D.   People like organic foods because they perceive "organic" to mean safer and healthier.

3. Which of these examples would the author be MOST LIKELY to use in his research paper?

    A.   a debate between diners at an organic foods restaurant

    B.   a list of brands which claim to be organic but are not

    C.   a timeline showing the history of organic food production in Greece

    D.   statistics showing the increase in sales of organic foods over the past 10 years

4. Which statement BEST describes the way the author feels about his topic?

    A.   He believes that organic foods are overrated.

    B.   He thinks that Americans have been slow to adopt organic foods.

    C.   He wants lawsuits brought against farmers who use pesticides.

    D.   He feels that consumers perceive organic foods as healthy.

PARAGRAPHS

After the introduction comes the body of the paper. This is a series of **paragraphs** in which the author supports the thesis by presenting ideas and evidence. A **paragraph** is a group of 3–6 sentences focusing on one idea. A well-constructed paragraph follows this structure:

> 1. Topic sentence
>
> 2. Supporting sentences
>
> 3. Concluding sentence

The **topic sentence** tells the reader what the paragraph will be about. It is often the first sentence in a paragraph.

Supporting sentences follow the topic sentence. Every sentence in a paragraph must support the topic sentence. Supporting sentences provide examples that support the idea in the topic sentence.

The **concluding sentence** is the final sentence in a paragraph. It sums up the main idea of the paragraph. In the concluding sentence, the author restates the topic sentence using different words and ties all of the ideas of the paragraph together.

Read the following paragraph about high diving as it is broken down into its three parts:

Topic sentence:

Learning to high dive is very exciting.

Supporting sentences:

It is thrilling to climb the tall ladder to the diving board. At the top, the board quivers a little as you walk to the end. As you stand preparing to dive, you look toward the pool far below. How can you leap out into space? Then you jump, twisting in the air and pointing head first to the oncoming water.

Concluding sentence:

As you swoosh into the pool, it is exhilarating to know that you had the daring and skill to do a perfect dive.

Notice that the topic sentence is the first sentence in the paragraph. Notice that each supporting sentence backs up the topic sentence by describing the thrills involved in high diving. The concluding sentence ties the examples into the topic sentence, finishing the description smoothly.

Practice 2: Identifying Topic Sentences, Supporting Sentences, and Concluding Sentences

Read the following paragraphs. Then answer the questions that follow each one.

Honey bees are important producers of two commonly used substances. Honey bees produce both honey and wax. Bees make honey by collecting and processing nectar, then storing it in honeycombs. Many people use honey when baking, as a spread for toast or in their tea. Bees also make wax, which they use to store the honey and construct their homes.   People use beeswax to make candles, cosmetics, and shoe polish.

1.   Which of the following would be the BEST concluding sentence for this paragraph?

   A.   Honey bees are important contributors to many commonly used products and foods.
   B.   Honey bees sting, and some people are extremely allergic to bee stings.
   C.   Beeswax melts at about 145 degrees F, which makes it a good preservative.
   D.   Honey bees begin their lives as eggs, and when they hatch, they can fly right away.

2. Which of these is a supporting sentence found in the paragraph?
   A. Many people use honey when baking, as a spread for toast or in their tea.
   B. Honey bees are important producers of two commonly used substances.
   C. People use beeswax to make candles, cosmetics, and shoe polish.
   D. Both A and C

 Volcanic ash is just as dangerous as lava. While some people think of a volcano as spewing lava which endangers nearby residents, volcanic ash can affect not only people living close to the volcano but also those living farther away. Ash is made up of fine rock and mineral particles. Ash mixes with air and drifts farther from the volcano than lava can reach. Inhaled ash can damage the lungs. Volcanic ash is especially dangerous to those who have breathing conditions such as asthma. In addition, ash mixed with rocks and gases can flow in an avalanche down a volcano's sides, moving faster than people can run.

3. What is the topic sentence in this paragraph?
   A. Volcanic ash is especially dangerous to those who have breathing conditions such as asthma
   B. In addition, ash mixed with rocks and gases can flow in an avalanche down a volcano's sides, moving faster than people can run.
   C. Ash mixes with air and drifts farther from the volcano than lava can reach.
   D. Volcanic ash is just as dangerous as lava.

4. Which of the following would be the BEST concluding sentence for this paragraph?
   A. Volcanic ash can make the air smell like sulfur.
   B. Volcanic ash in the air can create beautiful sunsets.
   C. Volcanic ash can have deadly consequences.
   D. A volcano is an opening in the earth's surface.

_____. In Greek mythology, a rainbow was considered a path between Heaven and Earth. The Bible shows the rainbow as symbolic of God's promise to Noah to never again flood the entire Earth. Irish leprechauns are said to hide their pots of gold at the end of rainbows. Many cultures used legends to explain the beautiful phenomenon of rainbows.

5. Which of the following would be the BEST topic sentence to add to the blank line at the start of this paragraph?
    A. For years, people have debated the existence of rainbows.
    B. Rainbows are multicolored arcs in the sky.
    C. Rainbows have been the subject of legends for centuries.
    D. Occasionally, a double rainbow forms.

6. Which of these is the concluding sentence in this paragraph?
    A. Many cultures used legends to explain the beautiful phenomenon of rainbows.
    B. In Greek mythology, a rainbow was considered a path between Heaven and Earth.
    C. Irish leprechauns are said to hide their pots of gold at the end of rainbows.
    D. The Bible shows the rainbow as symbolic of God's promise to Noah to never again flood the entire Earth.

George Washington Carver was a botanist and professor who made lasting discoveries and contributions involving peanuts. _____. He is also credited with using peanuts to help farmers improve poor-quality soil. Carver taught southern farmers that growing peanuts would help enrich soil with nitrogen which would, in turn, help other crops grow.

7. Which of the following would be a logical supporting sentence to add to the blank line in this paragraph?
    A. The year of Carver's birth is subject to debate.
    B. Carver taught for years at Alabama's Tuskegee University.
    C. Carver is famous for developing hundreds of uses for peanuts.
    D. After discovering a variety of ways to use peanuts, Carver died in 1943.

8. Which of the following would make the BEST concluding sentence for this paragraph?
    A. George Washington Carver was famous during his lifetime.
    B. He left few formulas of procedures written down for people to use later.
    C. George Washington Carver was born into slavery in Missouri.
    D. Many of Carver's uses for peanuts continue to be used today.

FOOTNOTES

An author can use **footnotes**, which are notes at the bottom of pages, in several ways. The definition of specific words can appear in footnotes. They might also explain complex ideas or unfamiliar terms.

When researching a topic for a paper, an author might use statistics, historical documents, surveys, and other research articles. An author uses this information in his paper to prove his thesis statement. When using facts or opinions of others, an author can give the source of this information by using footnotes.

Footnotes are numbered. Within the text, a number is written in superscript format just after the part of the text the footnote is referencing. The corresponding number is then written at the bottom of the page.

When an author uses footnotes for citations, the specific information about the source follows this number. Then a reader has this information and can go to the original source if he wants more information.

Read the paragraph about baby-naming trends in America. Note the superscripted "1" within the text.

> Baby-naming trends tend to last a few years before other names start to become more popular. For example, from 1999 to 2005, Jacob was the most popular boy's name in the United States.[1] Based on past trends, it was replaced in a few years by the boy's name that is currently most popular.

Here is how the footnote would appear at the bottom of the page:

[1] Social Security Administration's Baby Names Page, 4 Jan. 2007, Social Security Administration, 25 Feb. 2007 <http://www.ssa.gov/cgi-bin/babyname.cgi>.

There are a few different formats used for footnotes. The examples here are shown in Modern Language Association (MLA) style. You can visit www.mla.org for more information on this style. When writing your own research paper, you can ask your teacher which style to use.

Footnotes follow a very specific format. The format depends on what type of source an author is referencing. Here are some common sources and the format for citing each.

Book with one author or editor:

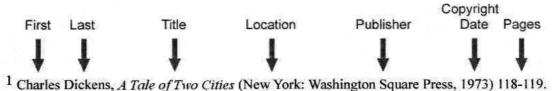

[1] Charles Dickens, *A Tale of Two Cities* (New York: Washington Square Press, 1973) 118-119.

Article from a magazine, journal, or newspaper with one or more authors:

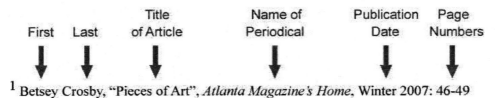

[1] Betsey Crosby, "Pieces of Art", *Atlanta Magazine's Home*, Winter 2007: 46-49

Interview:

[1] Adeline Smith, Personal Interview, 28 Feb. 2007.

Internet:

[1] "1968: Black Athletes Make Silent Protest", 17 Oct. 1968, bbc.co.uk, 25 Feb. 2007
<http://news.bbc.co.uk/onthisday/hi/dates/stories/october/17/news1d_3535000/3535348.stm>.

Web Address

Practice 3: Analyzing Footnotes

Read the footnotes below. Then answer the questions that follow.

[2] **Joanna Cole, *The Magic School Bus on the Ocean Floor* (: Scholastic, 1992).**

1. What piece of information is missing in this book's footnote?
    A. the location   C. the author
    B. the publisher   D. the date

2. What is the author's first name?
    A. Cole   B. Ocean   C. Scholastic   D. Joanna

[6] **Barnaby Feder, "In the Stent Era, Heart Bypasses Get a New Look," 25 Feb. 2007, New York Times, 27 Feb. 2007 <http://www.nytimes.com/2007/02/25/health/25bypass.html>.**

3. What is the title of this article that was found on the Internet?
    A. Barnaby Feder
    B. New York Times
    C. In the Stent Era, Heart Bypasses Get a New Look
    D. www.nytimes.com/2007/02/25/health/25bypass.html

4. On what date was the article published?
    A. February 26, 2006   C. August 12, 1995
    B. February 25, 2007   D. February 27, 2006

CONCLUSION

The **conclusion** is the final section of the research paper. In the conclusion, the author shows how his examples worked together to support his thesis. An author uses the conclusion to show why the paper he wrote was useful and meaningful.

Look back at the example of an introductory paragraph about cell phones at the beginning of this chapter. Here is the conclusion to the paper about cell phone use while driving.

> The statistics are overwhelming: driving while talking on a cell phone causes accidents. There is substantial evidence showing the increase in motor vehicle accidents when drivers are talking on cell phones. Lawmakers have a responsibility to enact legislation which bans cell phone use while driving. Cell phones are a convenient way to keep in touch, but their use should be limited to times when they will not endanger lives.

Notice how the conclusion echoes the introduction. Notice how the author sums up his argument (that cell phones are dangerous to use while driving) in light of the evidence he presented (he references the statistics he presented earlier in the paper).

Practice 4: Analyzing Conclusions

Read the conclusion paragraph to the paper about organic food. Then answer the questions that follow.

Laboratory testing has revealed pesticides in some of the most common conventional foods that we eat. New developments in genetically modified food have led many to ask what health implications these modified foods might have for consumers. Concern over the safety of conventional foods has led more and more Americans to demand safer foods. They see organic foods as a solution. The more stringent standards used for producing foods that are certified organic are leading many people to demand organic foods as a safe way to feed their families.

1. What evidence did the author LIKELY use to support the thesis in this research paper?
   A. an advertisement for a new kind of orange juice
   B. scientists' opinions on whether or not animals should be used for research
   C. a quote from a history book on the first crops grown in America
   D. results of testing for pesticide levels in common conventional foods

2. From reading the author's conclusion, what can you tell was the thesis for this paper?
   A. Many Americans see organic foods as a solution to declining food safety.
   B. Stringent production standards make conventional food safest.
   C. Genetically modified foods are just as safe as conventional foods.
   D. All conventional foods are dangerous to eat.

3. What does the author say has led many Americans to demand safer foods?
   A. Research about the pesticides used to keep worms out of apples.
   B. The opinions of farmers who can't afford to produce organic foods.
   C. Concern over the health implications of pesticides and genetically modified foods.
   D. Concern about cloned sheep.

4. According to the author, why do people believe organic foods to be safer than conventional foods?
   A. There is more variety of organic produce than conventional produce.
   B. Organic milk tastes best.
   C. More stringent standards are followed when producing organic foods.
   D. Organic food growers are lying to consumers.

BIBLIOGRAPHY

The **bibliography** is a separate section at the end of a research paper. A bibliography is a list of the sources the author used in his paper. As with footnotes, an author provides specific information in the bibliography about each source. Also like footnotes, bibliographies have a specific format. Every source listed in a footnote should appear in the bibliography. Bibliographies are presented in alphabetical order by author's last name. The following examples are shown using the MLA format.

Book with one author or editor:

Dickens, Charles. *A Tale of Two Cities*. New York: Washington Square Press, 1973.

Article from a magazine, journal, or newspaper with one or more authors:

Crosby, Betsey. "Pieces of Art." *Atlanta Magazine's Home.* Winter 2007: 46-49.

Interview:

Smith, Adeline. Interview. 28 Feb. 2007.

Internet

"1968:BlackAthletesMakeSilentProtest."17Oct.1968.Bbc.co.uk.25Feb.2007. <http://news.bbc.co.uk/onthisday/hi/dates/stories/october/17/newsid_3535000/3535348.stm>.

Notice how the format of entries in the bibliography is very similar to the format of footnotes. Notable differences include the use of the author's last name first, the lack of a footnote number at the beginning, and the replacement of periods.

Practice 5: Bibliographies

Read the bibliography entries below. Then answer the questions that follow.

McPherson, James M. *Battle Cry of Freedom: The Civil War Era*. New York: Oxford UP, 1988.

1. What is the title of the book listed in the entry above?

    A. *Battle Cry of Freedom: The Civil War Era*
    B. New York
    C. James McPherson
    D. The Civil War Era

2. In what year was the book written?
    A. 1998   B. 1988   C. Oxford   D. 1888

Gorman, Christine. "The Fight Over Food Labels." *TIME* **15 July 1991: 52-56.**

3. In what magazine did the above article appear?
    A. 15 July 1991   C. *The New York Times*
    B. "The Fight Over Food Labels"   D. *TIME*

4. In what month was this article published?
    A. January   B. July   C. June   D. September

5. If both of the above entries were listed in a bibliography, which would come first and why?
    A. Christine Gorman's, as entries are alphabetical by last name.
    B. James McPherson's, as books are more important than magazine articles.
    C. Christine Gorman's, as entries are alphabetical by first name.
    D. Christine Gorman's, as women authors are listed before men.

CHAPTER 3 SUMMARY

One way to present ideas or opinions about a topic is in a **research paper**. Research papers follow a logical order which helps an author keep ideas clear to the reader.

Sections of a research paper:

The **introduction** provides **background** and includes the **thesis statement**.

Paragraphs follow, in which the author presents **ideas** and **evidence**. Paragraphs follow this format:

- **Topic sentence**—tells what the paragraph is about
- **Supporting sentences**—provide examples that support the topic sentence
- **Concluding sentence**—sums up the main idea of the paragraph
- The **conclusion** demonstrates why the paper was useful and meaningful.
- **Footnotes** and **bibliographies** identify the sources an author consulted for the paper.

CHAPTER 3 REVIEW

Read the research paper. Then answer the questions that follow.

Smoking Should be Banned in Restaurants

Smoking causes a host of illnesses, from heart disease to emphysema to cancer. Studies have shown that smoking affects the health not only of smokers but also of nonsmokers who breathe in secondhand smoke. While many laws are in place prohibiting smoking in public places such as malls and offices, some areas have passed stricter smoking bans to include restaurants. Smoking should be banned in all restaurants in America. Smoking bans in restaurants will protect the health of nonsmokers who are unwillingly exposed to cigarette smoke.

Secondhand smoke is dangerous to nonsmokers. The Center for Disease Control in Atlanta states, "Each year, primarily because of exposure to secondhand smoke, an estimated 3,000 nonsmoking Americans die of lung cancer, and more than 35,000 die of heart disease."[1] In most areas of the country, restaurant diners are exposed to secondhand smoke whether they like it or not. When studies prove that secondhand smoke is dangerous, why should nonsmokers have to suffer the health risks of cigarette smoke while enjoying a restaurant meal?

Smoking bans in restaurants improve air quality and create a safer atmosphere for diners. A 2004 study showed that in New Jersey, restaurants had more than nine times the levels of indoor air pollution of neighboring New York City, which had enacted smoking bans.[2] According to Andrew Hyland, Ph.D., principal investigator for the study, "the results indicate that the levels of pollution in the New Jersey establishments were almost entirely caused by tobacco smoke."[3] Banning smoking in restaurants would eliminate the health risks to diners from polluting smoke.

Footnotes

[1] "Targeting Tobacco Use: The Nation's Leading Cause of Death," July 2006, Centers for Disease Control and Prevention, 26 Jan. 2007 < http://www.cdc.gov/nccdphp/publications/aag/osh.htm>

[2] "Study Finds That New Jersey Bars and Restaurants Have Nine Times More Air Pollution than Those in Smoke-Free New York," 14 Dec. 2004, University of Medicine & Dentistry of New Jersey, 1 March 2007 <http://www.umdnj.edu/about/news_events/releases/04/r041214_bars.htm>

[3] "Study Finds That New Jersey Bars and Restaurants Have Nine Times More Air Pollution than Those in Smoke-Free New York," 14 Dec. 2004, University of Medicine & Dentistry of New Jersey, 1 March 2007 <http://www.umdnj.edu/about/news_events/releases/04/r041214_bars.htm>

Opponents say that nonsmokers can choose to go to restaurants that voluntarily ban smoking. But why should nonsmokers have to limit where they eat out in order to avoid a dangerous substance? This is not fair to people who choose a healthier lifestyle. Many lawmakers agree and have passed laws to eliminate smoking in restaurants. As of January 1, 2003, there were 961 local ordinances across the country that restricted smoking in restaurants. [4] Nonsmokers have a right to be protected by law from hazardous substances.

Cigarette smoke is a hazardous substance. Studies have proven that secondhand smoke causes disease and that banning smoking can eliminate air pollution in restaurants. Lawmakers have a responsibility to protect nonsmokers from this dangerous substance by banning smoking in restaurants.

Footnote

[4]"Rights of Nonsmokers," January 2003, Americans for Nonsmokers' Rights, 12 Feb. 2007 <http://no-smoke.org/pdf/rights.pdf>

1. Which of these sentences from the introduction provides background information about the topic?

    A. Cigarette smoke is a hazardous substance.
    B. This is not fair to people who choose a healthier lifestyle.
    C. Smoking causes a host of illnesses, from heart disease to emphysema to cancer.
    D. Many lawmakers agree and have passed laws to eliminate smoking in restaurants.

2. Which of these sentences is the thesis statement?

    A. Smoking should be banned in all restaurants in America.
    B. Nonsmokers have a right to be protected by law from hazardous substances.
    C. Opponents say that nonsmokers can choose to go to restaurants that voluntarily ban smoking.
    D. This is not fair to people who choose a healthier lifestyle.

3. Which of these sentences is the topic sentence for the second paragraph?

    A. Cigarette smoke is a hazardous substance.
    B. Secondhand smoke is dangerous to nonsmokers.
    C. In most areas of the country, restaurant diners are exposed to secondhand smoke whether they like it or not.
    D. As of January 1, 2003, there were 961 local ordinances across the country that restricted smoking in restaurants [4].

4. Which of these sentences is a supporting sentence in the second paragraph?

    A. When studies prove that secondhand smoke is dangerous, why should nonsmokers have to suffer the health risks of cigarette smoke while enjoying a restaurant meal?

    B. While many laws are in place prohibiting smoking in public places such as malls and offices, some areas have passed stricter smoking bans to include restaurants.

    C. The Center for Disease Control in Atlanta states, "Each year, primarily because of exposure to secondhand smoke, an estimated 3,000 nonsmoking Americans die of lung cancer, and more than 35,000 die of heart disease.[1]"

    D. Nonsmokers have a right to be protected by law from hazardous substances.

5. Which of these statements BEST describes the topic of the third paragraph?

    A. Smoke poses health risks to everyone who breathes it in.

    B. Lawmakers have been slow to ban smoking in restaurants.

    C. It is unconstitutional to ban smoking in restaurants.

    D. Eliminating smoke in restaurants creates a safer atmosphere in the restaurant.

6. Which of the following sentences in the third paragraph has a footnote?

    A. Banning smoking in restaurants would eliminate the health risks to diners from polluting smoke.

    B. A 2004 study showed that in New Jersey, restaurants had more than nine times the levels of indoor air pollution of neighboring New York City, which had enacted smoking bans[2].

    C. Cigarette smoke is a hazardous substance.

    D. Smoking bans in restaurants improve air quality and create a safer atmosphere for diners.

7. What is the title of the article from which the first footnote comes?

    A. "Targeting Tobacco Use: The Nation's Leading Cause of Death"

    B. "Rights of Nonsmokers"

    C. Americans for Nonsmokers' Rights

    D. 26 Jan. 2007

8. Which of the following is the concluding sentence in the fourth paragraph?

    A. Smoking bans in restaurants will protect the health of nonsmokers who are unwillingly exposed to cigarette smoke.

    B. As of January 1, 2003, there were 961 local ordinances across the country that restricted smoking in restaurants[4].

    C. Nonsmokers have a right to be protected by law from hazardous substances.

    D. Cigarette smoke is a hazardous substance.

9. In the conclusion, which of the following is a point the author restates as support for his thesis?

    A. Cigarettes smell terrible.

    B. Cigarette smoke causes disease in nonsmokers.

    C. Cigarettes stain smokers' fingers.

    D. Lawmakers have overstepped their bounds in making anti-smoking laws.

10. Which of the following sources will the author list in the bibliography?

    A. Centers for Disease Control and Prevention

    B. University of Medicine & Dentistry of New Jersey

    C. Americans for Nonsmokers' Rights

    D. All of the above

Chapter 4
Analyzing the Author's Argument

This chapter covers the following Georgia standards.

ELA7R1	Recognize and trace the development of the author's argument for and against an issue.
	Identify evidence used to support an argument.
ELA7RC2	Examine the author's purpose in writing.

We encounter **persuasive** language almost every day. A commercial tries to persuade you to buy a new video game. Your mother tries to persuade you to spend more time studying rather than watching television. In **persuasive writing**, an author attempts to convince the reader that the author's viewpoint is correct or that the reader should take the course of action that the author recommends.

Persuasive writing follows a logical order using the following steps:

Step 1: The author states his opinion on an issue.

This is called making a claim.

Step 2: The author gives examples to support his opinion.

This is called proving a claim.

Step 3: The author discusses how the examples prove his point and addresses opposing viewpoints.

This is called building an argument.

PREPARE FOR YOUR END OF COURSE AND EXIT EXAMS!

Let us Diagnose your needs and Provide instruction with our EASY TO USE books!

tutor
Vista

World Class Tutoring,
A Click Away

Through a unique partnership with **TutorVista**, American Book Company now offers a **Diagnostic Test** that students can take **On-Line**. Test results are e-mailed to the teacher and the student and are graded with references to chapters in our book that will help reinforce the areas that are missed. It's 100% free, it takes the work out of hand grading, and it provides a specific prescription for improving students' performance on state and national assessments.

SIMPLY FOLLOW THESE 3 STEPS:

❶ Teachers, provide students with the book's ISBN number and your e-mail address. Then have them go to **www.americanbookcompany.com/tutorvista** and take the FREE On-Line Diagnostic Test.

❷ Teachers, determine the best way to use the Diagnostic Test results for your students and classes.

❸ Students can use their FREE 2 HOUR TutorVista session to address specific needs and maximize their learning.

We are very excited about this new avenue for test preparation and hope you join us in this opportunity to improve student learning. If you have any questions about TutorVista or the processes explained above, please feel free to contact a customer representative by e-mail at **info@tutorvista.com** or by phone at **1-866-617-6020**.

You may also go to **www.americanbookcompany.com/tutorvista/diagnostic** for ideas and suggestions on how to effectively use this service for students and schools.

PO Box 2638 ★ Woodstock, GA 30188-1383 ★ Phone: 1-888-264-5877 ★ Fax: 1-866-827-3240
Web Site: www.americanbookcompany.com ★ E-mail: contact@americanbookcompany.com

STEP 1: MAKING A CLAIM

When an author writes persuasively, his first step is to make a **claim**. In the video game commercial, the claim is that this new game is so fantastic that you must buy it and play it immediately. In your conversation with your mother, her claim is that your schoolwork is more important than television. In writing, the claim is the point the author wants you to agree with or action he wants you to take.

An author's claim is not merely a statement of fact. A claim is an author's **opinion** about an issue that not everyone agrees on. Whereas facts can easily be proven by looking in an encyclopedia or a textbook or by reading studies that have been done about the topic, claims are open for debate.

Here is an example of each type of statement.

Example: Fact

"I am 14 years old," said Steven.

This is a statement of fact. Steven can prove his statement by producing his birth certificate or by calling on his mother to support what he said.

Example: Claim

"Being 14 years old is better than being 15 years old," said Steven.

This is an opinion. Not everyone will agree with Steven. Others might have different opinions and different reasons for feeling as they do. While Steven can give reasons why he feels as he does, there is no quick and easy way to prove what he says.

Practice 1: Identifying a Claim

Read the following sentences. Then identify which sentences make a claim and which ones state a fact.

1. Spring is the best season.
    A.   fact   B.   claim

2. Spring is a time when many types of flowers begin to bloom.
    A.   fact   B.   claim

3. Math is easier than science.
    A.   fact   B.   claim

4. Math and science are both subjects that 7th graders study.
    A.   fact   B.   claim

5. Abraham Lincoln was the country's 16th president.
    A.   fact   B.   claim

6. Abraham Lincoln was America's greatest president.
    A.   fact   B.   claim

STEP 2: PROVING A CLAIM

Once an author makes a claim, he then must prove his claim. He does this by presenting **evidence** that he believes will make his readers agree with him. **Evidence** is the **proof** an author uses to support the claim he has made. The author's topic and audience dictate the best kind of proof to use. In a history paper, the author might use speeches or maps to support his claim. In a letter to the governor of Georgia about gun control, a constituent might use statistics to support a claim.

To choose the best evidence to support a claim, an author must consider and address the following issues:

Who is the audience?

Who is reading your paper? What will work best to convince them?

What evidence is best to use in this particular case?

What kind of evidence best supports your claim? Statistics? Surveys?

Quotes from experts on the topic?

Considering the audience

Who are you addressing in your persuasive paper, letter or conversation? Is it your parents? Your best friend? A teacher? The president of the United States? Whoever your answer is, that is your **audience**.

Who your audience is makes a difference when you are deciding the best way to prove your claim. Different audiences have different ideas about what is important. You will therefore need to use different types of evidence to convince different types of audiences. By defining who your audience is and anticipating what is important to them, you can choose the examples that will be most powerful in influencing their opinions.

For example, say you are trying to convince people to eat healthier. You want to persuade people that apples are a better snack choice than potato chips.

When addressing an adult, you might point out how apples are a good source of nutrients and fiber. You could add that the fat in potato chips puts people who eat them at greater risk of heart disease.

When addressing a teenager, you might point out that apples provide more energy than junk food like chips. You could also add that chips are bad for the complexion.

All of the evidence given in this example is true. The trick is to think about what evidence is going to persuade your audience. Adults generally are not as concerned about their complexions as teenagers are. Most teenagers don't care about the fiber content of their foods.

Practice 2: Considering the Audience

Read the following statements. Then decide which audience the speaker is addressing.

1. If I were elected student council president, I would give all students a say in the school lunch menu.

    A.   parents
    B.   school administrators
    C.   students
    D.   7th grade teachers

2. If I were elected student council president, I would work with students and teachers to make sure students understood why teachers make the rules they do, and I would encourage students to follow those rules.

    A.   teachers
    B.   students
    C.   younger siblings of the students
    D.   college administrators

3. School sports teams should be all-girl or all-boy, not coed. Coed teams are too competitive because boys always try to show off.

    A.   boys on the teams
    B.   girls on the teams
    C.   parents
    D.   referees

4. School sports teams should be all-girl or all-boy, not coed. Coed teams are harder to coach because the girls and the boys more likely to socialize when they are together.

    A.   boys on the teams
    B.   girls on the teams
    C.   coaches
    D.   referees

USING EVIDENCE

Once you have identified your audience and decided what is important to them, you must present valid **evidence** which shows that you are right. Strong evidence is specific. It is from reputable sources. Depending on the topic, the evidence you present might be statistics, experts' opinions, historical documents, survey results, or studies. Not all evidence works well to support a claim. Evidence must be relevant to your claims.

Strong Evidence	Weak Evidence
• relevant examples	• examples that don't support your opinion
• quotes from people who are experts on the topic	• generalizations
• studies and statistics that show you are right	• vague claims
• personal experience	• unsupported opinions

Read the following claim and the two pieces of evidence that follow. Which piece of evidence best supports the claim?

Claim:

- Athletes should abstain from steroid use to protect their own health.

Evidence:

- Misuse of steroids increases a person's chances of contracting hepatitis and developing cancer and psychiatric problems.
- It's not fair to athletes who don't use steroids to compete against those who do.

 If you chose **#1**, you are right. **#1** gives specific examples of how misuse of steroids harms a person's health. **#2** does not support the claim. While it is a valid point in regard to steroid use by athletes, it does not prove the claim that athletes should stop using steroids in order to protect their own health.

Practice 3: Using Evidence

Read the claims below. Then choose the best evidence to support the claim.

1. **Claim:** Bicycle helmets should be mandatory for bikers aged 14 and under.

   A. Bike helmets come in many colors and styles, so looking silly is not an excuse.
   B. Bike helmets are more comfortable than ever.
   C. Bicyclists aged 14 and under are at greater risk for injury than older cyclists.
   D. Everyone should wear bike helmets at all times.

2. **Claim:** School uniforms make schools safer.

   A. Having all students dress in the same colors makes it harder to recognize friends.
   B. In Long Beach, California, fights decreased by 51% after uniforms were mandated.
   C. Uniforms are more durable than regular clothes.
   D. Most parents support the idea of school uniforms.

3. **Claim:** Abraham Lincoln was America's greatest president in regard to his work against slavery.
   A. Lincoln was born in a log cabin.
   B. Lincoln issued the Emancipation Proclamation, declaring all slaves free.
   C. Lincoln began his political career in 1832, at age 23
   D. Lincoln did many great things to help the people of this country.

4. **Claim:** Dad, you should help me buy a car as soon as I am able to drive.
   A. I could then drive myself and my younger brother to school instead of you always having to do it.
   B. I've heard that everybody else's parents will buy them cars this year.
   C. I only speed some of the time and stop at red lights.
   D. The driver's education course is very expensive.

STEP 3: BUILDING AN ARGUMENT

Once the author has made his claim and provided examples that prove his claim, he then provides his reasoning as to why his claim is correct. This process is called **building an argument**. The **argument** is the part of persuasive writing in which an author defends his claim in light of the evidence he has presented.

A common way to make an argument is to argue **for and against** an issue. In this type of argument, an author claims that his viewpoint on a controversial issue is the right one. The author will present strong evidence to support his own point of view. He will also address the other side's argument and do his best to debunk it.

Here is an example of an author arguing **for** single-gender schools. His goal is to convince his audience that his point of view is correct. Notice how he states his claim in the first sentence. He then provides specific examples that support his claim and discusses how each example proves his claim. Next, he argues against his opponents, who feel that coed schools are better than single-sex schools. He does this by stating his opponents' viewpoint and providing reasons that it is not as valid as his own. He finishes his essay with a **conclusion** that sums up how his argument proved his claim.

Single-Gender Schools Are the Best

All-girls schools and all-boys schools are better learning environments than coed schools. Many studies done over the years have proven that students in single-gender environments outperform students in coed environments. An Australian study conducted in the 1990s showed that both girls and boys in single-gender schools scored higher on standardized tests than students in coeducational environments. Improving test scores is an important goal for school districts throughout the United States. If single-gender education has been proven to be an effective way to raise test scores, providing it would meet the goals of all school systems.

In addition, in 2006, U.S. Secretary of Education Margaret Spellings stated, "research shows that some students may learn better in single-gender education environments." As a result of this research, the U.S. Department of Education has developed new regulations which enable parents to choose single-gender public schools for their children. If the research was strong enough to convince the U.S. Secretary of Education to make provisions for students to attend single-gender schools, shouldn't we follow her lead?

Though single-gender schools have been proven to be better learning environments for students, there are some people who claim that creating single-gender environments is wrong because it promotes gender stereotyping. They say that coed education is the only way to provide exactly the same opportunities for boys and girls. They argue that an all-girls school would not offer activities like football and that an all-boys school would not offer activities like cheerleading. They feel that this would discriminate against girls who wanted to play football and boys who wanted to be cheerleaders. Let's face it—most students do not care to cross those gender lines. And if an exceptional one does, there are plenty of opportunities to participate in sports and other activities that are not sponsored by schools.

The primary goal of schools is to provide a strong education in academic subjects. Should we compromise academic performance by providing equal access to extracurricular activities that would not even be of interest to the majority of students? With so much talk about improving test scores as well as the overall quality of U.S. education, single-gender schools are a proven way to attain these goals.

Note the structure of the author's argument.

First, he makes his claim.

He claims that single-gender schools are better learning environments than coed schools.

Second, he provides proof of his claim using specific, relevant examples.

He uses the examples of the Australian study and the findings and subsequent action of the U.S. Department of Education.

Third, he makes his argument, discussing how his examples prove the claim.

He discusses how his examples prove that single-gender education is superior.

He also provides a claim argued by opponents of single-gender schools and does his best to convince readers that his points are more valid than those of his opponents.

Finally, the author finishes with a strong conclusion.

Here, the author briefly sums up how his argument for single-gender schools and against coed schools proved his claim.

Practice 4: Analyzing an Argument

Read the following essay in which a different author presents his viewpoint on single-gender and coeducational schools. Then answer the questions that follow. Use your own paper to respond.

Coed Schools Are the Best

Coeducational schools are better learning environments for students than single-gender schools. First of all, students prefer coed schools. Four out of five students surveyed here at Meridian Middle School said they would rather attend a coed school than a single-gender school. If student preference is for coed schools, how many would actually choose single-gender schools if offered the choice? Since schools are already coed, it seems that a lot of money could potentially be wasted creating new schools that students wouldn't want to attend anyway.

More importantly, single-gender education is discriminatory. In 1982, the Supreme Court ruled that denying males the right to enroll in the Mississippi University for Women School of Nursing violated the Equal Protection Clause of the Fourteenth Amendment. By not admitting men, the court decided that the school was discriminating against males who wanted to become nurses. It is doubtful that all-boy and all-girl schools would offer exactly the same activities. Wouldn't such schools be showing the same type of discrimination? It is unfair not to offer the same opportunities to each gender.

Opponents say that students in single-gender schools are more likely to participate in class than students in coed schools. However, there is no clear evidence or definitive studies that have proven this. In fact, boys and girls need to learn how to interact, whether through class participation or clubs or a drama production. The real world is coed—why should schools be any different? Coed schools provide an opportunity for socialization that single-gender schools cannot. Students need to learn how to get along with each other.

The answer is simple. Students clearly prefer to be in a coeducational environment. Given the discrimination that can occur in a single-gender school, the solution is clear—stick with coed schools.

1. What is the author's claim in this essay?

   A. Coed schools cost too much money.
   B. Coed schools are preferred by students.
   C. Single-gender schools are best for nursing studies.
   D. Single-gender schools discriminate against males.

2. Which is NOT a point the author makes in his argument for coed schools?

   A. Girls prefer coed schools more than boys do.
   B. Changing schools to single-gender would be expensive.
   C. Boys and girls need to learn to interact.
   D. According to a survey, students prefer coed schools.

3. What does the author say his opponents give as a reason for single-gender schools?
   A. Four out of five students prefer single-gender schools.
   B. Coed schools cannot teach kids how to get along.
   C. Students in single-gender schools participate more in class.
   D. Students clearly prefer single-gender schools.

4. Where does the author present his conclusion?
   A. the last sentence of paragraph 1
   B. the last two sentences of paragraph 2
   C. the second sentence of paragraph 3
   D. the last two sentences of paragraph 4

CHAPTER 4 SUMMARY

When an author wants to persuade his audience to agree with him on a controversial issue, he follows a series of logical steps. First, he **makes a claim**. Then, he **proves his claim** using specific examples that will be relevant to his audience. He provides an analysis of how the **evidence** he presented proves that his viewpoint on the issue is the most valid. Finally, the author **builds an argument** by stating a definite position on an issue and then defending it.

CHAPTER 4 REVIEW

Read the paragraph below. Then answer the questions that follow.

>   Cats make better pets than dogs for elderly people. Cats wash themselves and don't need to be taken out for exercise. Dogs need baths and must be taken on walks. Elderly people may have arthritis or other health problems that would make it difficult for them to keep a dog clean and to provide the dog with enough exercise. Cats don't require as much work and, therefore, make better pets for the elderly.

1. What is the claim the author makes in this paragraph?

    A. Cats wash themselves.
    B. Elderly people might have some health problems.
    C. Cats make better pets than dogs for elderly people.
    D. Dogs must be taken on walks.

2. What evidence does the author use to support his claim?

    A. Cats don't need outside exercise.   C.   Cats wash themselves.
    B. Dogs need outside exercise.   D.   all of the above

3. Which of the following statements would hurt the author's argument?

    A. Cats shed a lot, and their hair can get all over the house.
    B. Dogs have more health problems than cats.
    C. Pets have been shown to make their owners' lives longer.
    D. Cats are friendlier than dogs.

4. Why does the author say that cats ultimately make better pets for elderly people than dogs do?

    A. Cats don't require as much work.
    B. Cats are better behaved than dogs.
    C. Cats can sense when their owners are sick.
    D. Cats are hard to care for but are better than no pet at all.

Imagine that you want a later curfew. Read the discussions below and then answer the questions that follow.

Discussion #1

>   Can you believe my curfew is still 8:30? That is the earliest of anyone! I hate always being the one who has to leave first. I miss out on everything! Remember how last week I even had to walk out of the movie theatre to make my curfew?! I never did find out the end—what happened? My parents are so unreasonable. I've asked and asked, but they think 9:00 is too late. Anyway, I guess I'll see you tomorrow. Bye!

Discussion #2

I'd like to talk to you about the time of my curfew. My curfew is now 8:30, which is earlier than any of my friends. Everyone else has a 9:00 curfew. Would you consider extending my curfew to 9:00?

Making my 8:30 curfew means missing time with my friends. Last week, I even had to miss the end of a movie at the theatre to get home in time. I have never gotten into trouble while out with my friends, and I have never been late for my curfew. Could we try 9:00? I will prove by arriving on time and staying out of trouble that I can handle the added responsibility.

5. Who is the audience in **Discussion #1?**
   A. your parents
   B. your friend
   C. your teachers
   D. the school principal

6. Who is the audience is **Discussion #2?**
   A. an ambassador
   B. your friend
   C. your parents
   D. the movie theater manager

7. Which of the following statements used in Discussion #1 would you be sure NOT to use with your parents?
   A. "They are so unreasonable."
   B. "I never did find out the end—what happened?"
   C. "I miss out on everything!"
   D. "Anyway, I guess I'll see you tomorrow."

8. What would be a useful point to add in to the discussion with your parents?
   A. You have met all of my friends and think they are trustworthy.
   B. We can't even drive yet.
   C. All of the other parents are cooler than you.
   D. We didn't even get caught when we sprayed that graffiti last month.

Read the essay below. Then answer the questions that follow.

School Should Not Be Year-Round

Recently, there has been much discussion about switching from the traditional school schedule to year-round school. Switching to year-round school would be a big mistake. Summer vacation serves an important purpose for students. Aside from providing a much-needed break from school, summer vacations create a significant block of time for students to explore other interests. Summer is a time when kids can take art classes or try a new sport. The 12 million kids who go away to camp each year would no longer enjoy an experience that has been proven to promote independence and self-sufficiency.

Summer vacation is also a time that many students rely on to work. For many kids, working during the school year with its homework demands is not an option. They depend on the money they earn from summer jobs for spending money as well as savings for college. It would be a serious sacrifice for many students to give up this time during which to earn money.

Despite these important and positive aspects of summer vacation, there are some people who are arguing for year round school. The main reason these people have for moving to year-round school is their claim that much of what was learned during the school year is lost over the summer. They say that time is wasted re-teaching forgotten information in the fall. While this may be true to an extent, most teachers say that the amount of time spent re-teaching is in fact a very small portion of the school year. It is a small sacrifice to make to re-teach some material in order to preserve the benefits of having a summer vacation.

A traditional school schedule has served us well for generations. It provides a break to protect students from burnout while allowing students to develop new interests and maturity. Summer is also an important time for students to earn money. If an extra week or two of re-teaching is necessary to preserves the benefits of summer vacation, it is well worth it.

9. In which of the following sentences does the author state his claim in this essay?
   A. Camp provides lessons in independence and self-sufficiency that school cannot.
   B. Switching to year-round school would be a big mistake.
   C. They say that time is wasted re-teaching forgotten information in the fall.
   D. Summer vacation is also a time that many students rely on to work.

10. Which of the following does the author provide as proof that many kids would be affected by not being able to go to summer camp?
   A. It is a small sacrifice to re-teach some material in order to preserve the benefits of a summer vacation.
   B. Switching to year-round school would be a big mistake.
   C. Summer is an important time for students to earn money.
   D. About 12 million kids go away to camp each year.

11. In which of the following sentences does the author argue for the traditional school schedule?
   A. Despite these important and positive aspects of summer vacation, there are some people who are arguing for year round school.
   B. It would be a serious sacrifice for many students to give up this important time during which to earn money.
   C. They say that time is wasted re-teaching forgotten information in the fall.
   D. While this may be true to an extent, most teachers say that the amount of time spent re-teaching is in fact a very small portion of the school year.

12. In which of these statements does the author address the argument of his opponents?

    A. The main reason these people have for moving to year-round school is their claim that much of what was learned during the school year is lost over the summer.

    B. A traditional school schedule has served us well for generations.

    C. Summer is an important time for students to earn money.

    D. The 12 million kids that go away to camp each year would no longer enjoy an experience that has been proven to promote independence and self-sufficiency.

13. Which of these statements does the author use as part of his conclusion to sum up how his argument proved his claim?

    A. While this may be true to an extent, most teachers say that the amount of time spent re-teaching is in fact a very small portion of the school year

    B. Summer is a time when kids can take art classes or try a new sport.

    C. It provides a break to protect students from burnout while allowing students to develop new interests and maturity.

    D. Switching to year-round school would be a big mistake.

Chapter 5
Understanding Common Graphic
Features and Following Directions

This chapter covers the following Georgia standards.

ELA7R1	Identify and use knowledge of common graphic features to draw conclusions and make judgements (e.g., graphic organizers, diagrams, captions, illustrations).
	Understand and explain the use of a simple device by following technical directions.
ELA7RC2f	Recognize and use the features of disciplinary texts (e.g., charts, graphs, photos, maps, highlighted vocabulary).
ELA7LSV2	Determine how image and text in electronic journalism affect the reader.

Reading is a good way to learn new information. Sometimes, **graphics** can help explain ideas or show information more clearly than just using words can. Graphics are images like photographs, illustrations, pictures, diagrams, and organizational tools. Graphics are often used with words to help make information easier to understand.

GRAPHIC ORGANIZERS

A **graphic organizer** is a tool that allows you to organize information and see how information is related. One type of graphic organizer is a **Venn Diagram**. A Venn Diagram shows the relationship between two items. Look at the Venn Diagram below. Circle A represents the first item. Circle B represents the second item. The area where the two circles overlap shows what the two items have in common. The areas outside the overlap show properties that are unique to each item. If a teacher were to ask you to compare two items, a Venn Diagram would be a useful tool.

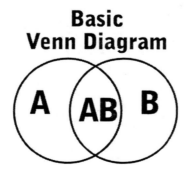

Practice 1: Venn Diagrams

Look at the Venn Diagram below. Then answer the questions that follow.

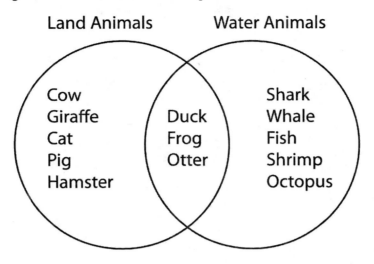

Land Animals   Water Animals

Cow
Giraffe
Cat
Pig
Hamster

Duck
Frog
Otter

Shark
Whale
Fish
Shrimp
Octopus

1. What are the two types of animals being compared in this Venn Diagram?
   A. cows and sharks
   B. ducks and frogs
   C. land animals and water animals
   D. land animals and all animals

2. Which of the following are two land animals shown in this diagram?
   A. pig and hamster
   B. cat and duck
   C. shark and whale
   D. frog and otter

3. Which of the following lists are water animals shown in this diagram?
   A. fish, duck, giraffe
   B. whale, shrimp, octopus
   C. frog, otter, hamster
   D. octopus, duck, cow

4. Which three animals listed in the diagram live both on land and in the water?
   A. shark, frog, pig
   B. frog, otter, duck
   C. whale, fish, shark
   D. pig, cat, giraffe

 Another type of graphic organizer is a **web**. A web shows how ideas are connected. Webs can be helpful when planning a writing assignment or studying for a test. The topic is shown in area A. Supporting ideas are shown in area B. Examples are shown in area C.

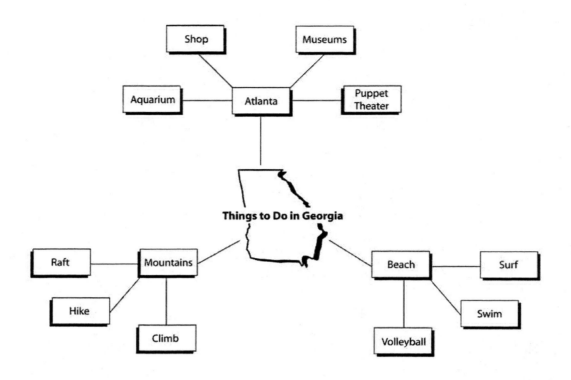

Practice 2: Webs

Study the web above. Then answer the questions.

1. What is the topic of this web?

   A. hiking
   B. going to the beach
   C. places to visit in Atlanta
   D. things to do in Georgia

2. What is one of the examples given in the web that visitors can do at the beach?
   A. swim   B. hike   C. jetski   D. sunbathe

3. Look at the "mountains" section. Besides the ideas written, which of these choices would be the best to add as an example?
   A. sail   B. camp   C. sunbathe   D. shop

4. Supporting ideas are shown in area B. What are the three supporting ideas shown in this web?

   A. swim, sail, hike
   B. symphony, hike, sail
   C. mountains, beach, Atlanta
   D. beach, swim, sail

DIAGRAM

A **diagram** is a drawing that shows where things are or how things work. A diagram often accompanies text to give a clear understanding of a concept. Diagrams can be found in textbooks and in magazine and newspaper articles.

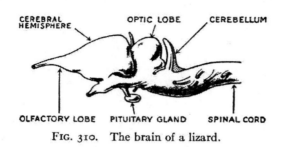

FIG. 310.   The brain of a lizard.

Practice 3:   Diagrams

Look at the diagram of the cell below and answer the questions that follow.

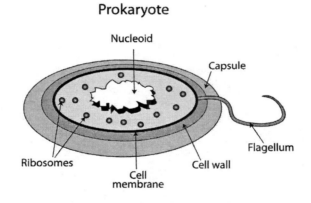

1.   What is the title of this diagram?

   A.   prokaryote   B.   nucleoid   C.   cell   D.   flagellum

2.   What is the name of the structure at the center of the cell?

   A.   capsule   C.   cell membrane
   B.   middle   D.   nucleoid

3.   What are the small circles called that are found throughout the cell?

   A.   cells   B.   ribosomes   C.   dots   D.   grains

4.   What part of the cell is found outside the capsule?

   A.   cell wall   B.   flagellum   C.   the edge   D.   prokaryote

CAPTIONS

A **caption** is a label that provides information about a photo or drawing. A caption names parts of an illustration or identifies images and explains why they are significant. Pictures with captions often accompany newspaper or magazine articles. The caption can provide new information not found in the article or can explain information more clearly.

Joseph Howard

Practice 4: Captions

Look at the two photographs below and read each caption. Then answer the questions that follow.

Image 1

The Washington Monument in early 2007. The flags are at half-staff as a sign of national mourning for the recent death of President Gerald Ford.

Image 2

The partially completed Washington Monument, photographed by Mathew Brady circa 1860

1. What monument is shown in each photograph?
   A. Gerald Ford Monument
   B. Mathew Brady Monument
   C. Washington Monument
   D. American Monument

2. In what year was Image 1 taken?
   A. 2007
   B. 1956
   C. The caption does not tell us this.
   D. 1860

3. In what year was Image 2 taken?
   A. 1860
   B. 2007
   C. 2006
   D. The caption does not tell us this.

4. Why might Mathew Brady have taken Image 2?
   A. to show construction in progress of a national monument
   B. to show how old the Washington Monument is
   C. because he recognized that this was an important American building
   D. all of the above

ILLUSTRATIONS

Illustrations are graphics, such as photographs or drawings, that enhance what is written in a text. Illustrations help us visualize what the text is about.

Take a look at this example of an article with an illustration.

Excerpt from "Playing It Safe with Eggs"

To avoid the possibility of foodborne illness, fresh eggs must be handled carefully. Even eggs with clean, uncracked shells may occasionally contain bacteria called *Salmonella* that can cause an intestinal infection. The most effective way to prevent egg-related illness is by knowing how to buy, store, handle and cook eggs—or foods that contain them—safely. That is why the US Food and Drug Administration (FDA) requires all cartons of shell eggs that have not been treated to destroy *Salmonella* must carry the following safe handling statement:

Safe Handling Instructions: To prevent illness from bacteria: keep eggs refrigerated, cook eggs until yolks are firm, and cook foods containing eggs thoroughly.

The photograph that illustrates this article is of eggs, including a raw egg out of its shell in a glass. How well does this picture add to your understanding of the text? Could a different illustration be used and, if so, what should it be? Think about these questions as you read passages that are illustrated.

Practice 5: Illustrations

The Balm from Gilead?

Can you name the material that can be used as an antiseptic salve, a treatment for stomach ulcers, an embalming fluid, and a great tasting topping for your morning toast? No such thing, you say? Be ready to be surprised. The answer is honey! The sticky, sweet, super-saturated sugar is all those things and more. The use of honey through the ages has met both medicinal and nutritional needs. Many cultures have used honey as a balm for wounds. Now, scientists have proven that the high level of sugar in honey prevents bacterial growth, and the fluid has moisturizing properties that promote healing. Honey works as a healing balm also for stomach ulcers when eaten by itself, with some foods, or added to herbal teas. As for embalming, the Greeks, Romans, and Egyptians all used honey to preserve the corpses of their revered dead. Alexander the Great's body, it is said, was shipped in a wooden cask filled with honey to his home in Greece for burial. Some of Alexander's funeral foods were most likely prepared with honey to sweeten and to thicken them. So, tomorrow morning take a jar of sourwood honey (my favorite though there are many other types) and pour the golden drops of bee-ripened nectar on your biscuit or into your tea. You'll see that honey is truly one of nature's sweetest surprises on earth.

1. How well does this picture illustrate the text?

   A. It is not a good illustration because it does not show someone being embalmed.
   B. It is a good illustration, as the main topic of the text is honey.
   C. It is not appropriate because the text is more about embalming.
   D. It should be a picture of a bee because bees make honey.

2. Which of these other possible illustrations would BEST add to your understanding of the text?

   A. a timeline showing when honey was used for embalming
   B. a photograph of a coffin
   C. a picture of someone eating honey
   D. a map of Greece

Doc Holliday

John Henry Holliday was born in 1851 in Griffin, Georgia, with a cleft palate and a cleft lip. His uncle was a surgeon and corrected the birth defects. The child had to be fed carefully or he could choke to death, so he was given liquids from a shot glass. By the age of 22, John Holliday had his Doctor of Dental Surgery degree. He had also contracted tuberculosis and was told that he had only a few months to live. Heeding the advice of his uncle to move to a drier climate, Doctor John Holliday boarded a train for Dallas. The year was 1873.

"Doc" Holiday began to practice in Dallas. But his disease continued to wrack his body. He would be overcome by coughing spells at the most embarrassing times, as in the middle of working on a patient. His dental practice declined, and Doc turned to gambling for a living. In the old west, a gambler stood alone and had to defend himself. Doc Holliday was well aware of this and religiously practiced with six-guns and knives. He was a hot-tempered southern gentleman that would step aside for no man. This led to one confrontation after another. After sending many bullies and gunmen to meet their maker, Doc moved from one western town to another, narrowly avoiding being hanged.

By the time he reached Tombstone, Arizona, Doc Holliday had a reputation as one of the fastest guns in the west. His trail was littered with the bodies of dead men who had underestimated his skill. In Tombstone, he was reunited with his old friend and lawman, Wyatt Earp. After the well-known gun fight at the OK Corral, Doc Holliday, Wyatt Earp and a few deputies hunted down the remaining members of the outlaw cowboy gang for the murder and maiming of Wyatt's two brothers. Over twenty outlaws died in Wyatt's ride of revenge, many at the end of Holliday's smoking pistol.

Doc Holliday had come west knowing that he was living on borrowed time. He always thought he would die by a bullet, a knife in his ribs, at the end of a rope, or by drinking himself to death. He maintained that he would not die in bed of a coughing fit. Yet, that is what fate had in store for him. May of 1887 found him in a convalescent hospital in Glenwood Springs, Colorado, dying of tuberculosis. He spent his last 57 days in bed, delirious for the last two weeks. On November 8, he woke up clear-eyed and asked for a shot of whiskey. He drank it down with great relish. Then looking at his condition and the irony of his life, he said, "This is funny," and died.

3. Which of these would BEST illustrate the first paragraph of this text?
    A. a map of Griffin, Georgia
    B. a picture of the house in which John Holliday grew up
    C. an illustration of how a cleft palate is corrected
    D. a photograph of Doc Holliday

4. What would be the MOST appropriate illustration for paragraph 3?
    A. a picture of the sign welcoming people to Tombstone, Arizona
    B. a photograph of Wyatt Earp and his deputies at the OK Coral
    C. a poster for a movie about Wyatt Earp
    D. a drawing of a smoking gun

ELECTRONIC NEWS

The **Internet** is a great place to find news and features about various topics. Many newspapers and magazines today have an electronic component. This means that, besides their printed version, they have many stories online.

The Internet can be a student's greatest resource or biggest waste of time. There are so many sites to explore. You can easily lose track of your original topic. You have to know how to find the right information by using **keywords**. Once you find material on the topic you want, you need to evaluate, or check, that it will be helpful to you.

Keywords are tools for finding the most useful sites. The results of a search depend entirely on what keywords you enter. First, decide what search engine to use, like Yahoo! or Google. Next, type in one or two keywords for the subject you want. The engine scans for sites that match the keyword(s) you entered and lists all the results. Searching by a single keyword will usually give you more results than you need. Limit your search by carefully choosing your keywords(s).

For example, let's say you are doing a report about the Bengal Tiger. If you just type "tiger" into a search engine, you will get millions of sites. There could be links to everything from endangered species of tigers, to software called Tiger, to articles about golfer Tiger Woods! Try typing more specific words. Of course, "Bengal Tiger" will bring more focused results. You can narrow your search even further, depending on what your report will cover. For instance, you could search for "Bengal Tiger habitat," "Bengal Tiger life cycle," and "Bengal Tiger diet." Remember that the pictures and maps on these sites will be very helpful also.

If you are looking for a story or news item about something, you can search the same way: Use keywords in a search engine. You could enter "volcano eruption" to find stories in various publications about a volcano that just came to life in the South Pacific. Another way to search is through the news sites. Try searching on the site of a well-known and trusted news organization, like *TIME*, *CNN*, or your city's local newspaper.

Once you find items that you searched for, the illustrations can be helpful. As you learned in the last section of this chapter, illustrations can make the text more clear. Look at these examples. Maura searched for news about the latest Mars mission. Here are two sites with news that came up.

Mars Tracks: The Mars Rover Info Site   Page 1 of 1

NEWS ▸

IMAGES

PRODUCTS

JOIN US

LINKS

EXPLORING THE
SOLAR SYSTEM

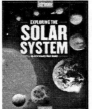

Click Here for the Best in Astronomy!

Source (http://athena.cornell.edu/the_mission/index.html)

On June 10, 2003, the single greatest event in the history of mankind will have occurred. On that date the first Mars Exploration Rover (MER) spacecraft was launched on a Delta II rocket from Cape Canaveral, Florida. After a seven month flight, it will enter the martian atmosphere in January 2004. A second lander and rover will follow a short time later. When landing, a parachute will deploy to slow the Rover spacecraft. Then a group of airbags will inflate around the vehicle to cushion the shock of impact. The first bounce on the martian surface will reach more than one hundred feet into the air. The airbags will bounce about a dozen times, and could roll as far as one kilometer (0.6 miles). When the spacecraft finally comes to a stop, it will use its sophisticated computer system to turn itself to an upright position so that the rover can deploy properly. The airbags will deflate and retract. Three flower-like "petals" will open to reveal a tightly folded rover. Piece by piece the rover will take shape, deploying its camera mast, antennas, wheels, and solar arrays. This exploration will definitely either prove or disprove the existence of life on Mars.

We will keep you posted on the latest news, so keep checking back!

ROVER POSTERS AVAILABLE HERE!

http://www.marstracks.net/news.html   6/16/04

This Web page is an example of a site that has the right type of information. It has a news story about a Mars mission. However, it is not recent. It also has pictures that are clear and interesting. But some are pictures of products sold on the site. This is a commercial site and not a very good news course.

Mars
The Red Planet

NEWS | IMAGES | LINKS | PICTURES

NEWS

NASA Readies Mars Lander for August Launch to Icy Site
by NASA

July 9, 2007

NASA's next Mars mission will look beneath a frigid arctic landscape for conditions favorable to past or present life.

Instead of roving to hills or craters, NASA's Phoenix Mars Lander will claw down into the icy soil of the Red Planet's northern plains. The robot will investigate whether frozen water near the Martian surface might periodically melt enough to sustain a livable environment for microbes. To accomplish that and other key goals, Phoenix will carry a set of advanced research tools never before used on Mars.

First, however, it must launch from Florida during a three-week period beginning Aug. 3, then survive a risky descent and landing on Mars next spring.

Artist's concept of Phoenix lander on Mars.
Image credit: NASA/JPL/UA/Lockheed Martin

For more information:
NASA's Mars Fact Sheet
Mars at Wikipedia

For other information about Mars, click the "LINKS" button above.

http://www.marstheredplanet.edu/facts.html

This site does not sell anything. That makes it more reliable as a news source. It features a more recent story about Mars exploration.

Practice 6: Electronic News

Use the Mars sites you just read to answer the following questions.

1. What is the name of the first site on page 96?

    A.   Mars News   C.   Solar System
    B.   Mars Tracks   D.   Mars Rover

2. Judging by the text and pictures, what is this page mainly about?

    A.   Mars history and geography
    B.   books and posters of the universe
    C.   tracks that have been left on Mars
    D.   the first Mars exploration mission

3. Looking at the second site on page 97, what makes it seem more "official"?

    A.   There is a link to more information from NASA.
    B.   There is a real photograph of the planet Mars.
    C.   It has a picture of the Phoenix lander by an artist.
    D.   It specifically identifies Mars as the Red Planet.

4. How is the story on this page more trustworthy as news?

    A.   It is more recent, whereas the story on the first Internet site was old news.
    B.   It presents just facts, while the first site's story expressed a strong opinion.
    C.   It is mostly about the planet Mars, but the first site was more about the mission.
    D.   It is written by a famous journalist, and the first article does not say who wrote it.

5. Why is the graphic of the Phoenix lander an artist's concept (idea) rather than a photograph?

    A.   The Phoenix lander has not yet been built.
    B.   There is no such things as the Phoenix lander.
    C.   The picture shows it on Mars, which hasn't happened yet.
    D.   It is against the law to take pictures of NASA space probes.

Using Technical Directions

There are times that we need instructions in order to learn how things work. You might need to read instructions to learn how to use your new DVD player, program numbers into a mobile phone, or assemble a motorized scooter. These types of directions are called **technical directions**. Technical directions explain the steps you must take in order to do what you want to do. Technical directions may use pictures, words or both. The illustrations that accompany technical writing tend to show actions rather than just the objects. Words *list* the steps in the order they should be done. Graphics *show* the steps in the order they should be done.

Practice 7:   Using Technical Directions

Read the technical directions below. Then answer the questions that follow.

Cooking Technique: Creaming Butter

Creaming combines sugar with butter or margarine. The sugar's sharp particles cut into the butter, introducing air bubbles. It is the most important step for cookies and cakes because it allows them to rise.

Cut the butter into small pieces before following these steps.

1. Use hand beaters to soften the butter, first on low, then increase to medium.

2. Add in sugar, eggs, and vanilla or cream of tartar, in this order. Scrape the sides often.

3. Beat until the mixture has changed color and texture (don't overbeat!)

1. Cut the butter into smaller pieces.

2. Begin to beat (with sugar).

3. Butter changes color.

1. What is the first thing the instructions tell you to do after cutting the butter into small pieces?

    A. Use hand beaters to soften the butter.
    B. Scrape the sides often.
    C. Beat until the mixture has changed color.
    D. Combine the butter and sugar.

2. What is the caption of illustration number 3?

    A. "Begin to beat."   C. "Butter changes color."
    B. "Add the sugar, eggs, and vanilla."   D. "Cut the butter into smaller pieces."

3. According to the directions, on what speed should you start the beaters?

    A. high
    B. medium
    C. low
    D. extra-low

4. When do the instructions say to stop beating the mixture?

    A. when the beaters stop spinning
    B. when the cookies are done
    C. when the butter is in small enough pieces
    D. when the mixture has changed color and texture

Read the information and study the illustration. Then, answer the questions that follow.

Imagine that you are assembling a new bicycle. You have followed the instructions that came in the box. This illustration shows the final step: putting on the reflectors.

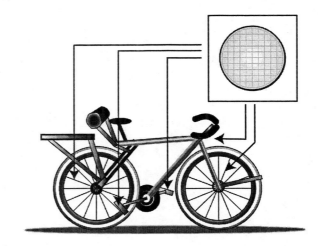

5. How many reflector areas are labeled in the illustration?

    A. 3
    B. 5
    C. 10
    D. 7

6. Which areas of the bicycle should have reflectors?

    A. the spokes of the front wheel   C. the spokes of the back wheel
    B. the pedals   D. all of the above

7. Which area should NOT have a reflector?
    A. the top of the seat
    B. the spokes
    C. in the front, below the handlebars
    D. the pedals

8. According to the illustration, what color should the pedal reflectors be?
    A. yellow
    B. red
    C. orange
    D. The illustration does not show the color.

CHAPTER 5 SUMMARY

Graphics can help us understand information and instructions. They can help a reader to better understand how to do something, how something fits together, or where something is.

Electronic news sources use text and graphics to provide the latest information. It is important to know how to search for and evaluate electronic news.

CHAPTER 5 REVIEW

Study the Venn Diagram below. Then answer the questions that follow.

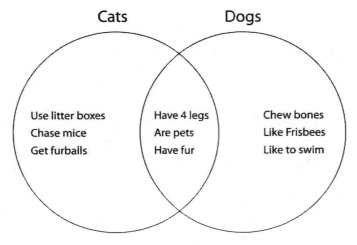

1. What is being compared in this Venn diagram?
   A. cats and mice
   B. cats and dogs
   C. cats and all other pets
   D. animals that live outside

2. Which of the following describes only dogs?
   A. chase mice
   B. have 4 legs
   C. chew bones
   D. have fur

3. Which of the following is something dogs and cats have in common?
   A. like to swim
   B. are pets
   C. like to dig holes
   D. use litter boxes

4. Create your own Venn Diagram comparing apples and grapes. Write at least three items in each of the three sections of the diagram.

Read the information below. Then study the diagram and read the captions. Answer the questions that follow.

The water cycle is the movement of water on and around the earth and its atmosphere. The sun heats water in the oceans, causing it to evaporate. Rising water vapor condenses into clouds. Cloud particles fall back to the earth in the form of precipitation, like rain or snow. The water then soaks into the ground and collects in rivers and lakes. As rivers empty into oceans, the cycle continues.

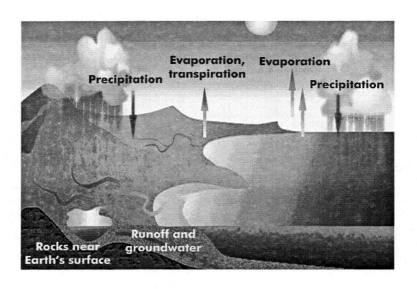

5. Where is one place that ground water discharge goes?
   A. clouds   B. oceans   C. snowballs   D. mountains

6. How does water leave oceans and get into the atmosphere?
   A. The sun evaporates it.   C. Clouds form underwater.
   B. The wind blows it.   D. It happens when it rains.

7. What is the process called when water returns to the earth?
   A. evaporation   B. precipitation   C. hail   D. condensation

8. Where does snowmelt runoff go?
   A. to streams   C. to the sun
   B. to clouds   D. back up the mountain

Read the information and study the illustration. Then answer the questions that follow.

The United States Consumer Product Safety Commission recommends that a working smoke alarm be installed on every level of the home, outside sleeping areas, and inside bedrooms.

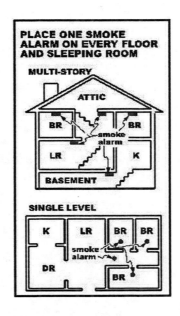

9. According to the instructions, which floors of a home should have working smoke alarms?
   A. the top floor
   B. the basement
   C. all floors
   D. the first floor

10. How many smoke alarms are shown in the multi-story house?
   A. 5   B. 4   C. 1   D. 10

11. According to the instructions, which room should always have a smoke alarm?
   A. kitchen   B. bedroom   C. attic   D. dining room

12. Why do you think an illustration is shown with these smoke alarm installation instructions?
   A. It shows that not all houses are built in the same way.
   B. It illustrates the need for alarms in attics and basements, if they exist.
   C. It helps a reader understand better where smoke alarms should be placed.
   D. It is required as part of the instruction from the Consumer Product Safety Commission.

Directions. Use the two sample Web pages that follow to answer the questions after the second one.

Web Page I

Welcome to Australia Travel!   Page 1 of 1

©2004 All Rights Reserved, Australia Travel

http://www.aussietravel.net

Web Page II

The Truth About Australia: History   Page 1 of 2

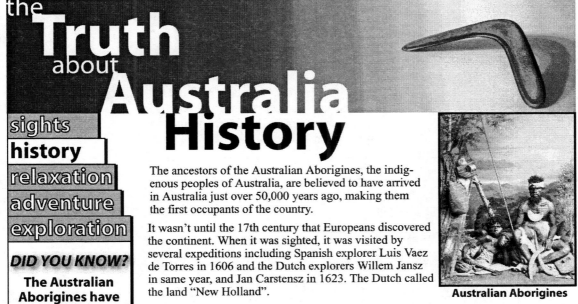

http://www.thetruthaboutaustrailia.org/history.html

13. Web page I would be a good resource for what type of information?
   A. geography of Australia   C. fun activities to do in Australia
   B. animals of Australia   D. population of Australia

14. Web page II would be a good resource for what type of information?
   A. famous people of Australia   C. places to stay in Australia
   B. size of Australia   D. movies made in Australia

15. Which statement indicates a major difference between the two Web pages?
   A. Page I was created by a business, and Page II was created by an organization.
   B. They are both about Australia.
   C. Page II is useful, but Page I has outdated information.
   D. Page I has tourist information, but Page II offers nothing for visitors.

Chapter 6
Understanding Literature

This chapter covers the following Georgia standard.

ELA7R1	For literary texts, identify the characteristics of various genres and produce evidence of understanding characterization, setting, and historical moment, theme (as distinguished from topic), and events that advance the plot.

Reading is a voyage.

Where will you journey today?

Who will you meet, where will you go as the narrator guides you away?

Across the seas, back in time,

You get lost somewhere; plots twist and unwind,

Stories of magic and fantasy,

Tales of horror and mystery…

Characters living dynamically are yours for the day.

Themes you learn as you journey,

Reading takes you away.

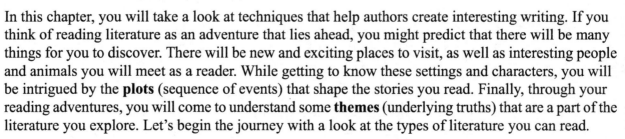

In this chapter, you will take a look at techniques that help authors create interesting writing. If you think of reading literature as an adventure that lies ahead, you might predict that there will be many things for you to discover. There will be new and exciting places to visit, as well as interesting people and animals you will meet as a reader. While getting to know these settings and characters, you will be intrigued by the **plots** (sequence of events) that shape the stories you read. Finally, through your reading adventures, you will come to understand some **themes** (underlying truths) that are a part of the literature you explore. Let's begin the journey with a look at the types of literature you can read.

LITERARY GENRES

There are different types of literature, which are called **genres**. The major genres into which writing fits are **nonfiction**, **fiction**, **poetry**, and **drama**. A genre is a type of literature with a similar style. For example, the genre of science fiction usually takes place in the future, and it might involve aliens or space travel.

Here are some of the literary genres:

Nonfiction is writing that is true and factual. It is about real people and real events.

- **Example genres within nonfiction:** autobiographies, biographies, historical accounts, informational articles, journals, letters to the editor, scientific explanations

- **Examples of works:**
    A Restless Spirit: The Story of Robert Frost by Natalie S. Bober (biography)

    Amistad: A Long Road to Freedom by Walter Dean Myers (historical account)

Fiction is narrative writing, which means it tells a story. A writer creates fiction from imagination rather than from history or fact. Fiction includes stories as short as one page all the way up to novels that are very long.

- **Example genres within fiction:** allegory, fable, fantasy, folk tale, legend, mystery, myth, romance, science fiction

- **Examples of works:**
    "A Rose for Emily" by William Faulkner (mystery)

    Invitation to the Game by Monica Hughes (science fiction)

    Greek Myths by Geraldine McCaughrean (myth)

Poetry is different from prose because it is written in lines and stanzas (rather than in sentences and paragraphs using Standard English construction). It usually has rhythm, sometimes rhymes, and can convey deep emotion or vivid descriptions.

- **Example genres within poetry:** epic, lyric, narrative, haiku, sonnet

- **Examples of works:**
    The Gargoyle on the Roof: Poems by Jack Prelutsky

    Good Luck Gold and Other Poems by Janet Wong

Drama is a story (fiction or nonfiction) told through action and dialogue. It is a play, short or long, that is meant to be acted out. You can see a play in a theater. You can also read a play. A screenplay, which is used to make a movie, is also a form of drama.

- **Example genres within drama:** comedy, tragedy, farce, melodrama

- **Examples of works:**
    Romeo and Juliet by William Shakespeare (tragedy)

    "Peggy, the Pint-Sized Pirate" by D. M. Bocaz-Larson (short comedy)

SETTING AND HISTORICAL MOMENT

Imagine that you have been given the task of writing your own life story. You are to describe your life, beginning with an explanation of where you live and a description of the time period in which you live. In doing this writing, it is important to consider not only the actual years and dates of your life, and the actual place you live, but the details of history that form a backdrop for your life. Do you live in a time of war or peace, prosperity or struggle? Is your home in the city or in a rural setting? How do people in your city or town live and think? What issues are important to the people of your era and generation?

These are all ideas that go into the creation of literature. In a story, novel, or drama, **setting** is the time and place in which the events of a story occur. Setting is important because it contributes many important details to the overall story. It affects the way the characters think and behave and contributes to the story's sequence of events. Setting is often described early on in a work of literature. Sometimes, as in the case of a story where a character struggles against nature, the setting is a major focus.

Historical moment is a part of setting. It refers to the historical backdrop of a work of literature. For example, if you consider a nonfiction work such as *The Diary of Anne Frank*, the historical moment would be the era of the Holocaust (the persecution and execution of Jews during World War II). The fact that the Holocaust is the time period in which the writing takes place contributes greatly to the writing. The events that take place—all the struggles that Anne Frank wrote about in her diary—happen because of the Holocaust.

YOM HASHOAH

"Remember the Holocaust"

Practice 1: Setting and Historical Moment

I was raised in a small town on the shores of Lake Erie. The big water was only three blocks away from my house, and as a young boy I spent much of my time fishing from its shore with my two friends Sparky and Dave.

–from "Tough Times on the Farm" by Dennis Martin

1. In the narrative excerpt above, what is the setting of the story?

    A. somewhere in Europe
    B. a major metropolitan city
    C. a small town on the shores of Lake Erie
    D. the writer does not reveal a setting

> In the ancient city of London, on a certain autumn day in the second quarter of
> the sixteenth century, a boy was born to a poor family of the name of Canty, who did
> not want him.

2. In the excerpt above, from Mark Twain's *The Prince and the Pauper*, which of the following
   is the physical setting and historical period of the story?
   A. Chicago, late 1800s
   B. London, early to mid 1500s
   C. Paris, mid 1900s
   D. Quebec, late 1700s

PLOT

What is **plot**? Often, after you have read a work of literature, your teacher or
your textbook will ask you to recount the important events that happened in
the story. You are being asked to discuss the plot, or storyline, of the story.
Plot refers to all the related events that move from the story's beginning to
its end. A plot shapes a work of literature. Other literary elements, like
characters and setting, fill in around the action and events that are driving the
storyline.

Take a moment to discuss with a classmate the plot of a book or short story
that you recently read. How did it start? Did the plot move slowly or quickly?
What was the **climax** (the highest point of action)? What was the conclusion?

EVENTS THAT ADVANCE PLOT

When you are reading for an understanding of plot, there are some important ideas
to consider. **First**, look for events in a story that advance the plot. For example, a
story might have a **climax** that features a piano recital. The events leading up to the
recital, such as practices, would be important **rising action** elements of plot.

PLOT EVENTS THAT EXPLAIN HOW CHARACTERS BEHAVE

Next, notice that plot events often explain the way a character has acted in the past
or behaves now. For example, a main character is fearful of traveling by plane. The
plot details could reveal through **flashback** that this character's best friend was lost
in a plane crash.

PLOT EVENTS THAT FORESHADOW

Finally, note that elements of plot **foreshadow**, which means they provide clues for events coming
later on in a story. For example, a character might commit petty thefts at the beginning of the story.
This could foreshadow or predict that this character will be responsible for the big crime that happens
later on in the story.

Practice 2: Plot

The Town Mouse and the Country Mouse

Once upon a time, a Town Mouse went on a visit to his cousin in the country. This Country Mouse was rough and ready, but he loved his town friend and made him heartily welcome. Beans and bacon, cheese and bread were all he had to offer, but he offered them freely.

The Town Mouse rather turned up his long nose at this country fare and said: "I cannot understand, Cousin, how you can put up with such poor food as this. But, of course, you cannot expect anything better in the country. Come with me, and I will show you how to live. When you have been in town a week, you will wonder how you could ever have stood a country life."

No sooner said than done, the two mice set off for the town and arrived at the Town Mouse's residence late at night. "You will want some refreshment after our long journey," said the polite Town Mouse, and took his friend into the grand dining room. There they found the remains of a fine feast, and soon the two mice were eating up jellies and cakes and all that was nice.

Suddenly, they heard growling and barking. "What is that?" said the Country Mouse. "It is only the dogs of the house," answered the other. "Only!" said the Country Mouse. "I do not like that music at my dinner." Just at that moment the door flew open, in came two huge mastiffs, and the two mice had to scamper down and run off. "Good-bye, Cousin," said the Country Mouse, "What! going so soon?" said the other. "Yes," he replied...

"Better beans and bacon in peace than cakes and ale in fear."

–from Aesop's fables

1. Which of the following BEST explains the plot of the above fable?

    A. A Town Mouse goes to visit his country cousin and invites the Country Mouse to the city. The Country Mouse visits the city and hastily returns to his country home, disturbed by all of the sights, sounds, and dangers of the fast-paced city life.

    B. A Country Mouse goes to visit his town cousin and invites the Town Mouse to the country. The town Mouse visits the country and returns hastily to his city home, disturbed by all of the slow-paced events of the country.

    C. A Town Mouse goes to visit his country cousin and invites the Country Mouse to the city. The Country Mouse visits the city, finds himself intrigued by the fast life, and decides to remain in the city.

    D. A Country Mouse goes to visit his town cousin and invites the Town Mouse to the country. The Town Mouse visits the country, finds himself intrigued by the slow-paced events of the country, and decides to remain in the country.

Mark woke up with a start, and he wondered why all was quiet in the house. Rolling over in bed, he saw that it was already 8:30 a.m. He had overslept and would be late for school! Jumping out of bed in a hurry, Mark tripped over his sneakers that were tossed carelessly on the floor. When he hopped into the shower, the hot water scalded him. "Ouch!" he grimaced. Finally leaving the house and rushing in the direction of school, Mark realized that he had forgotten to study for his Algebra test. Today would not be a very good day, he thought to himself.

2. Based upon the details in the story, which plot event is foreshadowed?
   A. Mark will pass his Algebra test with flying colors and have a great day.
   B. Mark will most likely fail his Algebra test and continue to have a bad day.
   C. Mark will be excused from his test because he has had such a bad day so far.
   D. This passage does not contain foreshadowing elements.

Priya's toes traced the wet sand where the water had reached during the high tide, but she was afraid to go any farther into the water. She thought back to the first time she ever visited Monroe Beach.

3. When a character remembers past plot events, this memory is called
   A. reflection.   C. recall.
   B. foreshadowing   D. flashback.

CHARACTERS

Take a minute to think about the last time you met someone new. What was your first impression of that person, and why? How did you learn more about that person? Now, think of someone you have known for at least a year. What three words come to mind when you have to describe that person? Why would you choose those particular words?

Reading literature and meeting **characters** can be similar to meeting and experiencing people and places in the real world. In doing so, you are introduced to people who have certain qualities and live in a certain place and time.

The way an author introduces and presents a character throughout a work of literature is called **characterization**. In real life, we know people by their words, actions, thoughts, and behaviors. We also know them by their personalities, feelings, and what others say about them. The way we get to know literary characters is very similar.

CHARACTERIZATION THROUGH DIALOGUE AND DIALECT

In literature, an author often uses characterization in the form of characters' words and what others say about them.

Sometimes, readers learn about characters through conversations between characters in the novel or story. This is called **dialogue**. Read the following excerpt from Louisa May Alcott's *Little Women* for an example of characterization through dialogue. After reading, discuss what you predict each character is like based upon the dialogue you read.

Louisa May Alcott

> "Christmas won't be Christmas without any presents, "grumbled Jo, lying on the rug.

> "It's so dreadful to be poor!" sighed Meg, looking down at her old dress.

> "I don't think it's fair for some girls to have plenty of pretty things, and other girls nothing at all, "added Amy, with an injured sniff.

> "We've got Father and Mother, and each other, "said Beth contentedly from her corner.

In **drama**, dialogue is the main way that we learn about characters, along with the characters' actions. In **nonfiction** and **fiction**, it is one way of many methods, such as narration and description. And in **poetry**, dialogue—as described here—is not used very often.

Dialect is another way that an author uses words to create characters. Dialect is a way of speaking that is characteristic of a particular region or group of people. When a character speaks in a dialect, his speech is different from the Standard English we use to write. Differences will be in pronunciation, grammar, and vocabulary. When a character speaks in dialect, it helps the reader to know where the character lives or was born.

For example, in Mark Twain's novel, *The Adventures of Huckleberry Finn*, young Huck is the narrator of his own story. The dialect in his narration reflects that he is a Southerner. It also shows that he is uneducated. In the following passage from the book, notice Huck's speech patterns, word choices, and grammar errors.

> The widow she cried over me, and called me a poor lost lamb, and she called me a lot of other names, too, but she never meant no harm by it. She put me in them new clothes again, and I couldn't do nothing but sweat and sweat, and feel all cramped up. Well, then, the old thing commenced again. The widow rung a bell for supper, and you had to come to time. When you got to the table you couldn't go right to eating, but you had to wait for the widow to tuck down her head and grumble a little over the victuals, though there warn't really anything the matter with them,——that is, nothing only everything was cooked by itself. In a barrel of odds and ends it is different; things get mixed up, and the juice kind of swaps around, and the things go better.

CHARACTERIZATION THROUGH NARRATOR DESCRIPTION

Sometimes, you learn about a character through **narrator description**. The narrator talks directly about that character. An example of narrator description about a character is the following line from Guy de Maupassant's short story, "The Diamond Necklace."

> The girl was one of those pretty and charming young creatures who sometimes are born, as if by a slip of fate, into a family of clerks.

CHARACTERIZATION THROUGH ACTIONS

In real life, when you meet people, you form an opinion about them by seeing what they do. For example, if you meet a new classmate, and he never joins in a class discussion or participates in friendly conversation, perhaps you might conclude that he is shy. We also learn about literary characters based upon their **behaviors** or **actions**.

CHARACTERIZATION THROUGH TRAITS

Take a moment to think about yourself. What aspects of your personality stand out to you? Are you loyal, brave, or outspoken? Are you an athlete or do you play an instrument? Are you tall or short? Try making a quick list of your specific qualities.

Sometimes, characters have important physical and non-physical qualities. These are called **traits**. In literature, just like in real life, character traits help us to know what a character is like. They describe characters' personalities and appearance. Character traits can be strengths, flaws, or simply descriptors.

Here are some examples of character traits:

friendly/unfriendly	flamboyant/plain	quiet/bold
cheerful/sad	wise/foolish	selfish/unselfish
short/tall	serious/playful	leader/follower
mischievous/compliant	shy/outgoing	brave/cowardly
kind/unkind	compassionate/uncaring	honest/dishonest

CHARACTERIZATION THROUGH EMOTIONS AND MOTIVATIONS

Take a moment to think of some stories or novels that you have read. Talk to your classmates about **emotions** that you saw in the characters you met in your reading. Dig deep to remember how you learned about what the characters felt. Think about why they acted the way they did.

Similar to real life, characters in literature have definite feelings and emotions. Their feelings can range from confusion to excitement and far beyond. As a reader, you will use characters' emotions to understand who the characters are. You will also use characters' **motivations** (reasons) for their actions to better understand the characters.

Here is an example from the fantasy novel *Avalon High* by Meg Cabot. In the book, junior Ellie enrolls at Avalon High School. There she discovers that some of the students may be reincarnations of King Arthur and his court. She becomes more and more convinced, especially when she sees their lives mimicking the legend. But if that's true, then many of them will have tragic ends! Ellie decides she has to help them.

How do you think Ellie *feels* when she learns this? If she likes the tales of the Round Table, she is probably pretty excited! And what are her *motivations* for wanting to help her new friends? Well, she likes them, and she doesn't want to see them hurt.

Here are some of the needs or wants that motivate people to do things:

attention	friendship	fame	knowledge
fortune	freedom	love	privilege

STATIC AND DYNAMIC CHARACTERS

Have you ever known someone who changed? Perhaps this person was once mean but is now kind. Similar to people in real life, characters in literature can change in the course of the story, novel, play, or poem. Characters that change or grow are called **dynamic characters**. Charles Dickens' *A Christmas Carol* gives a good example of a dynamic character. The story's main character, Ebenezer Scrooge, starts out as a hard-hearted miser. After he is visited by the ghosts of Christmas, Ebenezer becomes a different man. His heart fills with compassion, and he is no longer stingy or bad tempered. Since Scrooge is not the same at the end of the story as he was at the beginning, he is a dynamic character.

Sometimes characters do not change as you read. Rather, they remain the same until the story's end. Characters that remain the same are known as **static characters**. Static characters are often minor characters who serve to point out qualities of more major characters. Sometimes static characters exist to stand for an ideal, such as goodness or evil. An example of a static character is the witch in the fairy tale *Snow White and the Seven Dwarfs*. The witch represents evil and remains the same scary menace to Snow White throughout the story. Unlike Scrooge, she does not become a "better person."

Practice 3: Characters

Read the following passage about Rikki-tikki-tavi taken from Rudyard Kipling's *The Jungle Book*. Pay attention to character traits. Some are directly stated, and others are implied. Answer the questions that follow.

Mongoose

It is the hardest thing in the world to frighten a mongoose, because he is eaten up from nose to tail with curiosity. The motto of all the mongoose family is "Run and find out," and Rikki-tikki was a true mongoose. He looked at the cotton wool, decided that it was not good to eat, ran all round the table, sat up and put his fur in order, scratched himself, and jumped on the small boy's shoulder.

1. Which of the following is NOT a trait that describes Rikki-tikki?
   A. curious   B. shy   C. active   D. smart

2. What physical trait describes the boy in the story?
   A. smart   B. weak   C. small   D. tall

Read the following passage. Pay attention to how the author creates character motivation and emotion.

Becca waited nervously in the car-rider area at the front of her middle school. Craning her neck a bit, she hoped to catch a glimpse of her mother's silver mini-van making its way around the crowded circular lane. Her eyes were squinted, not because of the sunshine on this cloudy Friday afternoon, but because of her anxious eyebrows that furrowed across the top of wire-rimmed eye glasses. In her left hand, Becca held her violin, careful to have remembered it for weekend practice. In her right hand, she clutched her social studies test, the one that she had aced with flying colors. Becca was hoping that her good deeds could get her a step closer to spending Saturday afternoon at the mall with her best friend, Min.

3. Which of the following emotions is NOT displayed by Becca in the passage?
   A. anxiety   B. anticipation   C. nervousness   D. anger

4. Which of the following BEST describes what motivates Becca's anxiety and her desire to please her mother?

    A.   She is afraid of being punished for leaving her violin at school and receiving a poor mark on her social studies test.

    B.   She is hoping to impress her mother and earn the privilege of spending Saturday afternoon at the mall with her friend.

    C.   She is hoping that her good deeds will earn her the privilege of riding in the front seat, instead of allowing her brother to ride there.

    D.   She is hoping to impress her friend, Min, by practicing her violin over the weekend and acing her social studies test.

THEME AND TOPIC

In addition to recognizing setting and characterization, identifying **theme** is an important part of understanding literature. Theme is the underlying meaning or point of a work of literature. It is the idea about life that is revealed through some aspect of the story. When you are looking for a literary theme, you might consider how the main character changes or learns in the course of the story. Other important ideas to consider are the title and important passages in the work. Generally, theme is not stated directly, but must be inferred, or figured out, by the reader.

Sometimes in a work of literature, there are ideas that are important but not large enough to be considered a theme of that literary work. We can think of these ideas as **topics**. It is important that in your reading, you are able to distinguish a theme, which is the underlying meaning that a work of literature reveals, from a topic, which is simply a subject that the work talks about.

Here is an example of how to recognize theme:

In the story of "The Ugly Duckling," by Hans Christian Andersen, a family of ducks raises a swan. No one knows it's a swan; when it is little, it just looks too big and gangly to be a pretty little duckling. Near the end of the story, a group of children come to feed the ducks, and they see the "ugly" duckling, which has now become a beautiful swan. Read the passage from the story, paying attention to major ideas. (You can also read the whole story in a book of fairytales or online at www.bartleby.com/17/3/1.html.)

> Into the garden came little children, who threw bread and corn into the water; and the youngest cried, "There is a new one!" and the other children shouted joyously, "Yes, a new one has arrived!" And they clapped their hands and danced about, and ran to their father and mother; and bread and cake were thrown into the water; and they all said, "The new one is the most beautiful of all! So young and handsome!" and the old swans bowed their heads before him.

Which of the following BEST describes the theme of "The Ugly Duckling"?

    A.   Swans are pretty birds.

    B.   Being different does not make someone ugly.

    C.   Children like to feed birds.

    D.   Ducks and swans can sometimes swim together.

Answer **B** is the statement that can be a **theme** of this story. It is a general truth about life that is revealed by the story. It also is a lesson that a reader might learn from this story.

Answers **A**, **C**, and **D** are all smaller **topics**. They might be true statements for a reader, but they are not big enough ideas about life to be themes.

Practice 4: Theme and Topic

Read this description. Then answer the questions that follow.

> The novel, *A Perfect Storm*, centers on the conflict between the crew members of a fishing boat and a storm that they must face while at sea. In the end, the storm is stronger than they are. It swallows up the boat and everyone in it.

1. A possible theme of this novel might be stated as which of the following?

    A. Death is an inevitable consequence of the constant struggle in life.
    B. Sometimes in a conflict between man and nature, nature prevails.
    C. Death is sad and depressing.
    D. The sea is scary and dangerous.

2. Which of these is probably NOT a topic mentioned in the book?

    A. sea ports that pirates used in the old days
    B. what to do if caught in a storm at sea
    C. the difficulty of predicting the weather
    D. equipment fisherman use when out to sea

> A Lamb was perched up on the top of a house, and looking down saw a Wolf passing under him. Immediately he began to revile and attack his enemy. "Murderer and thief," he cried, "What are you doing here, near honest folks' houses? How dare you make an appearance where your vile deeds are known?"
>
> –"The Wolf and the Lamb" by Aesop

3. In this short fable, which of the following statements could serve as the theme?

    A. Pride is a lamb's best friend.
    B. Speaking to a wolf is bravery.
    C. Calling someone names involves foolishness.
    D. It is easy to be brave from a safe distance.

4. Which of the following statements could serve as a topic?

    A. It is easy to be brave from a safe distance.
    B. It is unwise to walk in high places.
    C. Wolves sometimes walk through villages.
    D. It is never safe to taunt others.

Chapter 6 Summary

Setting is the time and place in which the events of a work of literature occur.

Historical moment refers to the historical backdrop of a work of literature.

Plot is "what happens" in the story—all the related events that move the story from beginning to end. The plot shapes a work of literature.

Characterization is the way that an author introduces a character, letting a reader get to know that character.

- **Actions** are what characters do in a work of literature.
- **Traits** are character qualities; they may be physical or non-physical.
- **Emotions** are feelings demonstrated by a character.
- **Motives/Motivations** are reasons that characters are driven to act and what characters seek to do or obtain.
- **Dynamic Character** is a character that changes within a work of literature. The character grows or learns somehow or becomes different as a result of an event in the story.
- **Static Character** is a character that stays the same from beginning to end.

Theme is the underlying meaning of a story, novel, play, or poem. It is usually a truth about human nature. The story's details and plot point to the theme, but you usually have to figure it out (it is not directly stated). Themes are distinguishable from topics because themes are large ideas that are carried throughout a work of literature.

Topic is an idea or subject that is important in a work of literature but is not as dominant as a theme.

Purpose is the author's reason for writing the work of literature.

CHAPTER 6 REVIEW

Directions: Read each of the passages and answer the questions that follow.

> The policeman on the beat moved up the avenue impressively. The impressiveness was habitual and not for show, for spectators were few. The time was barely 10 o'clock at night, but chilly gusts of wind with a taste of rain in them had well nigh depeopled the streets.
>
> Trying doors as he went, twirling his club with many intricate and artful movements, turning now and then to cast his watchful eye adown the pacific thoroughfare, the officer, with his stalwart form and slight swagger, made a fine picture of a guardian of the peace. The vicinity was one that kept early hours. Now and then you might see the lights of a cigar store or of an all-night lunch counter; but the majority of the doors belonged to business places that had long since been closed.
>
> –From O'Henry's "After Twenty Years"

1. Which of the following sets of traits BEST characterizes the patrolman in the passage above?

   A. worldly, fun-loving, risk-taking   C. wise, selfish, short

   B. dutiful, hardworking, focused   D. caring, ambitious, angry

> In the novel, *The Giver*, by Lois Lowry the main character, Jonas, begins the book as a normal 11-year-old boy. By the end of the novel, Jonas has not only matured in age, but he has been forced to mature emotionally and psychologically as well.

2. Jonas is an example of

   A. a hero's quest.   C. a man-against-nature conflict.

   B. a static character.   D. a dynamic character.

> In Madeline L'Engle's novel, *A Wrinkle in Time*, Calvin is an important character whose personality and qualities are the same at the end of the book as at the beginning of the book.

3. Calvin is an example of:

   A. a hero's quest.   C. a man-against-nature conflict.

   B. a static character.   D. a dynamic character.

4. In a short story or novel where the main character dies, a possible and likely topic of the story is

   A. cultural events.   C. comedy.

   B. hero's quest.   D. tragedy.

5. In a short story or novel where the plot centers around a main character who must make a long trip to discover a great truth, which of the following themes is LEAST applicable?

   A. Sometimes one must journey to find oneself.

   B. A hero's quest is often a long journey to find truth.

   C. Discovery is a result of journey for truth.

   D. Often, men must battle to find themselves.

6. In a story where the main character seeks to understand or solve a mystery, it might be said that this character is motivated by which of the following?

   A. a quest for fame   C. a quest for attention

   B. a quest for knowledge   D. a quest for love

7. Which of the following is NOT a physical character trait?

   A. beauty   B. humility   C. strength   D. baldness

   The room filled with silence. Everyone waited as Amy searched her mind for an answer to the teacher's question. Looking down at her open binder, she could feel the fluttering of nervous butterflies in her stomach. Her palms sweated, and she gulped back tears.

8. What is the setting of the story?

   A. the cafeteria   C. Amy's house

   B. the classroom   D. the library

9. A story in which characters live in log cabins and travel by horse in carriage is MOST likely placed in which historical setting?

   A. colonial America   C. ancient Egypt

   B. 1990s America   D. future Japan

   Four-year-old Maria peered at her mother with a mischievous glare. The girl knew that she had spent the day causing havoc. She had begun the morning by deliberately turning over the puppy feeding bowl, giggling menacingly as she had done so. By noon, Maria had managed to cover the nursery room wall with every color of the Crayola rainbow. With this, she had clapped and bounced at her ingenuity. Now that it was time for dinner, Maria had the table covered in a recipe of salt, pepper, and Elmer's glue. Her mother was fed up with the girl's naughty antics.

10. Based upon the actions, emotions, and narrator descriptions of the girl in the passage, what word would BEST describe her?

   A. well-behaved   B. docile   C. compliant   D. rebellious

11. Which one of the following could be stated as a story's theme?

   A. Tyrone's skateboard was shiny and new.
   B. Felisha got caught in a downpour.
   C. It is better to have loved and lost than never to have loved at all.
   D. Scrooge is a character in a novel by Charles Dickens.

Read this excerpt from the play Pygmalion by George Bernard Shaw. Pygmalion is the story of a professor who makes a bet that he can transform a poor, uneducated flower girl by teaching her to speak perfectly. The film My Fair Lady is based on this play. After reading the excerpt, answer the questions that follow.

THE FLOWER GIRL [to Pickering, as he passes her]. Buy a flower, kind gentleman. I'm short for my lodging.

PICKERING. I really haven't any change. I'm sorry [he goes away].

HIGGINS [shocked at girl's mendacity[1]]. Liar. You said you could change half-a-crown.

THE FLOWER GIRL [rising in desperation]. You ought to be stuffed with nails, you ought. [Flinging the basket at his feet.] Take the whole blooming basket for sixpence[2].

[The church clock strikes the second quarter.]

HIGGINS [hearing in it the voice of God, rebuking him for his Pharisaic want of charity to the poor girl]. A reminder. [He raises his hat solemnly; then throws a handful of money into the basket and follows Pickering.]

THE FLOWER GIRL [picking up a half-crown]. Ah-ow-ooh! [Picking up a couple of florins.] Aaah-ow-ooh! [Picking up several coins.] Aaaaaah-ow-ooh! [Picking up a half-sovereign.] Aaaaaaaaaaaah-ow-ooh!!!

FREDDY [springing out of a taxicab]. Got one at last. Hallo! [To the girl] Where are the two ladies that were here?

THE FLOWER GIRL. They walked to the bus when the rain stopped.

FREDDY. And left me with a cab on my hands. Damnation!

THE FLOWER GIRL [with grandeur]. Never you mind, young man. I'm going home in a taxi. [She sails off to the cab. The driver puts his hand behind him and holds the door firmly shut against her. Quite understanding his mistrust, she shows him her handful of money.] Eightpence ain't no object to me, Charlie. [He grins and opens the door.] Angel Court, Drury Lane, round the corner of Micklejohn's oil shop. Let's see how fast you can make her hop it. [She gets in and pulls the door to with a slam as the taxicab starts.]

---

1. mendacity: deception, dishonesty
2. sixpence: a coin that was used in Britain but hasn't been minted since the 1970s (equal to a little more than 10 cents American)

12. Based on clues provided in the excerpt and the footnotes, what is the setting of this play?
    A. New York City in the present day
    B. London in the early 20th century
    C. an alien planet in the future
    D. Rome in the time of the gladiators

13. What is the MOST likely motivation for Professor Higgins to teach the flower girl to speak well?
    A. to win the bet he's made
    B. to be admired for his good work
    C. to impress the flower girl
    D. to receive a promotion at work

14. Based on this example, how can you tell what characters are doing when you read a play?
    A. The narrator describes a scene before the characters begin speaking.
    B. You have to watch the play being acted on stage.
    C. Directions for the actions of each character are written in brackets.
    D. You have to imagine what each character might do.

15. Which of these lines spoken by the flower girl is an example of **dialect**?
    A. Buy a flower, kind gentleman.
    B. I'm short for my lodging.
    C. They walked to the bus when the rain stopped.
    D. Eightpence ain't no object to me, Charlie.

16. Based on this excerpt, which traits BEST describe the flower girl?
    A. shy and soft-spoken
    B. loud and forceful
    C. refined and polite
    D. impatient and scared

Chapter 7
Figurative Language, Tone, and Mood

This chapter covers the following Georgia standard.

ELA7R1	For literary texts, identify the characteristics of various genres, and produce evidence of understanding the effects of sound, form, figurative language, and graphics, as well as the author's use of words to create mood and tone.

In the last chapter, you learned about types of literature called genres. You also learned about elements of literature like setting, characters, and theme. These are like the floor, walls, and roof of a house. The structure of writing makes sure it has everything it needs so someone can read it—just as a house needs a floor, walls, and roof so someone can live in it.

Now, it's time to get some furniture and decorate that house! In this chapter, you will learn about ways in which an author make writing interesting and memorable. You will learn about the use of figurative language as well as the way that writers create tone and mood. These are all **literary devices** that help to shape the literature that we read.

All writing has words, but the way that the words are used makes each story, novel, poem, and play unique!

FIGURATIVE LANGUAGE

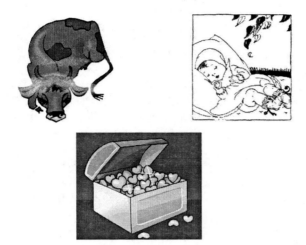

Have you ever heard a statement similar to one of these?

I am so hungry, I could eat a cow.

I slept like a baby last night.

She has a heart of gold.

Have you ever heard or tried to say a tongue twister?

Peter Piper picked a peck of pickled peppers.

These are all examples of **figurative language**. In literature, writers use figurative language to liven up their writing. They also use it to give precise expression to the ideas they wish to convey. Recognizing and understanding figurative language is an important part of reading literature.

Figurative language uses words or phrases that are not literally true. Often, one thing is described in terms of something else; to do this, the author uses imaginative comparisons. These descriptions can also be called **figures of speech**. The most common forms of figurative language are the following.

Simile:	A **simile** makes a comparison between two unlike things, using a word such as *like, as, than,* or *resembles*. **Similes** are commonly used to help writers express their ideas in a precise or imaginative manner.
	Example: *She was as fast as a cheetah. He is crazy like a fox. She is wiser than an owl.*
Metaphor:	A **metaphor** is an imaginative comparison between two unlike things in which one thing is said to be another thing. **Metaphors**, unlike similes, do not use words such as *like, as, than,* or *resembles*, to express comparisons.
	Example: He is a beast on the prowl. I am a monster on the soccer field. The roar of the engines was thunder, and the sparks flying on the speedway were its partner, lightning.
Analogy:	**Analogies** group words that are dissimilar by applying relationships between the words. The following word pairs are **analogies:** *Apple* is to *red* as *banana* is to *yellow*. (Here, each fruit is linked to its common color.) *Sandpaper* is to *rough* as *cotton balls* are to *soft*. (Each item is linked to its texture.) In literature, comparisons of unlike things can help readers understand concepts in new and creative ways.
	Example: *A child's life is like a piece of paper on which every person leaves a mark.* (The author is comparing the way in which people make impressions on a young child to the way that a pencil or pen writes on paper.)
Personification:	**Personification** is a figure of speech in which a nonhuman thing or quality is given human characteristics. Often, the use of **personified** objects in literature conjures up vivid mental images that readers can picture.
	Example: *The numbers danced off the page of my algebra test. My alarm clock screamed at me from the dresser. The television called out to me as I tried to concentrate on writing my essay.*
Hyperbole:	**Hyperbole** is the use of overstatement or exaggeration. It is a special type of figurative language that allows writers to infuse shades of meaning into their descriptions of characters and plots. Many **hyperboles** can be funny. For example, while a character could be described simply as strong, consider the power of describing him as having *the strength of a team of oxen*. Another example: *I was so hungry, I ate the entire house.*

Imagery:	**Imagery** is language that appeals to the senses. Most images are visual; they appeal to the sense of sight, creating pictures that readers can see in their minds. Other images appeal to the senses of touch, taste, hearing, or smell. Here is an example of **imagery** that uses the senses of smell, hearing, and sight: *Joey awoke to the smell of blueberry pancakes and bacon. He could hear the" sizzle pop" sound of the bacon frying in Grandma's iron skillet. Opening his eyes, he saw the floral pattern of the wallpaper that trimmed the tops of grandma's guest bedroom walls.*
Symbol	A **symbol** is a person, place, thing, or event that has its own meaning and stands for something beyond itself as well. **Symbols** are used in everyday life. For example, a red rose or a heart shape can symbolize love. An example of symbolism, appears in the novel *Lord of the Flies* by William Golding. In this novel, the young boys who are stranded on a deserted island come to fear "the beast" that they think inhabits the island. The idea of the beast is a symbol of the evil that is actually inside many of them.
Irony:	**Irony** is a contrast between expectation and reality. There are three common types of **irony**. • **Verbal irony** involves a contrast between what is said or written and what is meant. **Example:** After a day of mischief, little Juan was tired. With a smile, his mother put him down for a nap, cooing sweetly, "Now you can rest, *my little angel.*" • **Situational irony** occurs when what happens is very different from what is expected to happen. For example, in Aesop's fable, "The Tortoise and the Hare," a tortoise wins a race of speed against a hare. This surprise ending is an example of situational irony. • **Dramatic irony** occurs when the audience or the reader knows something a character does not know. For example, in reading a tragic novel where the main character is ill and going to die, the reader might learn that a character will die before the character actually realizes that death is near.
Paradox:	A **paradox** is a true statement that seems to contradict itself. For example, in Aesop's fable "The Wolf and the Lamb," which you read in the last chapter, a lamb makes bold insults to a wolf while standing out of the wolf's reach. This behavior could be described as "cowardly bravery." While the lamb shows that he is brave enough to stand up to the wolf, the lamb is only so brave because he is out of the wolf's reach. This means that the lamb's behavior is actually cowardly.

Practice 1: Figurative Language

Read the passages and answer the questions that follow.

A Book

by Emily Dickinson

He ate and drank the precious words,
His spirit grew robust;
He knew no more that he was poor,
Nor that his frame was dust.
He danced along the dingy days,
And this bequest of wings
Was but a book. What liberty
A loosened spirit brings!

1. In this poem, "he" refers to a book. This is an example of which form of figurative language?

   A. dramatic irony   C. hyperbole

   B. simile   D. personification

2. In this poem, the comparison of the book to a person is an example of which form of figurative language?

   A. situational irony   C. irony

   B. metaphor   D. paradox

   Upon the eighth night I was more than usually cautious in opening the door. A watch's minute hand moves more quickly than did nine.

   –from "The Tell-Tale Heart" by Edgar Allan Poe

3. Line 2 of this passage contains an example of which form of figurative language?

   A. simile   B. paradox   C. verbal irony   D. hyperbole

4. The following statement is an example of which form of figurative language?

   After returning from boot camp, the young man was as skinny as a rail.

   A. metaphor   B. symbolism   C. hyperbole   D. paradox

5. Complete this analogy: *Medical school* is to *doctors* as *law school* is to _____.

   A. paralegals   C. voters

   B. court stenographers   D. lawyers

Read this passage and answer the questions that follow.

Colin had been nervous all day. He had been practicing his history oral report for three weeks, yet he felt unprepared. He shuddered to think how he would feel standing in front of his classmates trying to remember details about the settlement of Savannah. Colin was so nervous about his speech that he had forgotten to write his name on his spelling quiz and made careless mistakes on his math test.

Now, as he sat at the lunch table, knowing the speech would be next period during social studies, Colin felt just like a newly hatched chick…he wanted to crawl right back into his shell. He ate his lunch slowly, lost in thought, going over the speech in his head. So consumed by worries about the coming speech, Colin forgot to grab a napkin and wipe his mouth after lunch. Unknowingly, he left the cafeteria and headed to social studies class with a milk moustache.

Finally, it was Colin's turn to speak about Savannah. He got up and walked slowly to the front of the classroom, turning to face the other students. A soft ripple of giggles made their way to him, starting with a small point-and-sniggle from Amy Tinsley in the back. When Mrs. Boles looked up from her grading notes to see what the children found so amusing, she had to hold back her own giggle. "Colin, dear," she said in her gentle way, "you are wearing a milk moustache."

6. What type of irony, if any, is used in this story?
   A.   Irony is not used.
   B.   Verbal irony is used.
   C.   Situational irony is used.
   D.   Dramatic irony is used.

7. What form of figurative language is used in this sentence from the passage:

   Now, as he sat at the lunch table, knowing the speech would be next period during social studies, Colin felt just like a newly hatched chick…and he wanted to crawl right back into his shell.

   A.   metaphor   B.   analogy   C.   paradox   D.   hyperbole

Read this passage. Then answer the questions that follow.

Sitting propped up by pillows in his bed, Kunal looked around his room. He saw his new computer system, complete with the latest technology and gadgets. It sat on the awesome new desk over to his left. The desk had been a surprise from his older brother who was away at college. On his right was Kunal's flat screen television that his parents had bought for him. The corkboard beside the TV had little space left; it was crowded by funny pictures and get-well cards from friends and family. Kunal could not help but think of himself as incredibly lucky and loved despite the cast that was heavy on his broken right leg. He would have lots of time to use his computer and watch his TV now that he could no longer compete in the sport he loved. He would no longer travel to all the state and regional tournaments with the basketball team. He had played as long as he could remember, perfecting his game, and now that he was so close, he might never get that scholarship he was hoping for. At least it would make sense, had he broken his leg playing…but he was in this cast because of taking a wrong step off a curb!

8. Which type of imagery is MOSTLY used in the following passage?
   A. sound   B. visual   C. taste   D. smell

9. What object could MOST be considered a symbol for Kunal not being able to play basketball?
   A. his room   C. the computer
   B. his new television   D. the cast on his leg

10. What type of irony, if any, is used in this passage?
   A. Irony is not used.   C. Situational irony is used.
   B. Verbal irony is used.   D. Dramatic irony is used.

SOUND

Have you ever had to recite a poem? Some forms of literature, such as poetry, are written to be read aloud. In these cases, special **sound devices** help to shape the writing of these literary forms. Writers use the following sound devices to give creativity and style to their writing.

Alliteration is the repetition of the same or very similar consonant sounds at the beginning of words. Alliteration helps emphasize words. It is used most often in poetry.

> **Example:** *The whisper of the wind-blown willows* (repeats the "w" sound).

Onomatopoeia refers to words that say the sound they are describing. Onomatopoeia helps to create the sound imagery of poetry.

> **Example:** *meow, buzz, tick-tock, boom*

Rhyme is the repetition of accented vowel sounds and all sounds following them in words close together in a poem.

> **Example:** *The cat in the hat sat on the mat* (*cat, hat, sat,* and *mat* all rhyme).

- Two types of rhymes are **internal rhyme** and **end rhyme**.
- **Internal rhyme** means that words within a line rhyme, like the example you just read, or like this example: *We **fight** with all our **might** to win by ten **tonight***
- **End rhyme** occurs at the end of lines.

> **Example:**
> 1 Here a star, and there a star,
> 2 Some lose their **way**.
> 3 Here a mist, and there a mist,
> 4 Afterwards – **day**!
> –Emily Dickinson

In this poem, **lines 2 and 4** use end rhyme.

The pattern of end rhymes in a poem is called a **rhyme scheme**. Readers use separate letters of the alphabet to identify each new sound in a poem's rhyme scheme. For example, the following quatrain (a poem with 4 lines in each stanza) has an *abab* rhyme scheme:

> Meg likes to read and eat. *a*
>
> She does not like to write. *b*
>
> She will devour a book or a tasty treat. *a*
>
> But she won't write her essay tonight. *b*

RHYTHM

Just like in music, **rhythm** refers to the beat and pace of written words. This is achieved by stressing certain syllables. Especially in poetry (in which meter is used to measure syllables), rhythm becomes important in the overall structure of the writing. Depending on how sounds are arranged, rhythm can be fast or slow, choppy or smooth, pleasant or harsh. Rhythm in prose (stories and novels) comes from repetitions of sounds and pauses.

Notice the rhythm of the excerpt from *The Song of Hiawatha* by Henry Wadsworth Longfellow:.

Example:

> By the shore of Gitchie Gumee,
>
> By the shining Big-Sea-Water,
>
> At the doorway of his wigwam,
>
> In the pleasant Summer morning,
>
> Hiawatha stood and waited.

Hiawatha

The rhythm is repetitive, with the stress on the same syllables in each line. So, it sounds almost like a Native American chant.

Practice 2: Sound

Read this except and then answer the questions about it.

> Once upon a midnight dreary, while I pondered, weak and weary,
> Over many a quaint and curious volume of forgotten **lore**,
> While I nodded, nearly napping, suddenly there came a tapping,
> As of some one gently rapping, rapping at my chamber **door**.
>
> "'Tis some visitor," I muttered, "tapping at my chamber **door**—
> Only this, and nothing **more**."

–from "The Raven" by Edgar Allan Poe

1. What literary sound device is used in the bolded words?
   - A. alliteration
   - B. onomatopoeia
   - C. end rhyme
   - D. internal rhyme

2. In this poem, which literary sound device is used in the line: *while I pondered, weak and weary,...?*
   - A. alliteration
   - B. onomatopoeia
   - C. end rhyme
   - D. internal rhyme

3. The rhythm of the poem is steady until the last line. Why does it MOST likely change then?
   - A. It trails off to show the reader that the narrator of the poem has left the room.
   - B. It ends abruptly to give an eerie, suspenseful feeling about what comes next.
   - C. It gets faster as the narrator becomes more frightened and his heart beats faster.
   - D. It slows down to show that it is late at night and the house is very quiet.

In another part of the poem, "The Raven," Poe writes:

> *Back into the chamber turning, all my soul within me burning.*

4. What literary sound device is used in the line above?
   - A. alliteration
   - B. onomatopoeia
   - C. end rhyme
   - D. internal rhyme

> The birds **buzzed**. The crickets **chirped**.

5. What literary sound device is used in the bolded words?
   - A. alliteration
   - B. onomatopoeia
   - C. end rhyme
   - D. internal rhyme

6. Which letter scheme below represents the rhyme scheme of the following poem?

> Glee! The great storm is over!
> Four have recovered the land;
> Forty gone down together
> Into the boiling sand.

–excerpt from "Life" by Emily Dickinson

   - A. abcc
   - B. abcb
   - C. abaa
   - D. abbc

GRAPHICS

In reading literature, especially poetry, there are some important graphic techniques to recognize. The way that poets use graphics such as **capital letters, line length, and word position** help to give readers important clues about the meaning of the poem.

Capital letters
In traditional poetry, the first word in a line is capitalized. Modern poetry does not always follow this traditional style.
Line length
Poets use line length to alter meaning, to create sounds and rhythm.
Word position
Choosing words in poetry is different than choosing words for other forms of literature. One way for poets to give creative style to their writing is to play around with a variety of wording positions.

Practice 3: Graphics

Read the following poem by Emily Dickinson, noticing the capitalization of the first word of each line, the variation of line lengths, and word position choices she uses.

Emily Dickinson

Success

Success is counted sweetest
By those who ne'er succeed.
To comprehend a nectar
Requires sorest need.

Not one of all the purple host
Who took the flag to-day
Can tell the definition,
So clear, of victory,

As he, defeated, dying,
On whose forbidden ear
The distant strains of triumph
Break, agonized and clear!

1. Discuss with a classmate how her use of graphic devices affects the overall poem. Write a list how each graphic element works in the poem, and share it with your teacher.

2. Sometimes words are positioned in the poem differently than how we would say them. Using this poem as an example, choose specific lines and figure out reasons why words are positioned as they are.

TONE AND MOOD

Tone in literature involves the attitude that a writer takes toward the audience, a subject, or a character. Tone is conveyed through the writer's choice of words and details.

Examples of Author's Tone			
serious	humorous	sarcastic	ironic
satirical	solemn	objective	angry
hysterical	desperate	tongue-in-cheek	light-hearted

Mood is closely related to tone, but slightly different. Rather than addressing how the writer, narrator, or speaker feels, mood is the overall emotion created by a work of literature. There are infinite possibilities for expressing literary tone and mood.

Examples of the Mood of a Work of Literature			
hopeful	horrific	sad	upbeat
joyful	scary	suspenseful	pensive

Practice 4: Tone and Mood

Read the following passages and answer the questions that follow.

The Camel's hump is an ugly lump
  Which well you may see at the Zoo;
But uglier yet is the hump we get
  From having too little to do.

Kiddies and grown-ups too-oo-oo,
If we haven't enough to do-oo-oo,
    We get the hump—
    Cameelious hump—
The hump that is black and blue!

–from Rudyard Kipling's "How the Camel Got His Hump"

1. Which of the following BEST describe the speaker's tone in the poem above?
    A. angry   B. humorous   C. confused   D. efficient

Without, the night was cold and wet, but in the small parlour of Laburnam Villa the blinds were drawn and the fire burned brightly. Father and son were at chess, the former, who possessed ideas about the game involving radical changes, putting his king into such sharp and unnecessary perils that it even provoked comment from the white-haired old lady knitting placidly by the fire.

"Hark at the wind," said Mr. White, who, having seen a fatal mistake after it was too late, was amiably desirous of preventing his son from seeing it.

"I'm listening," said the latter, grimly surveying the board as he stretched out his hand. "Check."

"I should hardly think that he'd come to-night," said his father, with his hand poised over the board.

–from "The Monkey's Paw" by W.W. Jacobs

2. In the above passage, which of the following BEST describes the mood?
   A. hopeful
   B. upbeat
   C. eerie
   D. sad

CHAPTER 7 SUMMARY

Figurative language uses words or phrases that describe one thing in terms of something else and are not literally true.

A **simile** makes a comparison between two unlike things, using a word such as like, as, than, or resembles. *Example: She was as quiet as a mouse.*

A **metaphor** is an imaginative comparison between two unlike things in which one thing is said to be another thing. Metaphors, unlike similes, do not use the words such as like, as, than, or resembles, to express comparisons. *Example: My love is a burning flame.*

Personification is a figure of speech in which a nonhuman thing or quality is given human characteristics. *Example: The couch moaned under the weight of the heavy dog.*

Hyperbole is the use of overstatement and/or exaggeration. *Example: She has the beauty of ten thousand princesses.*

Sound

Writers use sound in the form of literary devices to give creativity and style to their writing. **Alliteration** is the repetition of the same or very similar consonant sounds in words that are close together. *Example: Two tons of tangerines…*

Onomatopoeia is the use of words with sounds that echo their sense. *Ex. bark, buzz, boom*

Rhyme is the repetition of accented vowel sounds and all sounds following them in words close together in a poem. *Example: dog, frog*

- **End rhymes** are rhymes that occur at the end of a line.
- **Internal rhymes** are rhymes within a line.
- **Rhyme scheme** is the pattern of end rhymes in a poem. Readers use separate letters of the alphabet to identify rhyme scheme in a poem.

Graphics

In reading literature, especially poetry, there are some important graphic techniques to recognize.

> In traditional poetry, the first word in a line is **capitalized**. Modern poetry does not always follow this traditional style.
> Poets use **line length** to alter meaning, to create sounds and rhythm.
> One way for poets to give creative style to their writing is to use a variety of **word positions**.

Tone in literature involves the attitude that a writer takes toward the audience, a subject, or a character. Tone is conveyed through the writer's choice of words and details. **Mood** is the overall emotion created by a work of literature.

CHAPTER 7 REVIEW

Read each passage and answer the questions that follow.

> Let the world's sharpness like a clasping knife
> Shut in upon itself and do no harm
> In this close hand of Love, now soft and warm,
> And let us hear no sound of human strife
> After the click of the shutting. Life to life -   5
> I lean upon thee, Dear, without alarm,
> And feel as safe as guarded by a charm
> Against the stab of worldlings, who if rife
> Are weak to injure. Very whitely still
> The lilies of our lives may reassure   10
> Their blossoms from their roots, accessible
> Alone to heavenly dews that drop not fewer;
> Growing straight, out of man's reach, on the hill.
> God only, who made us rich, can make us poor.

–Elizabeth Barrett Browning

1. What literary sound device occurs in lines **2** and **3**?
    A.   alliteration   C.   end rhyme
    B.   onomatopoeia   D.   internal rhyme

2. What use of figurative language occurs in line **3** in the statement: *this close hand of Love*?
    A.   metaphor   B.   personification   C.   hyperbole   D.   sarcasm

3. Which of the following BEST describes the tone of the poem?
    A.   sarcastic   B.   humorous   C.   excited   D.   imploring

Sonnet 43

How do I love thee? Let me count the ways.
I love thee to the depth and breadth and height
My soul can reach, when feeling out of sight
For the ends of Being an Ideal Grace.
I love thee to the level of everyday's
Most quiet need, by sun and candle-light.
I love thee freely, as men strive for Right;
I love thee purely, as they turn from Praise.
I love thee with the passion put to use
In my old griefs, and with my childhood's faith.
I love thee with a love I seemed to lose
With my lost saints,—I love thee with the breath,
Smiles, tears, of all my life!—and, if God choose,
I shall but love thee better after death.

–Elizabeth Barrett Browning

4. In the first four lines what method of figurative language does the speaker of this poem use to describe the nature the love felt?
   A. simile
   B. hyperbole
   C. metaphor
   D. personification

5. Which of the following words BEST describes the tone of the poem?
   A. sarcastic   B. humorous   C. passionate   D. urgent

6. Which of the following sound devices is NOT used in this line: *I love thee with a love I seem to lose*?
   A. alliteration
   B. onomatopoeia
   C. rhythm
   D. internal rhyme

Read this poem. Then answer the question about it.

There are strange things done in the midnight sun
By the men who moil for gold;
The Arctic trails have their secret tales
That would make your blood run cold;
The Northern Lights have seen queer sights,
But the queerest they ever did see
Was that night on the marge of Lake Lebarge
 I cremated Sam McGee.

–from "The Cremation of Sam McGee" by Robert Service

7. Which of the following graphic devices is MOST important in creating the rhythm of the poem on the previous page?

   A. capitalization   C. word position

   B. line length   D. none of the above

> Well, he seemed so **low** that I couldn't say **no**; then he says with a sort of moan:
> "It's the cursed **cold**, and it's got right **hold** till I'm chilled clean through to the bone.

   –from "The Cremation of Sam McGee" by Robert Service

8. Which of the following sound devices do the **bolded** words represent?

   A. alliteration   C. end rhyme

   B. onomatopoeia   D. internal rhyme

9. Words like *yelp, scratch, and thud* make use of which sound device?

   A. alliteration   C. end rhyme

   B. onomatopoeia   D. internal rhyme

10. Which of the following sentences is an example of simile?

   A. Life is a sea.   C. Life is strife.

   B. Life is in the sea.   D. Life is like a sea.

11. Which of the following sentences is an example of metaphor?

   A. Life is a sea.   C. Life is strife.

   B. Life is in the sea.   D. Life is like a sea.

I slept the deepest sleep

(anonymous)

I slept
the deepest sleep of
      my life
before the wails of day
      turned to darkest night.

My father left me
      all alone.
My mother soothed
      my weary bones.

Three endless nights
      was I shrouded in white
      until father woke me
from deep sleep
      to new life.

12. Which of the following words BEST describes the mood of the poem?

   A. upbeat   B. confused   C. angry   D. excited

Read the following passage.

> A coffee shop customer who has been rudely treated pauses before leaving the store to say to the offending clerk, "Thank you for your outstanding customer service."

13. What type of irony, if any, does it contain?
    A. situational irony   C. dramatic irony
    B. verbal irony   D. no irony

14. Choose the kind of irony used in the following situation. In the "Three Little Pigs," the fact that one little pig outsmarts the Big Bad Wolf, getting him to fall into a kettle of boiling water, is an example of
    A. situational irony.   C. dramatic irony.
    B. verbal irony.   D. no irony.

15. What kind of irony, if any, is used in the novel described below?

> In the novel, *The Giver*, the reader understands that being assigned to be the next receiver of memories means that Jonas will have to hold the memories of society's social past. Jonas, however, does not understand his fate. While Jonas struggles through plot and conflict to understand his huge assignment, suspense builds while the reader waits.

    A. situational irony   C. dramatic irony
    B. verbal irony   D. no irony

16. In the fairy tale, "Cinderella," the poor stepdaughter (who has been treated as a housekeeper) is chosen as the prince's favorite over her pampered stepsisters (who have been given every advantage). This is an example of
    A. situational irony.   C. dramatic irony.
    B. verbal irony.   D. no irony.

17. Which line of the following poem contains a paradox?

> 1 Busy noises
> 2 People's voices
> 3 The sounds around me
> 4 Melt into one hum drum drone
> 5 As I sit on the corner stoop and think about
> 6 The noisy quiet of my city block

    A. line 1   B. line 3   C. line 5   D. line 6

18. This passage MOSTLY uses which form of imagery?
    A. smell   B. sight   C. taste   D. sound

19. In the fairy tale, "The Three Little Pigs," it might be said that the wolf is a symbol of
    A. anger.   B. hunger.   C. evil.   D. grief.

20. Which word best completes this analogy? *Horse* is to *barn* as *man* is to _____.
    A. car   B. house   C. school   D. office

21. Identify the rhyme scheme of the poetry lines below:

    Success is counted sweetest

    By those who ne'er succeed.

    To comprehend a nectar

    Requires sorest need.

    A. abcb   B. abab   C. abcd   D. aaab

Chapter 8
Literature across Cultures

This chapter covers the following Georgia standard.

ELA7R1	Identify the characteristics of various literary genres and identify and analyze similarities and differences in traditional literature from different cultures.

LITERATURE IN DIFFERENT CULTURES

Stories, poems, and plays are all forms of literature. Literature is used to tell stories. It also can be used to entertain, to inform, or to persuade. Literature also helps people remember events or ideas that are important in a culture.

Stories, poems, and plays can be found in every culture around the world. Greeks and Romans passed down myths with gods and goddesses. Africans songs and spirituals (which are types of poems) tell stories. European cultures have fables and fairytales that teach lessons. The list goes on and on.

Literature can help people understand their own culture, and it can help different cultures understand each other. Many cultures pass down their stories from one generation to another. This means that traditions will be remembered.

SIMILARITIES IN LITERATURE ACROSS CULTURES

A culture's stories come from the experiences of its people. People have the same experiences even if they live in different parts of the world.

For example, every culture has a story of how its people settled in a region. Every culture has a tale of a hero to remember and celebrate. Every culture has children's stories that teach lessons. These kinds of tales help different cultures connect through similar experiences.

In America today, you can find literature from many cultures. There are songs, fables, and fairytales from African history. There are poems and stories from Greek and Norse mythology. You can read stories and fables from all over Europe. Even though these cultures are spread out across the world, they have similar forms of literature, like stories, poems, and plays.

Here is an example of how literature is passed from one culture to another and is updated for each generation.

> Washington Irving wrote a famous story about a headless horseman. "The Legend of Sleepy Hollow" was published in America in 1818. But the idea for it came from many stories told in different cultures.
>
> For example, Ireland had stories about a "death coach" driven by a coachman without a head. Germany had stories about a headless horseman riding through the Black Forest.
>
> Today, we still read the story, "The Legend of Sleepy Hollow." And now, this story—inspired by tales from other cultures—inspires people to retell it in new ways. One example is the 1999 movie *Sleepy Hollow*.

THEME

The many uses of literature are similar across different cultures. Most stories, poems, and plays have themes. As you learned in chapter 6, a **theme** is the underlying meaning of a piece of literature. It is different from a simple topic discussed in writing. Read more about theme in chapter 6, Understanding Literature.

Themes can be found in the literature of every culture. For example, *The Adventures of Huckleberry Finn* by Mark Twain discusses racism and slavery—these are **topics** of the book. But a **theme** of the book is how slavery has negative effects on both the slave and the slave owner.

Literature can also do things like:

- help explain the beliefs in a culture.

- tell why a group of people settled in a certain place.

- explain mysteries like birth and death.

- explore the traditions and rules in a society.

LITERARY GENRES

As you know, literature is made up of **genres**. The big "umbrella" genres include the following:

Genres	
nonfiction	includes biographies and autobiographies
fiction	includes novels and short stories
drama	includes plays and screenplays
poetry	includes sonnets, lyric poems, haiku

Each big umbrella genre has its own **format** and **characteristics**. These include the language it uses, the characters in it, its themes, and its length, to name just a few.

- **Nonfiction** is full of real-life facts and people. It can be short, like an article in a newspaper, or long, like a biography about a famous person.

- **Fiction** has a made-up story and characters. A novel can be very long, while a short story can be as short as one page.

- **Poetry** is usually written in verses and sometimes rhymes. It is usually short. One exception is epic poems, which can be as long as novels!

- **Drama** is written with stage directions and dialog for the characters to say. There are short, one-act plays, which means they have only one act and might take only half an hour to act out. They can also be long, full-length plays with many acts that take hours. Screenplays from which movies are made are examples of drama.

Each umbrella genre also has smaller genres in it. For example, genres under the umbrella of fiction include myth, fairytale, fable, romance, mystery, science fiction, western, and others. Some of these—like myths, legends, and fairytales—are common in many cultures around the world. Others might be familiar, but people in another country might not know what they are. For example, they may have never read a western. They may not know about science fiction. Some genres are common in some cultures and not in others.

FICTION

This table explains some of the genres of **fiction** that are common in many cultures.

Fable: a short tale that teaches a moral or lesson, usually using animals as characters	**Example:** "The Tortoise and the Hare" by Aesop
Fairytale: a story that uses magical events and characters to solve problems or teach lessons	**Example:** "Little Red Riding Hood," "Beauty and the Beast"
Legend: a story written to celebrate a hero, usually related to a historic period in a culture	**Example:** *Iliad* and *Odyssey,* epic poems by Greek poet Homer, tell stories about the hero Achilles
Tall tale: a special kind of legend in which the hero is larger than life	**Example:** stories about Paul Bunyan and his giant ox, Babe
Myth: a story with supernatural characters and events that explains something in a culture	**Example:** the famous Greek myth of how Prometheus stole fire from gods and gave it to human beings
Parable: a brief story that has a moral or religious lesson	**Example:** parables in the Bible, like the story of the prodigal son (its lesson is that parents love their children no matter what mistakes they make)

Genres are similar to each other across cultures. For example, poems convey emotion and imagery, no matter what language they are written in. Most fiction has humans and/or animals as characters. Fables and fairytales include lessons for children to learn. Many ancient cultures, like the Greeks, Romans, and Egyptians, used stories and poems to pass down ideas from one generation to the next.

Practice 1: Similar Fiction across Cultures

Read the following excerpts and answer the questions.

A Story from Japan

A long time ago, all the elements—water, air, earth, and fire—were mixed together. A spirit of life lay inside. This spirit stirred everything around until the heavy parts began to settle and the lighter parts rose to the top. An ocean covered the whole earth, and from it began to grow a green shoot. It grew taller and bigger until it reached the clouds. There, it was transformed into a god. Other shoots grew into more gods. The last two gods created, Izanagi and Izanami, were the most remarkable.

The other gods all asked Izanagi and Izanami to create the first land. So the two descended to the watery earth. They wondered what they should do. Izanagi suggested to his companion that they try stirring the seas. He thrust his staff into the waters. When he pulled it back up, some clumps of mud fell back into the sea. They grew and became solid, and today they are the islands of Japan.

The two gods descended to these islands to explore, each going in a different direction. They created a variety of plants. When they met again they decided to marry and have children to inhabit the land. The first child Izanami bore, Amaterasu, was a girl of radiant beauty. The gods decided to put her up in the sky, and she became the sun. Their second daughter, Tsukuyomi, became the moon. Their third child, Susanoo, was an unruly son and was sentenced to the sea, where he creates storms.

Later, their first child, Amaterasu, bore a son who became the emperor of Japan. All the emperors since then have claimed to descend from him.

1. What genre of fiction is this?

    A.   a fairytale   B.   a myth   C.   a tall tale   D.   a parable

2. How do you know that it is this genre of fiction?

    A.   The story talks about a real-life hero and depicts a historical period.

    B.   It contains tales about a larger-than-life hero and his adventures.

    C.   The story has animal characters and gives readers a moral or lesson.

    D.   It has supernatural characters and explains how the world started.

Aesop was one of the most famous writers of fables. He lived in Greece in the 6th century B.C., so his stories have been around for a very long time. His fables include animal characters. Their adventures teach the reader some kind of lesson or moral.

–excerpt from Aesop's fable *The Lion and the Mouse*

Once, when a Lion was asleep, a little Mouse ran up and down upon him. This soon woke up the Lion. He placed his huge paw upon the Mouse and opened his big jaws to swallow him. "Pardon, O King," cried the little Mouse. "Forgive me this time, and I shall never forget it. Who knows—I may be able to do you a turn one of these days." The Lion was so tickled at the idea of the Mouse being able to help him that he lifted up his paw and let him go.

Some time later, the Lion was caught in a trap. The hunters, who wanted to carry him alive to the King, tied him to a tree while they searched for a wagon to carry him on. Just then, the little Mouse passed by. He saw the sad plight of the Lion. The Mouse came over and soon gnawed away the ropes that bound the King of the Beasts. "Was I not right?" said the little Mouse.

3. This fable is similar to which of the following?
    A. the fairytale of Snow White and the seven dwarves, in which Snow White has to hide from the evil queen but is rescued by the prince
    B. the fable of the tortoise and the hare, in which the tortoise's slow and steady pace proves to be the right way to win the race
    C. the parable of the Good Samaritan, in which a stranger helps an injured man, showing that your real neighbor and friend shows you love and compassion
    D. a story about fairies in the woods, who confuse the human beings who come into the forest by putting magic potions in their eyes

4. Fables and parables are similar in that they both
    A. teach a lesson.
    B. usually rhyme.
    C. have a narrator.
    D. have a villain.

POETRY

Poetry, like fiction, has its own **format** and **characteristics**. Poetry is very different from prose (fiction and nonfiction) because it is written in lines and stanzas, rather than sentences and paragraphs. Often, it does not use the same rules of grammar and punctuation as prose. Sometimes it rhymes, but not always.

These are some of the genres of poetry.

Epic poem:	a long narrative poem about a central character who is a hero on an adventure.
Example: *Iliad* and *Odyssey* by Homer	
Narrative poem:	a poem whose main purpose is to tell a story.
Example: "The Raven" by Edgar Allan Poe, which tells the story of a man in his study visited by a raven	
Lyric poem:	a poem whose main purpose is to convey intense emotion or deep thoughts. Lyric poetry does not tell a story.
Example: "A Child's Amaze" from *Leaves of Grass* by Walt Whitman Silent and amazed, even when a little boy, I remember I heard the preacher every Sunday put God in his statements, As contending against some being or influence.	

Sonnet:	a 14-line poem with a specific rhyme scheme and number of syllables per line.

	Example: "Sonnet 18" by William Shakespeare Shall I compare thee to a summer's day? Thou art more lovely and more temperate. Rough winds do shake the darling buds of May, And summer's lease hath all too short a date. Sometime too hot the eye of heaven shines, And often is his gold complexion dimm'd; And every fair from fair some time declines, By chance, or nature's changing course, untrimm'd; But thy eternal summer shall not fade Nor lose possession of that fair thou ow'st; Nor shall Death brag thou wand'rest in his shade, When in eternal lines to time thou grow'st: So long as men can breathe or eyes can see, So long lives this, and this gives life to thee.

Haiku:	a Japanese poem of three lines with a specific number of syllables per line.

	Example: Basho's traditional haiku Clouds appear and bring to men a chance to rest from looking at the moon.

Limerick:	a type of comical short poem, often with nonsense subject matter, that has a rhyme scheme of aabba.

	Example: poem from John Newbery's *A Little Pretty Pocket-Book* Hickory Dickory Dock The mouse ran up the clock The clock struck one The mouse ran down Hickory Dickory Dock

Many cultures use poems to explain things like:

- their religious beliefs.
- celebration rituals, like weddings and funerals.
- important events in history, like wars.
- phenomena in nature, like rainbows and storms.

Here is an example of how different cultures use poems to celebrate a person of importance:

In Old English, there is an epic poem about a warrior hero called Beowulf. He defeats the monster Grendel. He is remembered by his people and celebrated.

In Greek and Roman history, there is an epic poem called A*eneid* by Virgil. It tells about Aeneas. He is one of the heroes of the Trojan War. He founded the city that became Rome.

In Spanish history, there is an epic poem about a warrior hero called El Cid. He fought against invaders of Spain.

Practice 2: Similar Poetry across Cultures

Read the following excerpts and answer the questions.

Poem by Edward Lear

There was a Young Lady whose chin,

Resembled the point of a pin;

So she had it made sharp,

And purchased a harp,

And played several tunes with her chin.

1. What type of poem is this?

On my travels, stricken—
my dreams over the dry land
go on roving.

–Matsuo Basho

A. limerick   B. haiku   C. epic   D. sonnet

2. This haiku is similar to a lyric poem because
    A. it rhymes.
    B. it has 14 lines.
    C. it conveys feelings.
    D. it communicates a story.

Samuel Taylor Coleridge was an English poet. He lived in London. His poems use strange images and are often written as if part of a dream.

Read the following excerpt and answer the questions.

> At length did cross an Albatross:
> Through the fog it came;
> As if it had been a Christian soul,
> We hailed it in God's name.
>
> It ate the food it ne'er had eat,
> And round and round it flew.
> The ice did split with a thunder-fit;
> The helmsman steered us through!
>
> And a good south wind sprung up behind;
> The Albatross did follow,
> And every day, for food or play,
> Came to the mariners' hollo

–excerpt from Samuel Taylor Coleridge's *The Rime of the Ancient Mariner*

3. What genre of poem is this?
   A. a narrative poem
   B. a sonnet
   C. an epic poem
   D. a limerick

4. How do you know it is this genre of poetry?
   A. It does not rhyme.
   B. It is humorous.
   C. It tells a story.
   D. It has 3 lines.

5. This poem is similar to the Japanese haiku in question 1 because
   A. both tell a story.
   B. both talk about nature.
   C. both are about love.
   D. both have *aabba* rhyming.

DIFFERENCES IN LITERATURE ACROSS CULTURES

The experiences of cultures can sometimes be vastly different. These differences also can be seen in the literature of each culture. Some cultures use fables to teach children good behavior from bad. Some cultures use legends to teach adults the same lesson. Some cultures use myths to help young adults get ready for adulthood. Other cultures use folk tales or fairytales to explain why adults act in certain ways. Fables, legends, myths, and tales are types of fiction. However, each has its own specific purpose.

Practice 3: Identifying Differences in Literature across Cultures

Hans Christian Andersen was a Danish writer in the 1800s. He loved to write fantastic stories. His stories include humor and unlikely events.

"The Real Princess" by Hans Christian Andersen

There was once a Prince who wished to marry a Princess; but then she must be a real Princess. He traveled all over the world in hopes of finding such a lady; but there was always something wrong. Princesses he found in plenty; but whether they were real Princesses it was impossible for him to decide, for now one thing, now another, seemed to him not quite right about the ladies. At last he returned to his palace quite cast down, because he wished so much to have a real Princess for his wife.

One evening a fearful tempest arose, it thundered and lightened, and the rain poured down from the sky in torrents: besides, it was as dark as pitch. All at once there was heard a violent knocking at the door, and the old King, the Prince's father, went out himself to open it.

It was a Princess who was standing outside the door. What with the rain and the wind, she was in a sad condition; the water trickled down from her hair, and her clothes clung to her body. She said she was a real Princess.

"Ah! We shall soon see that!" thought the old Queen-mother; however, she said not a word of what she was going to do; but went quietly into the bedroom, took all the bed-clothes off the bed, and put three little peas on the bedstead. She then laid twenty mattresses one upon another over the three peas, and put twenty feather beds over the mattresses.

Upon this bed the Princess was to pass the night.

The next morning she was asked how she had slept. "Oh, very badly indeed!" she replied. "I have scarcely closed my eyes the whole night through. I do not know what was in my bed, but I had something hard under me, and am all over black and blue. It has hurt me so much!"

Now it was plain that the lady must be a real Princess, since she had been able to feel the three little peas through the twenty mattresses and twenty feather beds. None but a real Princess could have had such a delicate sense of feeling.

The Prince accordingly made her his wife; being now convinced that he had found a real Princess. The three peas were however put into the cabinet of curiosities, where they are still to be seen, provided they are not lost.

Wasn't this a lady of real delicacy?

1. What genre of fiction is this?
    A. a myth
    B. a tall tale
    C. a fable
    D. a fairytale

2. How do you know that it is this genre of fiction?
    A. because it tells story of how the first real princess came into existence
    B. because the characters have to solve the problem of whether the girl is a real princess
    C. because the real princess, the heroine of the story, is portrayed as larger than life
    D. because it teaches an important lesson about how to recognize someone's true nature

Now, read this story and answer the questions that follow.

–adapted from "The Toad and the Boy" in *Old Indian Legends* by Zitkala-Sa

It was the hunting season and the Indian men, with bows and arrows, were wading waist deep amid the wild rice. Near by, within their wigwams, the wives were roasting wild duck and making down pillows.

In the largest teepee sat a young mother. Beside her lay a black-eyed baby boy cooing and laughing. Remembering there were no willow sticks for the fire, she covered the baby with a blanket and hurried away toward the wooded ravine. She was strong and swung an ax skillfully. She soon brought back a bundle of long willows on her back and slipped back into the teepee.

In a moment, she came running out again, crying, "My son! My little son is gone!" There was nowhere any sign of the child. "We will search with you," said all her neighbors. They met the returning husbands, who turned about and joined in the hunt for the missing child. But he was nowhere to be found. After many days and nights, the search was given up. It was sad, indeed, to hear the mother wailing aloud for her little son.

Thus ten summers and winters came and went since the strange disappearance of the little child. Every autumn with the hunters came the unhappy parents of the lost baby to search again for him. Toward the end of the tenth season, the mother walked again along the lake shore weeping.

One evening, across the lake from where the crying woman stood, a pair of bright black eyes peered at her through the tall reeds and wild rice. A little wild boy stopped his play among the tall grasses. Crouching low, he listened to the wailing voice. As the voice grew to only hoarse sobs, the eyes of the wild boy grew dim and wet. When the moaning ceased, he sprang to his feet, ran like a nymph, and rushed into a small hut of reeds and grasses.

"Mother! Mother! Tell me what voice it was I heard which pleased my ears, but made my eyes grow wet!" said he, breathless.

"Han, my son," grunted a big, ugly toad. "It was the voice of a weeping woman you heard. My son, do not say you like it, "replied the great old toad. Inside, she thought: "The human child has heard and seen his real mother. I cannot keep him longer, I fear. Oh, no, I cannot give away the pretty creature I have taught to call me 'mother' all these many winters."

The old toad mother watched her stolen human son very closely. When by chance he started off alone, she shoved out one of her own children after him, saying: "Do not come back without your big brother."

One day an Indian hunter, wading in the deep waters, spied the boy. He had heard of the baby stolen long ago. "This is he!" murmured the hunter to himself as he ran to his wigwam. "I saw among the tall reeds a black-haired boy at play!" he shouted to the people.

At once the unhappy father and mother cried out, "Our boy!" Quickly he led them to the lake. Peeping through the wild rice, he pointed with unsteady finger toward the boy playing all unawares.

"It is he!" cried the mother, for she knew him.

In silence the hunter stood aside, while the happy father and mother caressed their baby boy grown tall.

3. What genre of fiction is this story MOST like?
    A. a legend   B. a fable   C. a parable   D. a tall tale

4. Both "The Toad and the Boy" and "The Real Princess" talk about finding out who someone really is. How are the two stories different?

    A. The Princess story has talking animal characters, and the Toad story includes several magical events.

    B. The first story is about real people at a specific time in history, while the second story is about imaginary people.

    C. The Princess story tells how to recognize a person's true nature, while the Toad story tells that one's true nature cannot be hidden.

    D. The first story shows the negative effects of fooling someone, whereas the second story shows the positive effects of telling the truth.

Read this poem, and then answer the questions that follow.

"Bright Star" by John Keats

Bright Star, would I were steadfast as thou art—
Not in lone splendor hung aloft the night,
And watching, with eternal lids apart,
Like Nature's patient sleepless Eremite,
The moving waters at their priest-like task
Of pure ablution round earth's human shores,
Or gazing on the new soft-fallen mask
Of snow upon the mountains and the moors—
No- yet still steadfast, still unchangeable,
Pillow'd upon my fair love's ripening breast,
To feel for ever its soft fall and swell,
Awake for ever in a sweet unrest,
Still, still to hear her tender-taken breath,
And so live ever- or else swoon to death.

5. What genre of poetry is this?
    A. a sonnet　　　　B. a limerick　　　　C. an epic poem　　　　D. a lyric poem

6. Review the sonnet by Shakespeare in the chart of poem types. How is "Bright Star" similar to "Sonnet 18"?
    A. Neither of them rhymes.
    B. Both are about nature and love.
    C. Both are very humorous poems.
    D. They both teach important lessons.

7. Which of the following is NOT a way in which this poem is similar to Japanese haiku?
    A. Both have deep feelings or thoughts.
    B. They both are kinds of lyric poetry.
    C. Both have the same number of lines.
    D. They both talk about nature.

CHAPTER 8 SUMMARY

People all around the world have traditions that make up their culture. Literature is one way people preserve and share their cultures. Just about every culture has **fiction** and **poetry**. Literature helps define a culture's history and beliefs.

Myths and **legends** are similar in different cultures. **Fables** and **fairytales** are also the same in different cultures. Some of the differences between cultures are found in the ways that stories are used or in the messages they contain.

In various cultures, poetry can be used to celebrate aspects of life or to explain religious beliefs.**Sonnets**, **epic poems**, **narrative poems**, and **lyric poems** have similar content and forms, no matter what culture they are found in.

Knowing how genres of literature are the same in different cultures helps people understand others. It also lets people see how very much alike they truly are. Knowing the differences among how cultures use literature helps understanding, too.

CHAPTER 8 REVIEW

Robert Louis Stevenson was a Scottish writer and poet in the later 1800s. He is famous for his novel Treasure Island *and the short book* The Strange Case of Dr. Jekyll and Mr. Hyde. *Here is a modern fable that he wrote.*

"The Man and His Friend" by Robert Louis Stevenson

A man quarreled with his friend.

"I have been much deceived in you," said the man.

And the friend made a face at him and went away.

A little after, they both died, and came together before the great white Justice of the Peace. It began to look black for the friend, but the man for a while had a clear character and was getting in good spirits.

"I find here some record of a quarrel," said the justice, looking in his notes. "Which of you was in the wrong?"

"He was," said the man. 'He spoke ill of me behind my back."

"Did he so?" said the justice. "And pray how did he speak about your neighbors?"

"Oh, he had always a nasty tongue," said the man.

"And you chose him for your friend?" cried the justice. "My good fellow, we have no use here for fools."

So the man was cast in the pit, and the friend laughed out aloud in the dark and remained to be tried on other charges.

1. Refer back to the fable you read earlier in this chapter, *The Lion and the Mouse* by Aesop. Then, answer the following question:

    How are these fables similar, even thought they are written hundreds of years apart and by authors of different cultures?

    A. Both talk about how lonely it is to be alone in the world.
    B. Both show the importance of treating people kindly.
    C. Both inform about the value of wisely choosing friends.
    D. Both tell readers how to make friends for a lifetime.

2. Which genre of poetry is most like the stories in fiction?
    A. narrative
    B. sonnet
    C. lyric poetry
    D. limerick

Here is an example of African American poetry. This poem is about the history of African Americans in early America. As slaves, they were not allowed to do many things. They could not speak about certain things or even practice their own religious beliefs. This poem refers to the spirituals that were sung by slaves. They used spirituals as a way to communicate and a way to practice their religious beliefs. This poet writes as if he is talking to his ancestors.

This idea of being a slave to another group of people can also be seen in the Bible in the book of Exodus. That is where Moses freed the slaves from the pharaoh. This is also similar to some writing of South Africa during the 50 years of apartheid, when the country's government was made up of people of a very different culture from the natives.

Read the following excerpts and answer the questions.

–excerpt from "O Black and Unknown Bards" by James Weldon Johnson

O Black and unknown bards of long ago,

How came your lips to touch the sacred fire?

How, in your darkness, did you come to know

The power and beauty of the minstrel's lyre?

Who first from midst his bonds lifted his eyes?

Who first from out the still watch, lone and long,

Feeling the ancient faith of prophets rise

Within his dark-kept soul, burst into song?

Heart of what slave poured out such melody

As "Steal away to Jesus"? On its strains

His spirit must have nightly floated free,

Though still about his hands he felt his chains.

Who heard great "Jordan roll"? Whose starward eye

Saw chariot "swing low"? And who was he

That breathed comforting, melodic sigh,

"Nobody knows de trouble I see"?

3. What genre of poetry is this poem?
   A. epic   B. sonnet   C. lyric   D. narrative

4. In what way is this poem similar to *The Rime of the Ancient Mariner* on page 152?
   A. It tells a story about unfortunate events.
   B. Both poems speak directly to the reader.
   C. It has the same rhyme scheme.
   D. Both poems are about slaves.

5. This poem is similar to the legend genre in fiction because
   A. it teaches a valuable lesson or moral.
   B. it shows heroes as being larger than life.
   C. it tells about a certain historical period.
   D. it shows how the first slave came to be.

Read the two stories below and then answer the questions that follow.

"Crow Brings Daylight"
An Inuit story

Long ago, when the world was just born, the Inuit people lived always in darkness. They thought it was dark everywhere. Then the crow came and told them that he had seen daylight on his long flights.

It sounded wonderful, and the people wanted some daylight. "We could hunt farther," they said, "and fish longer. We could see the bears and wolves before they could sneak up and attack us." They begged the crow to bring them daylight. Though it was far to fly, the crow finally agreed.

He flew and flew, and finally he came to a village where it was light. The daughter of the chief was walking to the river for water. Crow turned himself into a speck of dust and drifted onto her fur cloak. When she went back to her father's snowlodge, she carried him with her.

Inside the snowlodge, the girl took off her cloak and the speck of dust drifted into the ear of the chief's grandson, who was playing on the floor. The boy started to cry.

"What's wrong?" asked the chief, who was sitting by the fire.

"Tell him you want to play outside with a ball of daylight," whispered the dust.

The chief wanted his favorite grandson to be happy and told his daughter to fetch the box of daylight balls. She gave him a small one to play with and took him out in the snow.

When they were outside, the speck of dust turned back into crow. He grabbed the daylight ball in his talons and flew into the sky.

The crow reached the Inuit again and dropped the ball of daylight. It shattered and threw brilliant light everywhere. The sky was no longer dark. The people ran out and rejoiced.

"Look how far we can see! The sky is blue and bright. And there are mountains in the distance! Thank you, crow, for bringing the daylight.

He nodded, explaining that he could only carry a small ball of daylight. The trip was long, and he would not be able to make it often, so the Inuit would have daylight only half the year. The people were happy and said that was better than darkness all the time.

6. What genre of story is "Crow Brings Daylight"?
   A. legend   B. parable   C. fable   D. myth

7. Why does the Crow turn himself into a speck of dust?
   A. because he wants to get back to his village
   B. because he wants to see where the daylight is
   C. because he wants to travel on the ball of daylight
   D. because he wants to stay in the Chief's snowlodge

"The Forge of the Gods"
A Roman story

Among the perfect gods there was one who was quite ugly. His name was Vulcan. He was the son of Jupiter, the king of the gods, and his wife Juno. One day, Jupiter was angry, and Vulcan, trying to protect Juno, was thrown from the high mountain on which they lived. As a result, he also began to limp.

After this, Vulcan decided to live under ground. He made his home under a mountain and constructed a great forge (a shop with a furnace where blacksmiths work, heating metal and making it into useful things). His helpers were the one-eyed Cyclops. They were deformed, like he was, but he treated them well.

He became respected as the gentle God of the Forge. For Juno, he made a golden throne. For Jupiter, he hammered the great thunderbolts that the king of the gods used to light up the sky in battle. He made weapons for the other gods, but he did not fight himself. He was kind and peaceful and married the most beautiful goddess in the heavens, Venus.

Every time people see fire come from the top of the mountain, they know that Vulcan is hammering at his forge.

8. What genre of story is "The Forge of the Gods"?
   A. parable   B. fable   C. myth   D. epic

9. What phenomenon does "The Forge of the Gods" explain?
   A. volcanoes   C. earthquakes
   B. forest fires   D. thunderstorms

10. Which of the following expresses a similarity between the "The Forge of the Gods" and "Crow Brings Daylight"?
   A. Both stories are from the same culture.
   B. They both relate a moral or lesson to the reader.
   C. Both tell how the earth came to have light.
   D. They both explain things that happen in nature.

11. From these two stories, you can conclude that both cultures thought that light or fire was something
    A. that was not needed by most people.
    C. that was powerful and beautiful.
    B. that was very easily contained.
    D. that was not as good as darkness.

Read the story below and answer the questions that follow.

"How the World Was Made"
–from *Philippine Folklore Stories,* by John Maurice Miller

Thousands of years ago there was no land nor sun nor moon nor stars, and the world was only a great sea of water, above which stretched the sky. The water was the kingdom of the god Maguayan, and the sky was ruled by the great god Captan.

Maguayan had a daughter called Lidagat, the sea, and Captan had a son known as Lihangin, the wind. The gods agreed to the marriage of their children, so the sea became the bride of the wind.

Three sons and a daughter were born to them. The sons were called Licalibutan, Liadlao, and Libulan, and the daughter received the name of Lisuga.

Licalibutan had a body of rock and was strong and brave; Liadlao was formed of gold and was always happy; Libulan was made of copper and was weak and timid; and the beautiful Lisuga had a body of pure silver and was sweet and gentle. Their parents were very fond of them, and nothing was wanting to make them happy.

After a time, Lihangin died and left the control of the winds to his eldest son Licalibutan…Licalibutan, proud of his power over the winds, resolved to gain more power, and asked his brothers to join him in an attack on Captan in the sky above. At first they refused; but when Licalibutan became angry with them, the amiable Liadlao, not wishing to offend his brother, agreed to help. Then together they induced the timid Libulan to join in the plan.

When all was ready the three brothers rushed at the sky, but they could not beat down the gates of steel that guarded the entrance. Then Licalibutan let loose the strongest winds and blew the bars in every direction. The brothers rushed into the opening, but were met by the angry god Captan. So terrible did he look that they turned and ran in terror; but Captan, furious at the destruction of his gates, sent three bolts of lightning after them.

The first struck the copper Libulan and melted him into a ball. The second struck the golden Liadlao, and he too was melted. The third bolt struck Licalibutan, and his rocky body broke into many pieces and fell into the sea. So huge was he that parts of his body stuck out above the water and became what is known as land.

In the meantime, the gentle Lisuga had missed her brothers and started to look for them. She went toward the sky, but as she approached the broken gates, Captan, blind with anger, struck her too with lightning, and her silver body broke into thousands of pieces.

Captan then came down from the sky and tore the sea apart, calling on Maguayan to come to him and accusing him of ordering the attack on the sky. Soon Maguayan appeared and answered that he knew nothing of the plot as he had been asleep far down in the sea. After a time, he succeeded in calming the angry Captan. Together they wept at the loss of their grandchildren, especially the gentle and beautiful Lisuga; but with all their power they could not restore the dead to life. However, they gave to each body a beautiful light that will shine forever.

And so it was that golden Liadlao became the sun and copper Libulan the moon, while the thousands of pieces of silver Lisuga shine as the stars of heaven. To wicked Licalibutan, the gods gave no light, but resolved to make his body support a new race of people. So Captan gave Maguayan a seed, and he planted it on the land, which, as you will remember, was part of Licalibutan's huge body. Soon a bamboo tree grew up, and from the hollow of one of its branches a man and a woman came out. The man's name was Sicalac, and the woman was called Sicabay. They were the parents of the human race. Their first child was a son whom they called Libo; afterwards they had a daughter who was known as Saman. Pandaguan was a younger son and he had a son called Arion…

…And so the world came to be made and peopled. The sun and moon shine in the sky and the beautiful stars light up the night. All over the land, on the body of the envious Licalibutan, the children of Sicalac and Sicabay have grown great in numbers. May they live forever in peace and brotherly love!

12. Which of the following is NOT explained or described in the story?
   A.   the formation of land
   B.   the creation of the sun
   C.   the creation of animals
   D.   the creation of the moon

13. This story is a
   A.   fable
   B.   legend
   C.   myth
   D.   fairytale

Read the story below and answer the questions that follow.

excerpt from "Ali Hafed's Quest" by Orison Swett Marden
–from *Story Hour Readings, Seventh Year* by E. C. Hartwell

Happy and contented was the good Ali Hafed, when one evening a learned priest of Buddha, journeying along the banks of the Indus, stopped for rest and refreshment at his home, where all wayfarers were hospitably welcomed and treated as honored guests.

After the evening meal, the farmer and his family with the priest in their midst gathered around the fireside, the chilly mountain air of the late autumn making a fire desirable. The disciple of Buddha entertained his kind hosts with various legends and myths, and last of all with the story of the creation.

He told his wondering listeners how in the beginning the solid earth on which they lived was not solid at all, but a mere bank of fog. "The Great Spirit," said he, "thrust his finger into the bank of fog and began slowly describing a circle in its midst, increasing the speed gradually until the fog went whirling round his finger so rapidly that it was transformed into a glowing ball of fire. Then the Creative Spirit hurled the fiery ball from his hand, and it shot through the universe, burning its way through other banks of fog and condensing them into rain, which fell in great floods, cooling the surface of the immense ball.

Flames then bursting from the interior through the cooled outer crust, threw up the hills and mountain ranges and made the beautiful fertile valleys. In the flood of rain that followed this fiery upheaval, the substance that cooled very quickly formed granite, that which cooled less rapidly became copper, the next in degree cooled down into silver, and the last became gold. But the most beautiful substance of all, the diamond, was formed by the first beams of sunlight condensed on the earth's surface.

14. What kind of story is this?
    A.   a religious parable
    B.   an amusing fairytale
    C.   a creation myth
    D.   an incredible fable

15. Which of the other stories in this chapter review is LEAST like "Ali Hafed's Quest"?
    A.   "The Forge of the Gods"
    B.   "The Man and His Friend"
    C.   "Crow Brings Daylight"
    D.   "How the World Was Made"

Chapter 9
Reading across Subject Areas

This chapter covers the following Georgia standards.

ELA7R1	Identify the characteristics of various genres and produce evidence of reading that distinguishes between the concepts of theme in a literary work and the author's purpose in an expository text.
ELA7R2	Identify messages and themes from books in all subject areas. Respond to a variety of texts in multiple modes of discourse. Relate messages and themes from one subject area to those in another area. Evaluate the merits of texts in every subject discipline.

Reading is a skill that applies to every subject. Math word problems, timelines in history, the periodic table of elements in science, and a playbook for football all involve reading. In this chapter, you will learn some ways to get more out of what you read. Whether you are reading your favorite magazine or a social studies textbook, there are things to look for when you read that can give the words more meaning.

MODES OF DISCOURSE

Information is everywhere. Disc jockeys tell us what the most popular songs are by playing them repeatedly. Television advertisements show us the newest video games. Product manuals tell us how to assemble a scooter. A football player speaks at assembly about not using drugs. How do you respond to these various presentations? Do you know who is presenting the information and how the person wants you to respond? Be assured that the presenter has thought about your response. Have you?

Read the advertisement below.

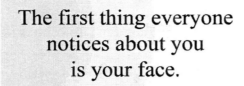

The first thing everyone notices about you is your face.

Is your face covered with pimples?
Do you want to have clear skin that everyone notices?

Acme Acne Soap is the solution.
Acme beats all of the leading brands at
knocking out acne.

Try it today!!

Stop and think for a moment. Who is presenting this information? Does this ad apply to you? Do you agree that acne is unsightly? Should you treat it yourself? Should you use soap or another kind of treatment? Do you believe that this particular soap is the best product for the job? Will you buy it?

The company presenting this advertisement is trying to get you to act a certain way. As you probably know, just because something appears in print or on TV does not mean it is true. It may well be true, but asking questions lets you find out for yourself. The questions you will ask will depend on the situation, but there are a few main questions that you can always begin with.

Questions to ask about presentations:

- **Who** is writing or speaking?
- Is this person an expert in the field? Is it an advertiser? A teacher? A doctor?
- **Why** is the person writing?
- **What** is the author's **purpose**? Does he want to teach you something? Does he want you to buy something? Does he want you to agree with him?

An author's **purpose** is important to uncover when you are decoding information. When writing or speaking, authors have **three main purposes:**

- **To inform:** An author can write with the purpose of teaching the audience. A textbook informs you about the water cycle; an owner's manual informs you how to program your cell phone. A research paper that you write is also done to inform. Informational writing should be done by an expert, or someone who has a good deal of experience with the topic, or who has done a good deal of research on the topic.

    Example: A doctor presents a paper that shows the benefits of a new kind of surgery he has developed at a medical convention.

- **To entertain:** An author can write with the purpose of entertaining the audience. A movie can be entertaining, as can a concert or a comic routine. Authors can also use entertainment in other kinds of presentations. For instance, say you are on a field trip to the Atlanta History Center. A guide there may tell an entertaining story from history to get your attention before beginning a more serious lecture.

  Example: A politician tells a funny story about when she was a child to get the audience's attention during a debate.

- **To persuade:** An author can write to convince the audience to think as he does and act as he recommends. Perhaps the author works for a shoe company that wants to sell sneakers. Perhaps the author is an animal rights activist who wants people to stop eating meat. The author presents evidence (proof and examples) to try to convince the audience that he is right.

  Example: An environmental conservationist is interviewed on public radio and tells the host why it is important to stop polluting the Chattahoochee River.

Once you determine who is speaking and for what purpose, you can decide how the author's beliefs match up with your own. Knowing the author's purpose will help you make sense of the information that you read, watch, and hear.

Practice 1: Evaluating Modes of Discourse

With a partner, read paragraphs A and B that follow. For each question, determine **who** is speaking and his **purpose** in speaking. Then share your answers with the class.

A. The following excerpt is taken from a speech made by a 7th grade class representative.

Junk food and desserts should be banned from the school cafeteria. While I like cookies and chips as much as the next kid, we all know that those foods are not as healthy as fruits and vegetables. Everyone has heard about childhood obesity. Let's show people that our school is different and that our student body supports and demands a healthier menu.

1. Who is speaking?

    A. a student
    B. a teacher

    C. a school administrator
    D. a parent

2. What is the speaker's purpose?

    A. to get Americans to eat healthy foods
    B. to have snack vending machines installed at school
    C. to convince everyone at school to have only healthy food in the cafeteria
    D. to invite others to submit their suggestions for new menu items in the cafeteria

3. Who is the audience?

   A. the President of the United States

   B. the student body

   C. the cafeteria staff members

   D. the local TV news

4. How do you think the audience will respond?

5. How would you respond?

B. The following is an excerpt from a lecture given during a field trip to the salt marsh.

Students, if you look around you, what do you see? Grasses, mud, salt water? These are all components of the salt marsh you are standing in right now. You'll notice that there is not much variety in the type of foliage we have here because plants must be tolerant of both the salt and being at least partly submerged in water. That spiky looking bush over there is a glasswort. This taller clump of green foliage I am standing next to is cordgrass. Now let's walk over to that little patch of purple and I'll show you a flower that can actually bloom in these conditions.

1. Who is speaking?

   A. a police officer   C. an electrician

   B. a science teacher   D. the bus driver

2. What is the speaker's purpose?

   A. to inform those on the field trip about the environment

   B. to entertain everyone while they wait for the bus

   C. to persuade the listeners that this is a great place to live

   D. to show everyone how pollution has affected this environment

3. Who is the audience?

   A. biology professors

   B. people concerned about conservation

   C. the students in the class

   D. residents who want advice about lawn care

4. How do you think the audience will respond?

5. How would you respond?

THEME AND MESSAGE

THEME IN FICTION

Theme is an important element of literature. You learned about theme and other elements of literature in chapter 6. Review that chapter if you need to.

Theme is an author's underlying message in a piece of fiction. Theme shows the author's view about life.

As you read in chapter 6, there is a difference between **theme** and **topic**. While the **theme** is an author's message, the **topic** is what the piece of writing is about. The topic of an essay you write might be what you did during your summer vacation. The topic of a newspaper article you read might be how knee injuries affect football players. A theme has deep meaning and is a way for an author to comment on an aspect of life that most people can relate to.

An easy way to see how an author uses theme is to read a fable. Fables are stories that are intended to teach a lesson. In a fable, this lesson is also the theme. Read the fable by the famous Greek author Aesop.

Aesop

The Dog and the Shadow

It happened that a dog had got a piece of meat and was carrying it home in his mouth to eat it in peace. Now on his way home he had to cross a plank lying across a running brook. As he crossed, he looked down and saw his own shadow reflected in the water beneath. Thinking it was another dog with another piece of meat, he made up his mind to have that also. So he made a snap at the shadow in the water, but as he opened his mouth the piece of meat fell out, dropped into the water and was never seen more.

The theme, or lesson, of this fable is: when you are greedy, you can lose everything.

Hints for finding the theme:

Look for clues in the title.
Look for how the author uses symbols.
Look at the wording the author uses.
Then, write one sentence that sums up the author's message.

ACTIVITY: FINDING THEME

Read another of Aesop's fables. With a classmate, see if you can figure out the theme. Share your answer with the class.

The Fox and the Crow

A Fox once saw a Crow fly off with a piece of cheese in its beak and settle on a branch of a tree. "That's for me, as I am a Fox," said Master Reynard, and he walked up to the foot of the tree. "Good-day, Mistress Crow," he cried. "How well you are looking to-day: how glossy your feathers; how bright your eye. I feel sure your voice must surpass that of other birds, just as your figure does. Let me hear but one song from you that I may greet you as the Queen of Birds." The Crow lifted up her head and began to caw her best, but the moment she opened her mouth, the piece of cheese fell to the ground, only to be snapped up by Master Fox. "That will do," said he. "That was all I wanted."

What is the theme of this passage?

MESSAGE IN NONFICTION

Nonfiction writing can also have a message. While in fiction this message is called a theme, in nonfiction this message is called, simply, the **message**. In nonfiction, the message is the underlying meaning in the writing. The message in nonfiction writing often shows the author's **point of view** on a topic. For example, Martin Luther King, Jr.'s message in his speech "I Have a Dream" was that it was time for blacks and whites to be treated equally.

Whether you are reading an assignment for science or social studies, being able to find the message of a passage is important for understanding what the passage is about and why it is important.

Read the following passage about Abraham Lincoln.

Abraham Lincoln

Abraham Lincoln showed great character from an early age. There is a story about when young Abe borrowed a book from a neighbor. To keep the book safe, Abe would store it in a crack in the cabin. One night it rained, soaking the book through. Abe went to his neighbor right away, told him what had happened and offered to pay for the book. The neighbor was happy that Abe had told him the truth and had taken responsibility for what had happened. Because of events like this, Abe was known for much of his life as "Honest Abe."

The message of this passage is the value of honesty. Notice that the author does not state directly, "People respected Abe Lincoln because he was honest." Instead, the author shows how Abe's honest actions won him respect. It is up to the reader to make the connection between what the author says, how he says it, and the details he includes to tell the story.

Practice 2: Finding Themes and Messages

Read the following paragraphs. Then choose the answer that BEST describes the theme in the fiction passages and the message in the nonfiction passages.

Egyptian pharaohs were viewed as both kings and gods. To show their power, they had scribes write stories about the great things they had done. They had slaves build enormous monuments to honor them. They had workers carve images of their faces in stone. People did what the pharaoh commanded, no matter how much work it involved.

1. Which of the following statements BEST describes the message of this paragraph?
   A. It was important to pharaohs to show their power.
   B. Many of the Pharaohs had false modesty.
   C. Many people felt the pharaohs were too powerful.
   D. Some people rebelled against the pharaoh's power.

French artist Claude Monet liked to use color in his paintings. One of his paintings, *Tulips in Holland*, depicts a field of flowers on a sunlit day. The warm reds and yellows Monet uses give us an impression of the warmth of the sun.

2. Which of the following statements BEST describes the message of this paragraph?
   A. Monet's colors were too bright.
   B. People liked Monet's work better than paintings by other artists.
   C. Using too much color can ruin a painting.
   D. Color can contribute to the feel of a painting.

No one is certain why dinosaurs became extinct. Some people say a comet hitting Earth was responsible. Others say it was a climate change. Still others claim that disease played a part.

3. Which of the following statements BEST describes the message of this paragraph?
   A. Scientists are not sharing the real reason dinosaurs became extinct.
   B. There are several possibilities why the dinosaurs became extinct.
   C. Some day we will know for sure what caused the dinosaurs' extinction.
   D. The cause of the dinosaurs' extinction is not worth looking into further.

He had had a nice, good, idle time all the while—plenty of company—and the fence had three coats of whitewash on it! If he hadn't run out of whitewash he would have bankrupted every boy in the village.

Tom said to himself that it was not such a hollow world, after all. He had discovered a great law of human action, without knowing it—namely, that in order to make a man or a boy covet a thing, it is only necessary to make the thing difficult to attain.

–from *The Adventures of Tom Sawyer*, by Mark Twain

4. Which of the following statements BEST describes the theme of this paragraph?

    A.   A fence can have too much whitewash on it.

    B.   People can be easily fooled by a child.

    C.   People want what they cannot have.

    D.   The world is not hollow.

THEMES AND MESSAGES ACROSS SUBJECT AREAS

Different pieces of literature can have the same theme. In fact, some themes, especially those related to love, war, and courage, are so popular that people have been writing about them for hundreds of years. Read the two passages that follow to see how two different authors write using the same theme.

Author #1: Hans Christian Andersen

Hans Christian Andersen

Type of Literature: Short story

Theme: Selfishness is a negative human trait

Many years ago, there was an Emperor, who was so excessively fond of new clothes, that he spent all his money in dress. He did not trouble himself in the least about his soldiers; nor did he care to go either to the theatre or the chase, except for the opportunities then afforded him for displaying his new clothes. He had a different suit for each hour of the day; and as of any other king or emperor, one is accustomed to say, "he is sitting in council," it was always said of him, "The Emperor is sitting in his wardrobe."

–from "The Emperor's New Clothes" by Hans Christian Andersen

Author #2: Charles Dickens

Type of Literature: Novel

Charles Dickens

Theme: Selfishness is a negative human trait

The door of Scrooge's counting-house was open that he might keep his eye upon his clerk, who in a dismal little cell beyond, a sort of tank, was copying letters. Scrooge had a very small fire, but the clerk's fire was so very much smaller that it looked like one coal. But he couldn't replenish it, for Scrooge kept the coal-box in his own room; and so surely as the clerk came in with the shovel, the master predicted that it would be necessary for them to part. Wherefore the clerk put on his white comforter, and tried to warm himself at the candle; in which effort, not being a man of a strong imagination, he failed.

–from *A Christmas Carol* by Charles Dickens

Notice that neither author came right out and said that his character was selfish. Instead, each author gave us this information by describing his character's actions and attitudes. In "The Emperor's New Clothes," we can tell from what the emperor chooses to spend his money on (or not spend his money on) that his own personal comfort is the most important thing to him. In *A Christmas Carol*, we can tell by who gets the bigger fire who Scrooge values more.

Theme is not specific to one kind of writing or even to one subject. For instance, a poet may deal with the *theme* of war being devastating emotionally in a poem while a historian may deal with the *message* of war being devastating economically in a research paper. How a theme or a message is treated depends on the subject and the person handling it.

Let's look at how two different writers work with a similar **theme** and **message** in two different subjects.

Edgar Allan Poe

Author #1: Edgar Allan Poe

Type of writing: Fiction

Subject: Literature

Theme: Money and power cannot help someone escape a dreaded disease

    The "Red Death" had long devastated the country. No pestilence had ever been so fatal, or so hideous. Blood was its Avatar and its seal—the redness and the horror of blood. There were sharp pains, and sudden dizziness, and then profuse bleeding at the pores, with dissolution. The scarlet stains upon the body and especially upon the face of the victim, were the pest ban which shut him out from the aid and from the sympathy of his fellow-men. And the whole seizure, progress, and termination of the disease, were the incidents of half an hour.

In the rest of the story, rich Prince Prospero isolates himself and his court in his palace. He hopes to escape the fate of the rest of the land. But someone dressed as the Red Death comes to the party. The Prince is shocked and makes him remove his mask. It turns out to be death. Through symbolism, the story shows that one cannot use money or power to escape disease.

–from "The Masque of the Red Death," by Edgar Allan Poe

Author #2: A scientist

Type of writing: Nonfiction

Subject: Science

Message: Disease

Tuberculosis is an infection of the lungs. It can be transmitted from one person to another when an infected person sneezes, coughs, or even speaks. People with tuberculosis often have a bloody cough, fever, and listlessness. Tuberculosis can be prevented by vaccines and treated by antibiotics.

A Scientist

Note that Poe's examination of disease includes emotional words, like "hideous" and "sympathy." Poe shows the fear and horror that goes along with the infectious disease. By contrast, the scientist's description of a similar disease, tuberculosis, is more clinical. It describes the facts that relate to the disease: what it is, how it is transmitted, what the symptoms are, and how it is treated. It does not show emotion, because that is not the purpose of a scientific report. While literature tends to use description and imagination, science relies on fact. Therefore, a similar theme and message are treated differently in these types of writing.

Practice 3: Identifying Themes and Messages across Subject Areas

Read the excerpts below. Then answer the questions that follow.

Rosa Parks on Bus

Rosa Parks is famous for her refusal on December 1, 1955, to obey bus driver James Blake's demand that she relinquish her seat to a white man. Her subsequent arrest and trial for this act of civil disobedience triggered the Montgomery Bus Boycott, one of the largest and most successful mass movements against racial segregation in history, and launched Martin Luther King, Jr., one of the organizers of the boycott, to the forefront of the civil rights movement. Her role in American history earned her an iconic status in American culture, and her actions have left an enduring legacy for civil rights movements around the world.

(from http://en.wikipedia.org/wiki/Rosa_parks)

The following are two of Georgia's Jim Crow laws that were enforced from the 1880s to 1960s:

Restaurants: "All persons licensed to conduct a restaurant, shall serve either white people exclusively or colored people exclusively and shall not sell to the two races within the same room or serve the two races anywhere under the same license."

Baseball: "It shall be unlawful for any amateur white baseball team to play baseball on any vacant lot or baseball diamond within two blocks of a playground devoted to the Negro race, and it shall be unlawful for any amateur colored baseball team to play baseball in any vacant lot or baseball diamond within two blocks of any playground devoted to the white race."

(from http://www.nps.gov/archive/malu/documents/jim_crow_laws.htm)

1. Where would you MOST likely read the account of Rosa Parks?
    A. in a science book
    B. in a history book
    C. in a literature book
    D. in a math book

2. Where would you MOST likely read the Jim Crow laws?
    A. in an art book
    B. in a law book
    C. in a novel
    D. in a science book

3. Which excerpt includes an analysis of how the historical event shaped history?
    A. the account of Rosa Parks
    B. the Jim Crow laws
    C. both excerpts
    D. neither excerpt

4. Which of the following BEST describes the topic of both excerpts?
    A. racial segregation
    B. bus rules
    C. the separation of church and state
    D. the glory of nature

5. How does the message of the two excerpts differ?
    A. The first text has a message about women being strong leaders, while the second has a message that eating and sports should be strictly regulated.
    B. The first text has a message of disobedience if someone is being mistreated, and the second has a message of tolerance.
    C. The first text shows what happens when people begin breaking rules, while the second tells people how to behave to keep peace in the community.
    D. The first text tells how a brave woman helped change unfair laws, while the second sends the message that blacks and whites must be separated everywhere.

EVALUATING THE MERITS OF TEXTS

What makes writing good? If a story is supposed to be entertaining, it should be. If an article is supposed to teach us about President Andrew Jackson, it should do so. We can evaluate books and other writing to see if they accomplish their purpose. If they do, what makes them successful? If they don't, what's missing?

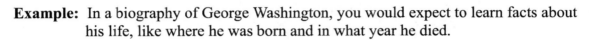

First, does the writing cover what it is supposed to?

A novel's purpose might be to entertain you. In a math book, you would expect to see math problems as well as an explanation for how to do them. On a science program, we expect to hear the narrator tell us facts about science and show us some demonstrations of experiments. An American history documentary should provide facts about American history. A poetry book should be full of poems.

> **Example:** In a biography of George Washington, you would expect to learn facts about his life, like where he was born and in what year he died.

Second, does the writing present the information effectively?

Writing, especially nonfiction, should proceed in a logical order, and it should give plenty of examples. Does the science book include diagrams that show you how to do complicated experiments? Does the online encyclopedia article give you important dates? Does the psychology speech explain why some people act as they do?

> **Example:** In a math book, you would expect to learn addition before division.

Finally, how does this book fit in with what you know about the world around you?

Mona Lisa

Good writing can help you understand the world around you. Maybe a grammar textbook does a good job of making grammar interesting. Maybe a movie got you interested in a president that you hadn't known much about before. After observing a classmate's science fair project on volcanoes, maybe now you can name a type of lava. After reading an art book, maybe now you understand what people mean when they talk about a "Mona Lisa smile."

> **Example:** After reading a science Web site about trees, can you identify any of the trees you see on a nature walk?

By examining the information writing covers and how it covers it, we can determine how effective the writing is and how it relates to our lives.

Practice 4: Evaluating the Merits of Texts

Read the excerpts. Then answer the questions that follow.

Dolphins are mammals that live in water. Dolphins are carnivores and eat mainly fish and squid. They have excellent hearing and eyesight. They are considered to be intelligent, playful, and friendly, and for this reason, people are interested in studying them. Dolphins have even been used by the U.S. military to find mines and recover equipment.

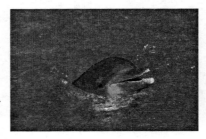

1. In what kind of book would you expect to find this paragraph?

   A. a history book about the U.S. military
   B. a science book about dolphins
   C. a math book about geometry
   D. an English book about famous authors

2. Which of the following is a reason the author gives that people are interested in studying dolphins?

   A. Dolphins are mammals that live in water.
   B. Dolphins eat mainly fish and squid.
   C. Dolphins are intelligent, playful, and friendly.
   D. Dolphins have excellent hearing and eyesight.

In 1838 the U.S. government forced thousands of Native Americans from the Cherokee tribe to move west to Indian Territory from their homes in the South. _____. Soldiers rounded up Cherokees from Georgia, North Carolina, Tennessee, and Alabama and forced them to travel, mainly on foot, approximately 1,200 miles. Thousands of Cherokees died along the way, mostly from disease.

3. In what kind of book would you expect to find this paragraph?

   A. in a history book about Native Americans
   B. in a science book about the plague
   C. in a math book about distance
   D. in a novel

4. Which of the following sentences best fits into the blank in the paragraph?

   A. Today, there is a trail that commemorates this journey.
   B. This relocation was called the Trail of Tears.
   C. They passed many types of plants that were new to them on the journey.
   D. Slavery was still legal at that time.

The use of *its* and *it's* is confusing for many people. People see the apostrophe and think it means that the word is possessive. Here is a simple rule so you will always know which word to use:

Use *it's* only when you mean *it is*. Otherwise, use *its*.

5. In what kind of book would you expect to find this paragraph?
   A.   in a book of poetry
   B.   in a dictionary
   C.   in a social studies textbook
   D.   in a grammar handbook

6. Who would benefit MOST from reading this paragraph?
   A.   a school principal
   B.   the PTA of a high school
   C.   college students who are taking writing courses
   D.   anyone who is confused about how to use *it's* and *its*

CHAPTER 9 SUMMARY

When reading, seeing, and hearing information, it is important to know **who** is presenting the information and for what **purpose.** An author's purpose might be **to inform, to entertain,** or **to persuade.** Knowing this can help us understand the presenter's message and how it applies to us.

Theme is an author's underlying message in a piece of fiction. In nonfiction, this is called the author's **message.** Different kinds of writing can have the same theme or the same message. A science book and a history book might cover the same message but will do so in different ways.

There are questions you can ask to see how well a piece of writing does its job. **First,** does it cover what it is supposed to? **Second,** does it do so effectively? **Third,** does it help you make better sense of the world around you?

CHAPTER 9 REVIEW

Read the passages and answer the questions that follow.

Dear Congressman,

(1)I am a constituent living in your district. Like many hikers, I enjoy walking the trails through the North Georgia Mountains. Like many hikers, I am horrified by the trash I am constantly finding along the trails. I am writing to urge you to propose legislation that enforces the littering policy currently in place.

(2)I know that enforcing the law will cost money, and I am willing to have my taxes increased to pay for it. I am willing to give my time for this cause. Already, I spend most weekends walking the trails with a trash bag, cleaning up after other hikers. I spend many of my evenings hosting neighborhood meetings to address this issue, drafting petitions, and writing letters, all in an attempt to solve this problem. Our trails are a natural beauty as well as a tourist attraction. Keeping them clean will preserve our environment and keep tourists coming to our mountains as well.

Sincerely,

Michael Jones

1. Who is writing this letter?

    A. a congressman
    B. a citizen
    C. a tourist
    D. a cruise director

2. Which of the following best describes the message of paragraph 2 of the letter?
    A. I am willing to work hard and sacrifice for what I believe in.
    B. Trash stinks and should not be allowed on nature trails.
    C. Taxes are unconstitutional, but we all have to pay them.
    D. People need to be responsible for their actions.

3. What evidence does the writer give to show he is willing to give his own time to this cause?
    A. I am a constituent living in your district.
    B. I know that enforcing the law will cost money, and I am willing to have my taxes increased to pay for it.
    C. I spend most weekends walking the trails with a trash bag, cleaning up after other hikers.
    D. Our trails are a natural beauty as well as a tourist attraction.

4. What is Michael's purpose in writing this letter?
    A. to get more time to clean up the trails
    B. to make his congressman upset
    C. to tell on his neighbors
    D. to get government to help keep the trails clean

The Pilgrims faced many challenges when they decided to leave England to pursue religious freedom in America. They encountered dissent among themselves, cold weather, and uncertainty with the Native Americans. The Pilgrims suffered from disease and hunger. Many died. In America, they faced an unfamiliar landscape and had to learn to cultivate the unfamiliar land. Along with that came uncertainty about what crops to grow and how to grow them. However, despite these challenges and setbacks, the Pilgrim colony survived and eventually flourished.

5. In what subject would you expect to read this account?
   A. English   B. math   C. science   D. social studies

6. Who is most likely writing this account?
   A. a Pilgrim   C. a scientist
   B. a historian   D. a Native American

7. What best describes the message of this passage?
   A. The Pilgrims would not have survived without Native Americans helping them.
   B. The Pilgrims were willing to work hard and sacrifice for what they believed in.
   C. Many Pilgrims gave up because of all the hardships in the New World.
   D. The Pilgrims wished they had not made the trip.

8. What is one example the author uses to show how the Pilgrims suffered?
   A. The Pilgrims suffered from disease and hunger.
   B. The Pilgrims learned about the new land.
   C. The Pilgrims decided to leave England to pursue religious freedom in America.
   D. The Pilgrims did not agree with the rules in England.

9. What is the author's purpose in writing?
   A. to inform   C. to entertain
   B. to persuade   D. to make the Pilgrims feel better

The Code of Hammurabi was a set of laws for the ancient civilization of Mesopotamia. These laws were written in 1760 B.C. Law number 22 states, "If anyone is committing a robbery and is caught, then he shall be put to death."

The Jim Crow laws we looked at earlier in this chapter were enforced in the southern United States from 1876–1965. One law from Florida reads, "All marriages between a white person and a negro, or between a white person and a person of negro descent to the fourth generation inclusive, are hereby forever prohibited."

10. Where would you expect to read these laws?
    A. in an algebra book   C. in an English book
    B. in a biography   D. in a social studies book

11. Which is the BEST reason to study the Code of Hammurabi today?

    A.   It shows what laws we should have in the United States today.

    B.   It shows the differences between their civilization and ours.

    C.   It is much more lenient than our laws.

    D.   It is the same as our laws.

12. Which is the BEST reason to study the Jim Crow laws today?

    A.   They show what our laws are like now.

    B.   They show how an ancient civilization lived.

    C.   They show why having laws is important in a civilized society.

    D.   They show how our country has progressed in terms of race relations.

> Fellow students,
>
> As you may know, there has been a lot of graffiti on the school recently. We've seen it on the walls, in the bathrooms, and on the sidewalks. While the administration works to find the offenders, I'd like to ask for your help.
>
> First, if you see anybody defacing the school, tell a teacher. You can help us have a cleaner campus.
>
> Second, if you are the one doing the defacing, stop. Dealing with this issue takes time from other issues, and it makes our school look trashy. You should also know that the principal just announced that offenders will spend a week in in-school suspension for each offense.
>
> With everyone's help and cooperation, we can have a school to be proud of. Thank you.

13. What issue does the speaker intend to address in this speech?

    A.   too much homework   C.   graffiti in the school

    B.   study habits   D.   in-school suspension

14. Which points support what the speaker intended to address in this speech?

    A.   the fact that administrators are working on the problem

    B.   what students should do if they see someone defacing the school

    C.   consequences for defacing school property

    D.   all of the above

15. What new information did students learn in this speech that might affect them?

    A.   the penalty for defacing school property

    B.   the color of the graffiti on the walls

    C.   who is doing the graffiti

    D.   the principal's name

Chapter 10
Extending Meaning

ELA7RC4	Establish a context for information acquired by reading across subject areas, explore life experiences related to subject area content, and understand how words and concepts relate to multiple subjects.

In the earlier chapters, you reviewed strategies for reading and understanding a variety of texts. You learned to:

- understand new vocabulary
- look at how the text is organized
- analyze the features of different texts
- use graphics to help you understand writing
- get more from the literature you read by knowing how authors use genres, literary devices, figurative language, and other elements
- recognize how authors write for purpose in various subject areas and even in different cultures

Now, we will go a step further by **extending the meaning** of a text. When you read, it is your interaction with the text that gives it a specific meaning. That's why a story or an article can mean one thing to you and another to your classmate.

One way to extend meaning to yourself is to think about your life experiences and how they might relate to what you are reading. For example, if you are reading about different types of snakes found in Georgia, you can think back to any snakes that you have seen in your own yard, while hiking, and anywhere else.

In addition to what a text means to you personally, its ideas and issues also relate (sometimes strongly, sometimes not) to the current society and time in which we live. As you read, also think about what point a text makes that is important to today's society.

LITERAL MEANING, AUTHOR'S PURPOSE, AND CONTEXT

- First, make sure you understand the **literal meaning** of the text you are reading. Use the reading strategies from previous chapters to help you get the full meaning. For example, if you are reading an old novel with old-fashioned words or an article with technical terms, look up any words you don't know in a dictionary.

- Next, figure out the **author's purpose** for writing the text. What style and devices are used? Is the text meant to inform, persuade, or entertain?

- Finally, consider the **context** of when, where, and by whom the text was written. How is the history of the time reflected, or how might it affect the author? What impact might culture make on the ideas in the text? Is there anything about the author's background that might play into how the text is written?

EXTENDING MEANING TO YOURSELF AND TO SOCIETY

As you know, authors have a purpose for writing a text, and so they usually intend for readers to have some thoughts or ideas or take some action after reading it. Consider the following example.

---

excerpt from *Walden* by Henry David Thoreau

I went to the woods because I wished to live deliberately, to front only the essential facts of life, and see if I could not learn what it had to teach, and not, when I came to die, discover that I had not lived. I did not wish to live what was not life, living is so dear; nor did I wish to practice resignation, unless it was quite necessary. I wanted to live deep and suck out all the marrow of life, to live so sturdily and Spartan-like as to put to rout all that was not life, to cut a broad swath and shave close, to drive life into a corner, and reduce it to its lowest terms, and, if it proved to be mean, why then to get the whole and genuine meanness of it, and publish its meanness to the world; or if it were sublime, to know it by experience, and be able to give a true account of it in my next excursion. For most men, it appears to me, are in a strange uncertainty about it, whether it is of the devil or of God, and have *somewhat hastily* concluded that it is the chief end of man here to "glorify God and enjoy him forever."

Literal meaning: From reading the passage carefully, you see that the author describes wanting to live simply and naturally and find out what life is truly about.

Author's purpose: Thoreau was writing about nature and people's relationship to it. He felt people took it for granted in his time. He wanted to show that a person could get more out of life if he or she connected again with nature. He uses imagery in "suck out all the marrow of life" to show how he wanted more out of life than what society offered. He also uses personification when he says he wants to "drive life into a corner, and reduce it to its lowest terms." Using these devices, Thoreau paints a picture of the enthusiasm behind his ideas.

Context: Thoreau moved to the woods to be close to nature and live without many of the limitations or the luxuries of his society. He studied nature. His goal was to bring others to a better understand how we all are connected to and depend on the natural world. He also felt that many people lived only to serve God; he felt this was an admirable ideal, but that it needed consideration and a broader look at how one can do that. He asked important questions of people in his time, like what does it cost to exist; what is the best way to live; and do we really need what we think we need?

Extend meaning to the reader: Decide what the passage means to you. Think about your opinions as you read. What is your reaction to Thoreau's words and his ideas? What are your ideas in general about the topics he writes about?

Extend reading to contemporary society: Just as in Thoreau's time (perhaps more), we can forget about the world around us. We sometimes overlook that things are happening around us that don't revolve around our own everyday life. Suddenly, we might hear about something that reminds us how connected nature is to the man-made world. What meaning do Thoreau's words have for people in today's society?

When you extend the meaning of any text that you read, you apply what you learn to yourself and today's society. Taking the example above, what would be the BEST answers for the following questions?

After reading this text, a reader would MOST likely conclude that:

    A.   the author is depressed.

    B.   the author is not a religious man.

    C.   the author thinks country living is easier than city living.

    D.   the author feels that many of our daily activities are not really living.

Answer *A* is not supported; the language and style show that the author is excited, not depressed. Answer *B* also is not supported, as Thoreau never says he is against religion but encourages a thoughtful decision about how to live life. Answer *C* is not mentioned in the text; the author talks about some advantages of living in the woods, but he never says that it is easier. **Answer *D* is the best choice of answer for this question.** It states one of the reasons that Thoreau left society to live in the woods: he wanted to "live deliberately" and not discover later that he "had not lived."

Practice 1: Extending Meaning to Yourself and Society

Read the following passages. Then choose the best answer to each question.

> **—excerpt from *Apple Growing* by M.C. Burritt**
>
> The apple has long been the most popular of our tree fruits, but the last few years have seen a steady growth in its appreciation and use. This is probably due in a large measure to a better knowledge of its value and to the development of new methods of preparation for consumption. Few fruits can be utilized in as many ways as can the apple. In addition to the common use of the fresh fruit out of hand and of the fresh, sweet juice as cider, this "King of Fruits" can be cooked, baked, dried, canned, and made into jellies and other appetizing dishes, to enumerate all of which would be to prepare a list pages long. Few who have tasted once want to be without their apple sauce and apple pies in season, not to mention the crisp, juicy specimens to eat out of hand by the open fireplace in the long winter evenings. Apples thus served call up pleasant memories to most of us, but only recently have the culinary possibilities of the apple, especially as a dessert fruit, been fully realized.

1. In what way, if any, is the information in this text relevant in today's society?

   A. Everyone eats apples, so it offers useful information.

   B. No one has time to cook or bake these days, so it's not much use.

   C. With today's focus on healthy eating, this text offers ways to use a healthy food.

   D. People today have many choices of fruit, making this passage too narrow for modern audiences.

2. This passage would MOST likely encourage a reader to

   A. consider ways to prepare and eat apples more often.

   B. read further about the history of the apple.

   C. make a chart about types of apples.

   D. eat an apple pie.

—excerpt from "The Spirit of 1906" by George W. Brooks,
an eyewitness to the San Francisco earthquake

The first natural impulse of a human being in an earthquake is to get out into the open, and as I and those who were with me were at that particular moment decidedly human in both mold and temperament, we dressed hastily and joined the group of excited neighbors gathered on the street. Pale faced, nervous and excited, we chattered like daws until the next happening intervened, which was the approach of a man on horseback who shouted as he "Revere-d" past us the startling news that numerous fires had started in various parts of the city, that the Spring Valley Water Company's feed main had been broken by the quake, that there was no water and that the city was doomed.

This was the spur I needed. Fires and no water! It was a call to duty. The urge to get downtown and to the office of the "California" enveloped me to such an extent that my terror left me. Activity dominated all other sensations and I started for the office. As all street car lines and methods of transportation had ceased to operate it meant a hike of about two miles.

---

3. What aspect of human nature, true in the past as it is now, is expressed by the author?
   A. Without water, no one can put out a fire.
   B. Faced with danger, many people overcome fear and take action.
   C. People continue to move to California even thought it's not safe.
   D. It's important to get outside in an earthquake.

4. This passage would MOST likely encourage a reader to
   A. think about what he or she would do during a natural disaster.
   B. consider how his or her town would withstand a disaster.
   C. read the history of the San Francisco fire.
   D. dream about moving to California.

EXTENDING MEANING ACROSS SUBJECT AREAS

In previous chapters, you leaned about understanding different kinds of informational texts. You also learned about a variety of literature. Whenever you read something new, no matter what it is, you can think about what you already know that relates to the new topic. The meaning of a new word or idea in one subject might be *similar* to what you already know from other subject areas.

For example, you have read novels that have their own plots and characters but also include historical events and real people. The more you know about history, the more you will understand such books. Say you learn in social studies about the American Revolution. You read about the events that led up to it. You find out why the colonists wanted to separate from Britain. And you learn how the revolution affected people. Now, suppose you read a novel about a fictional character living in that time period. Because you already know about the American Revolution, you will quickly understand the problems he or she faces. You will have background about a historical period that will help the novel make more sense.

 The other side of the coin to extending meaning across subjects is that the meaning of a new word or idea could be quite *different* from other subjects in which you have seen it. For example, consider the words below:

Theory:

In science: a reasonable or acceptable principle that explains something
"Einstein's theory of relativity so far has not been disproved."

In social studies: a hypothesis (educated guess) is made so that investigation can continue
"She decided to test her theory about who had been taking the cookies. She told the Baxter twins to wait in the kitchen, and then she peeked through the keyhole."

Revolution:

In science: the motion of something around a center or axis
"Earth revolves around the Sun."

In social studies: a major change in political organization, such as the American Revolution or the French Revolution

---

Trial:

In science: one of repetition of an experiment
"They did many trials to prove that the results would be the same every time."

In social studies: a legal proceeding to decide whether an accused criminal is guilty or not guilty. "When the evidence was found, the thief knew his trial would not go well."

> **Culture:**
>
> **In science:** in biology, a culture is a group of bacteria , usually in a dish for a scientist to use in experiments, "Dr. Ramsey put a sample of the culture of each glass slide. Then we looked at it under our microscopes."
>
> **In social studies:** the beliefs, practices, and social norms of a racial, religious, or social group "Noemi was fascinated by the wedding. Wedding ceremonies were very different in her culture."

From individual words all the way to big ideas, you can use your past experiences to help you understand new material.

Practice 2: Extending Meaning across Subject Areas

Read this passage from a chemistry textbook. Look at how you can use what you know to extend meaning to this subject area. The answer to the first question has been done as an example for you.

> A chemical equation is a symbolic representation of a chemical reaction and information about the state of the reactants and products. The coefficients next to the symbols and formulae of entities are the absolute values of the stoichiometric numbers. In a chemical reaction, the quantity of each element does not change, so each side of the equation must represent the same quantities in order to be balanced.

What are the BEST definitions for the following words from this excerpt?

1. *reaction*

    A.   reverse movement

    B.   political conservatism

    C.   chemical change

    D.   decline in the market

The excerpt does not talk about a reverse in direction, so A is out. Answers B and D both sound like a definition for a different subject area (namely, politics and economics). This leaves us with answer C, which gives us a big hint by having the word *chemical* in it. Also, remember that when you observe reactions in science class experiments, you are observing *changes* (for example, a substance changing from liquid to solid form). **C is the correct choice.**

2. *element*
    A. part of a whole
    B. a simple substance
    C. natural environment
    D. atmospheric force

3. *balanced*
    A. having like distribution
    B. sane and calm
    C. same amount of debits and credits
    D. symmetrically proportioned

4. Now, say that you are reading a fictional story for an English class. The teacher tells you to look for symbolism in the story. How can you BEST use knowledge of the "symbolic representation" mentioned in the chemistry book to better understand symbolism in fiction?
    A. Understanding the interactions of the elements in chemistry helps a reader to know how characters in fiction interact with one another in the storyline.
    B. Just like the symbolic representation of the formula in chemistry, a fictional story has a formula through which the plot, setting, and characters are presented.
    C. The wording of a chemical equation to show what happens in a chemical reaction is very similar to wording an author uses to portray characters and plot.
    D. Seeing how the letters and numbers in a chemical equation stand for a chemical reaction helps you see how a thing or person in fiction can represent a bigger idea.

COMPARING AND CONTRASTING TO EXTEND MEANING

As you have learned, when you extend meaning, it helps to think about how a new idea might be like something you already know. Doing this means you are looking at how something new is the same or different from something you already know, or something in another subject area. This means you are comparing and contrasting.

Comparing and **contrasting** means you look for similarities and differences between two or more texts and the ideas in them. It is one way to analyze ideas and issues in a text or across texts.

When you use this process, be sure to look for similarities or differences within the same category. This means you have to make sure you are comparing "apples to apples" and "oranges to oranges" but not "apples to oranges." For example, consider this sentence:

This candy is tangy and sweet, but that candy is green.

This statement compares flavor and color which are two unrelated categories. We may be able to conclude that the writer likes sweet candy and does not like green candy, but we can't adequately compare the two candies because we don't know the color of the sweet candy, and we don't know the flavor of the green candy. Therefore, when comparing or contrasting two things or ideas, stay in the same category.

COMPARING AND CONTRASTING IDEAS

Sometimes, finding similarities and differences in a passage or in several texts about the same thing can help you extend meaning. But finding comparisons and contrasts in texts is not always easy. A strategy that can help you is to look for signal words.

As you read a passage in order to answer questions about comparing and contrasting ideas, you can look for **signal words** that point to similarities or differences. Study the following list of signal words.

Signal Words for Similarities and Differences			
Similarities			
again	both	like	similar too
also	in a related way	likewise	similarly
as	in the same way	once more	the same
as well as	just as . . so too	parallel	too
Differences			
although	even though	neither	still
but	however	nevertheless	though
contrary to	in contrast	not as/not like	unlike
conversely	in opposition	on the contrary	whereas
despite	in spite of	on the other hand	while
different from	instead	regardless	yet

Practice 3: Comparing and Contrasting Ideas

Read the following passage. In the questions that follow, identify the signal words and whether they point to similarities or differences.

The French and English Colonies

The (1)main interest of 17th century French colonizers in North America was trade in animal furs. Some furs were used for hats that were (2)very popular in France at the time. The Native Americans were valuable trading partners to the French, supplying animal pelts from beaver, otter, muskrat, and mink. (3)Consequently, the French saw no need to try to conquer them. (4)Likewise, the French did not destroy the forests because they wanted to maintain the habitat of the animals they valued so much. Because the northern areas of North America, where the French colonized, were sparsely populated, epidemics took less of a toll. **(5)**Similarly, the French **(6)**tended to see native peoples as equals, and they accepted intermarriage. The Native Americans were **(7)**also valuable to the French as allies in wars against the British.

     (8) In contrast, the English colonies may be called "colonies of settlement" where settlers **(9)**tried to establish English society in the New World. They took control of the land and brought their own political and economic systems, **(10)**as well as crops and animals. The English came to the New World in much **(11)**greater numbers than the French, and they wanted control of more and more land, thus displacing great numbers of Native Americans. The Native Americans were **(12)**not as beneficial economically to the English as to the French, so the English saw them, **(13)**instead, as an obstacle to progress **(14)**and a nuisance.

1. A. compares   B. contrasts   C. neither
2. A. compares   B. contrasts   C. neither
3. A. compares   B. contrasts   C. neither
4. A. compares   B. contrasts   C. neither
5. A. compares   B. contrasts   C. neither
6. A. compares   B. contrasts   C. neither
7. A. compares   B. contrasts   C. neither
8. A. compares   B. contrasts   C. neither
9. A. compares   B. contrasts   C. neither
10. A. compares   B. contrasts   C. neither
11. A. compares   B. contrasts   C. neither
12. A. compares   B. contrasts   C. neither
13. A. compares   B. contrasts   C. neither
14. A. compares   B. contrasts   C. neither

15. Based on reading the passage as a whole, which statement is true?
    A. The entire passage focuses on similarities.
    B. The whole passage discusses differences.
    C. The first paragraph shows similarities, while the second introduces differences.
    D. The first paragraph talks mainly about differences, while the second explores similarities

Practice 4: Comparing and Contrasting to Extend Meaning

Life in a Sod House Was No Fun at All

The Homestead Act of 1862 offered free farm land to any settler over the age of 21 who built a dwelling at least 12 x 14 feet. This act ushered in a rush of pioneers and farmers onto the Great Plains.

When the settlers reached states like Nebraska and the Dakotas, they were startled to find mostly wide open seas of grassy prairie land. Without the presence of wood or brick or stone, settlers were forced to build their homes from sod. They plowed up the earth and cut it into rectangular pieces measuring six inches thick and two feet long by one foot wide. These blocks of sod were then stacked one on top of the other, grass side down, to form a makeshift house.

Some settlers sang the praise of their sod homes, claiming that they were not only dirt cheap, that but due to the thickness of the walls they were cool in the summer and warm in the winter. Others claimed that the sod house was good at keeping the stove's heat well contained. But most inhabitants of these sod homes, or "soddies" as they were called, quickly found how hard the living could be in one of these shelters.

The shallow roofs were never really waterproof and sometimes caved in. In a heavy downpour, they would leak from one end to the other and continue to leak for days after a rain. Extra care had to be taken to keep lids tight on the skillets to prevent mud from falling into the food. During the winter, snow came streaming in through every crevice. It was usually so cold inside the earthen dwelling that people got frostbite even though they would be sitting by the stove wrapped in a quilt. The floors were compacted dirt, and if straw was brought in to cover them, so too came an army of fleas. Mice and rats burrowed into the walls and were so ever-present that settlers constantly had to kick them out of the way.

Living in a sod house was a never-ending battle just to keep the outside out! All things considered, as one prairie woman said: "Life is too short to be spent under a sod roof."

1. What American ideal does the passage refer to which also can be seen in stories from other periods in our history?
    A.   freedom of speech
    B.   taking inspiration from nature
    C.   creativity in architecture
    D.   survival in a new environment

2. What contrasting idea can help a reader understand this passage?
    A.   considering the advantages of carpeting
    B.   looking at life in hilly or mountainous areas
    C.   thinking about the comforts of a modern home
    D.   reflecting on how settlers journeyed across the plains

3. After reading this passage, which of the following concepts would you MOST likely understand better?

   A. The veterinarian telling someone that a pet has fleas.

   B. A neighbor saying he will place new sod in his yard.

   C. An advertisement for a company that does roof repair.

   D. A newspaper article about the increase in heating costs.

4. How are the last two passages, "The French and English Colonies" and "Life in a Sod House Was No Fun at All," MOST similar?

   A. Both passages recount events from American history.

   B. Both talk about sad times in the lives of American settlers.

   C. Both passages tell about oppression of early immigrants.

   D. Both inform readers about how settlers made money.

CHAPTER 10 SUMMARY

- **Extending the meaning** of a text means that you understand and then apply the ideas to yourself and to current society. Think about your life experiences as they pertain to any subject area in which you are reading.

- You can also **extend meaning across subject areas**. Words and concepts that you learn in one subject can help you understand others. Take care to see that some words and ideas are *similar* across subjects, while other words and ideas are very *different* from one subject to another.

- **Comparing** and **contrasting** is the process of looking for similarities and differences between two or more objects, characters, or ideas. One of the most important aspects of comparing and contrasting is to look for similarities or differences **within the same category**.

CHAPTER 10 REVIEW

Read the passages that follow. Answer the questions after each passage. Some questions relate to more than one of the passages.

"In the Eye of the Shark" editorial by B. A. Wares

Here's a new idea: put yourself into a shark's skin. Do you dare to enter the world where they must glide alone and hungry? Imagine you feel the emptiness of a creature for whom there is no free lunch, no supermarket, and no way to beg for even a single fish scale. You're that animal.

Cast your gaze through the waters: the waters that grow dimmer and lose oxygen every day. You, as the shark, don't realize that it is pollution from some very profitable corporations that is suffocating and blinding you. You only know hunger. Now you feel the tugs and swishes in the water which signal food, life. You move with silent purpose towards the food. You feel the weight of the water moving against your skin as the food bobs in front of your eyes. Your eyes see little through the murky water, little but the food you must have to live, and the urge to live is stronger than the pull of tides.

Now the moment is here, and you open your mouth to grasp the food that comes from your place in the ocean; as a meat-eater your place is to eat the weak and misshapen. Your eyes must close against the struggling food. You see even less than before. There are flashes of pain as you hold on to food that will sustain your life. The ache of hunger is gone, and you move to deeper, clearer water.

Listen people: fearing and condemning sharks won't change their needs or their natures. We, as intelligent beings, must simply take our chances or stay out of the water.

---

1. Why did the author write this editorial?
   A. He wants the big, profitable corporations to stop polluting the oceans.
   B. He says sharks do what comes naturally, and it's up to people to avoid them.
   C. He is advocating better safety measures at beaches to prevent shark attacks.
   D. He thinks more food should be provided for sharks so they will not attack people.

2. When was this editorial MOST likely written? How can you tell?
   A. It was written long ago. Shark attacks do not happen anymore today.
   B. It was written some time ago, when newspapers printed long editorials.
   C. It was written recently. Large-scale polluting of oceans is a recent event.
   D. There is no way to tell when this editorial was written.

3. What is a reader MOST likely to do after reading this passage?

   A. Take up scuba diving to see sharks firsthand.

   B. Make a promise to never swim in the ocean.

   C. Consider the interaction of people and ocean life.

   D. Write an editorial about animals to a newspaper.

4. The author includes a comparison-contrast signal word in the last sentence. It tells readers that there are two different options for dealing with sharks. What are these options?

   A. 1) Realize that sharks might attack you; 2) stay out of the water.

   B. 1) Carry a weapon; 2) cloud the water around you to blind the shark.

   C. 1) Tell big corporations to stop polluting; 2) get ready for mutant sharks.

   D. 1) Wear protective gear when you swim; 2) do not ever go swimming again.

Southeast Regional Beach Safety Guide

Do swim at beaches patrolled by lifeguards or beach patrol organizations.

Do Not swim alone, ever.

Do wait to swim one half-hour after eating food or drinking alcohol.

Do Not struggle if gripped by a cramp, only raise your voice and one arm up for help, float, and keep as still as possible.

Do swim in late morning to afternoon hours when sharks are less active.

Do Not panic if caught in a rip current or undertow; raise your voice and one arm for help while floating.

Do watch for sudden drop offs; look for boundary flags.

Do Not rely on flotation devices for safety; know how to swim well.

Do swim only when the beach is open and surf conditions are good.

Do Not swim if danger signals (red flags) are raised.

Post on All Public Beaches–2007

---

5. What relevant information does this notice provide for people who are concerned about shark attacks?

   A. Sharks only attack in the early morning hours.

   B. Sharks never attack a person swimming alone.

   C. Sharks usually can smell food you have eaten.

   D. Sharks are less active in the middle of the day.

6. Look back at the editorial about sharks. Would the author of the editorial agree with the beach safety guide rules?

   A. He would agree because the rules help prevent water pollution.

   B. He would agree because the rules put the responsibility on people.

   C. He would disagree because the warning about sharks is too strong.

   D. He would disagree because there is not enough warning about sharks.

—excerpt from encyclopedia entry for *shark*

Sharks are fish, and there are many different kinds of them. There are tiny ones like the pygmy shark (about the size of your hand) all the way to giant ones like the whale shark. As the largest fish, the whale shark can grow up to almost 40 feet in length. Sharks have a streamlined body and a skeleton made of cartilage rather than bone. They breathe through gill slits. Sharks have a covering of special scales to protect their skin from damage and parasites. These scales also helps them glide through the water. Unlike people, who get just two sets of teeth for a lifetime, sharks can grow new teeth whenever they lose them.

7. In this context, what is the BEST definition for the word *streamlined*?

A. designed to offer the least resistance to fluid flow

B. reduced to essentials, lacking anything extra

C. improved in appearance and efficiency

D. effectively organized

—excerpt from *The Pirate Shark* by Elliott Whitney

"Are you goin' hunting with us?" shot out Mart. "Tiger hunting?"

"That depends, lad, that depends," and Jerry wagged his head solemnly. "I never killed a tiger yet. I've killed whales, though, aye, and tiger sharks! Think of the mystery of the sea, lads— wave after wave, with the fish down below and us up here above! Fish tell no tales, lads, fish tell no tales. There's strange things out where we be bound for."

"What?" asked Bob eagerly. "Sharks?"

The quartermaster nodded. For a moment he seemed to hesitate, then turned to Mart and laid a hand on the boy's knee.

"Lads, did you ever hear tell o' the Pirate Shark?"

Mart thrilled at the name, and the tone of the old man's voice gave him a creepy feeling, as it often did.

"No!" he exclaimed delightedly, scenting a yarn. "What about him?"

(SECTION OF STORY REMOVED)

"The Pirate Shark," answered old Jerry slowly. "Yes, I'll tell you about it, lads. There ain't many as knows where the Pirate Shark is, but old Jerry Smith, he knows. He's a big shark, he is—mighty big, an' a man-killer. He come up first at Thursday Island, years ago, an' caught half a dozen Jap pearlers. Then he showed up in the Flores Sea, an' for a year the fishers didn't dare visit the pearlin' beds. After that he went over to the Sulu Islands, down to Java, back to the Chiny Sea—always killin' men, natives or white. Then he vanished for a while—mystery o' the sea, lads, wave after wave—"

[1]**pearlers** fishermen who harvest pearls from oysters

8. What is the author's purpose for writing this passage?
   A.   to recount a historical event
   B.   to educate people about sharks
   C.   to warn people about where sharks are active
   D.   to entertain with a suspenseful tale about a shark

9. What MOST makes old Jerry's story about the Pirate Shark so scary for readers?
   A.   Readers can tell that Jerry is an evil character who will put the whole crew in danger.
   B.   The atmosphere of the story is dark and ominous, with the ship headed for disaster.
   C.   People know that sharks truly can become man-eaters if they are hungry enough.
   D.   We know that every movie or book with pirates in it contains frightening events.

10. Which of these three passages would help you avoid sharks if you went to the beach on vacation?
   A.   the editorial   C.   the encyclopedia entry
   B.   the beach safety guide   D.   *The Pirate Shark*

11. Which, if any, of these three passages could you use if you were writing a paper about the changing environment that sharks live in today?
   A.   the editorial   C.   the encyclopedia entry
   B.   the beach safety guide   D.   *The Pirate Shark*

12. Think again about the editorial and the story in *The Pirate Shark*. What similar idea do these two passages contain?
   A.   People imagine that sharks do terrible things. They really are just innocent fish.
   B.   Sharks are carnivorous. They will naturally try to eat people when they see them.
   C.   Sharks can be dangerous eating machines. People have to be careful around them.
   D.   It is hard for sharks to see near the shore. Stay near the shore to avoid shark attacks.

Passing the Georgia 7th Grade CRCT
CRCT in Reading Practice Test 1

The purpose of this practice test is to measure your knowledge in reading comprehension. This practice test is based on the GPS-based CRCT standards for reading and adheres to the sample question format provided by the Georgia Department of Education.

General Directions:

1. Read all directions carefully.

2. Read each question or sample. Then choose the best answer.

3. Choose only one answer for each question. If you change an answer, be sure to erase your original answer completely.

The following poem, written by Emma Lazarus in 1883, is about the Statue of Liberty. In 1903, the poem was engraved on a plaque and mounted inside the pedestal that supports the Statue of Liberty. The title of the poem refers to the Colossus of Rhodes, which was an enormous statue of the Greek god Helios. It was built on the Greek island of Rhodes in ancient times. The Colossus of Rhodes fell after an earthquake in 226 BC. This was only 56 years after it had been erected.

The New Colossus

1   Not like the brazen giant of Greek fame,

     With conquering limbs astride from land to land;

     Here at our sea-washed, sunset gates shall stand

     A mighty woman with a torch, whose flame

5   Is the imprisoned lightning, and her name

     Mother of Exiles. From her beacon-hand

     Glows world-wide welcome; her mild eyes command

     The air-bridged harbor that twin cities frame.

     "Keep ancient lands, your storied pomp!" cries she

10   With silent lips. "Give me your tired, your poor,

     Your huddled masses yearning to breathe free,

     The wretched refuse of your teeming shore.

     Send these, the homeless, tempest-tost to me,

     I lift my lamp beside the golden door!"

1. What type of figurative language is   R1-G
used in the words "sea-washed,"
"sunset," "shall" and "stand" in this
poem?

   A.   assonance

   B.   alliteration

   C.   irony

   D.   personification

2. Which of the following BEST   R1-G
reflects the main idea of lines 9
through 13?

   A.   The ancient world should keep its
tradition of favoring the rich.

   B.   The ancient world is rich with cere-
mony and art.

   C.   The statue welcomes those rejected
elsewhere.

   D.   The air is better in the United States.

3. The phrase "the wretched refuse of your teeming shore" means   R1-G

   A. the garbage from your beaches.

   B. people who desperately search for a better life.

   C. the excess seafood that is spoiled and left on the beach.

   D. the toxic waste that flows from the rivers into the sea.

4. The mood of the poem is BEST described as   R1-H

   A. sad.

   B. hopeful.

   C. gloomy.

   D. mysterious.

5. Based on context clues, the word astride means   R2-A

   A. on top of.

   B. close to.

   C. on both sides of.

   D. near.

> *"Give me your tired, your poor,*
>
> *Your huddled masses yearning to breathe free..."*

6. The "huddled masses" described in the quote above are MOST likely   RC2-C R1-C

   A. people leaving America.

   B. citizens of Greece.

   C. the Colossus of Rhodes.

   D. immigrants coming to America.

7. The Statue of Liberty could be considered a "New Colossus" because   RC2-C R1-C

   A. it was a gift from Greece.

   B. it was constructed by a Greek artist.

   C. it is incredibly large, like the Colossus of Rhodes.

   D. it represents oppression, like the Colossus of Rhodes.

excerpt from "Dracula's Guest" by Bram Stoker

I stopped, for there was a sudden stillness. The storm had passed; and, perhaps in sympathy with nature's silence, my heart seemed to cease to beat. But this was only momentarily; for suddenly the moonlight broke through the clouds showing me that I was in a graveyard and that the square object before me was a great massive tomb of marble, as white as the snow that lay on and all around it. With the moonlight there came a fierce sigh of the storm which appeared to resume its course with a long, low howl, as of many dogs or wolves. I was awed and shocked, and I felt the cold perceptibly grow upon me till it seemed to grip me by the heart. Then while the flood of moonlight still fell on the marble tomb, the storm gave further evidence of renewing, as though it were returning on its track. Impelled by some sort of fascination, I approached the sepulchre to see what it was and why such a thing stood alone in such a place. I walked around it and read, over the Doric door, in German—

COUNTESS DOLINGEN OF GRATZ

IN STYRIA

SOUGHT AND FOUND DEATH

1801

On the top of the tomb, seemingly driven through the solid marble — for the structure was composed of a few vast blocks of stone—was a great iron spike or stake. On going to the back I saw, graven in great Russian letters: "The dead travel fast."

There was something so weird and uncanny about the whole thing that it gave me a turn and made me feel quite faint. I began to wish, for the first time, that I had taken Johann's advice. Here a thought struck me, which came under almost mysterious circumstances and with a terrible shock. This was Walpurgis Night!

Walpurgis Night was when, according to the belief of millions of people, the devil was abroad—when the graves were opened and the dead came forth and walked. When all evil things of earth and air and water held revel. This very place the driver had specially shunned. This was the depopulated village of centuries ago. This was where the suicide lay; and this was the place where I was alone—unmanned, shivering with cold in a shroud of snow with a wild storm gathering again upon me! It took all my philosophy, all the religion I had been taught, all my courage, not to collapse in a paroxysm of fright.

And now a perfect tornado burst upon me. The ground shook as though thousands of horses thundered across it; and this time the storm bore on its icy wings, not snow, but great hailstones which drove with such violence that they might have come from the thongs of Balearic slingers—hailstones that beat down leaf and branch and made the shelter of the cypresses of no more avail than though their stems were standing corn. At the first I had rushed to the nearest tree; but I was soon fain to leave it and seek the only spot that seemed to afford refuge, the deep Doric doorway of the marble tomb. There, crouching against the massive bronze door, I gained a certain amount of protection from the beating of the hailstones, for now they only drove against me as they ricochetted from the ground and the side of the marble.

As I leaned against the door, it moved slightly and opened inwards. The shelter of even a tomb was welcome in that pitiless tempest and I was about to enter it when there came a flash of forked lightning that lit up the whole expanse of the heavens. In the instant, as I am a living man, I saw, as my eyes turned into the darkness of the tomb, a beautiful woman with rounded cheeks and red lips, seemingly sleeping on a bier. As the thunder broke overhead, I was grasped as by the hand of a giant and hurled out into the storm. The whole thing was so sudden that, before I could realize the shock, moral as well as physical, I found the hailstones beating me down. At the same time I had a strange, dominating feeling that I was not alone. I looked towards the tomb. Just then there came another blinding flash which seemed to strike the iron stake that surmounted the tomb and to pour through to the earth, blasting and crumbling the marble, as in a burst of flame. The dead woman rose for a moment of agony while she was lapped in the flame, and her bitter scream of pain was drowned in the thundercrash. The last thing I heard was this mingling of dreadful sound, as again I was seized in the giant grasp and dragged away, while the hailstones beat on me and the air around seemed reverberant with the howling of wolves. The last sight that I remembered was a vague, white, moving mass, as if all the graves around me had sent out the phantoms of their sheeted dead, and that they were closing in on me through the white cloudiness of the driving hail.

8. What is the setting of this passage?   R1-C

   A. the woods

   B. the town of Walpurgis

   C. a graveyard

   D. a small European cottage

9. The tone of this passage is BEST   R1-H
   described as

   A. romantic and sweet.

   B. lighthearted and comedic.

   C. cold and sinister.

   D. serious but optimistic.

10. What is the author's MAIN purpose   RC2-E
    for writing this passage?

   A. to create suspense and terror in the reader

   B. to explain the dangers of hailstorms

   C. to describe Walpurgis Night to tourists

   D. to convince readers never to travel to Europe

11. Which of the following quotes from the passage LEAST advances the plot? R1-E

   A. "Here a thought struck me, which came under almost mysterious circumstances and with a terrible shock. This was Walpurgis Night!"

   B. "The shelter of even a tomb was welcome in that pitiless tempest and I was about to enter it when there came a flash of forked lightning that lit up the whole expanse of the heavens."

   C. "It took all my philosophy, all the religion I had been taught, all my courage, not to collapse in a paroxysm of fright."

   D. "Impelled by some sort of fascination, I approached the sepulchre to see what it was and why such a thing stood alone in such a place."

12. Which of the following quotes from the passage BEST communicates the narrator's feelings? R1-F

   A. "On going to the back I saw, graven in great Russian letters: "The dead travel fast."

   B. "With the moonlight there came a fierce sigh of the storm which appeared to resume its course with a long, low howl, as of many dogs or wolves."

   C. "I was awed and shocked, and I felt the cold perceptibly grow upon me till it seemed to grip me by the heart."

   D. "The last thing I heard was this mingling of dreadful sound, as again I was seized in the giant grasp and dragged away, while the hailstones beat on me and the air around seemed reverberant with the howling of wolves."

Read the following sentences from the passage:

> "At the same time I had a strange, dominating feeling that I was not alone. I looked towards the tomb. Just then there came another blinding flash which seemed to strike the iron stake that surmounted the tomb and to pour through to the earth, blasting and crumbling the marble, as in a burst of flame."

13. Which plot component do these sentences best represent? R1-E

   A. resolution

   B. climax

   C. falling action

   D. introduction

Read the following sentences from the passage:

> "There was something so weird and uncanny about the whole thing that it gave me a turn and made me feel quite faint. I began to wish, for the first time, that I had taken Johann's advice."

14. Based on these sentences, we can infer that the narrator R1-F

   A. has changed his mind about the situation.

   B. feels guilty about his actions.

   C. is uncertain about his health.

   D. is concerned about Johann.

15. Based on the author's description, we can conclude the narrator is R1-B

   A. foolish and silly.

   B. brave but frightened.

   C. angry and mean spirited.

   D. a superstitious villager.

You do not need to refer to the passage to answer questions 16 – 20.

16. Which of the following statements about theme in literature is NOT correct? R1-A

    A. Theme is the underlying meaning of a story.

    B. Theme is the main topic of a work of literature.

    C. A story's theme is usually a truth about human nature of the world.

    D. The reader must often infer what the theme of a work is.

17. An author's reason for writing an expository text is its R1-A

    A. theme.

    B. evidence.

    C. purpose.

    D. idea.

18. What should you add to the word stated to make it mean "stated again"? R2-B

    A. pre   C. re

    B. post   D. de

19. If you wanted to add a brief explanation to a photograph for a magazine article, you would MOST likely use a R1-B

    A. diagram.

    B. caption.

    C. illustration.

    D. graphic organizer.

20. Which of the following words contains a suffix that means *without*? R1-B

    A. unable

    B. cheerful

    C. easily

    D. thoughtless

The stories that follow are from two different cultures. Read each story. Then answer the questions.

Walks All Over the Sky ~ A Traditional Native American Folktale

Long ago, there was a chief that ruled the sky. He had two sons and a daughter to help him. During this time, life was very peaceful for the people and animals of the Earth. However, there was no light in the sky, so everyone was forced to live out their days in darkness.

One day, the younger son, who was named Walks-All-Over-the-Sky, looked down at the dark world and thought about how beautiful the world would be if it had light. The people of Earth would be so happy! He decided to do something about the darkness that covered the world.

As he was gathering wood in the forest of the sky with his older brother one day, the younger son made a mask out of cedar wood and placed it over his face. Then, he lit the mask on fire and began to walk east, leaving his bewildered brother standing alone. As the younger son walked, flames shot from his mask and illuminated the Earth. He started running faster towards the east, and the flames grew brighter. He looked down and saw that the people of the Earth were joyously celebrating the light. Because he saw how happy the people were, the younger son knew that he had given them a great gift. So, every day, the son ran east to west so that he could continue to light up the Earth. Later, Walks-All-Over-the-Sky decided to sleep. While he slept, sparks flew out of his mouth and turned into stars.

The older brother, Walking-About-Early, wanted to offer something to the people of the world as well. One night, as his younger brother was sleeping, Walking-About-Early rubbed charcoal and fat on his face. With his face shining, he began walking east. Walking-About-Early shed light over the world, much like his brother, except this time the light was soft and not quite as bright as the sun. Nevertheless, the people were happy to have this little bit of light with them while the younger brother was sleeping. In this way, the world was never completely dark. All the people of the Earth praised the chief and his children for bringing the gifts of the sun, moon, and stars to the world.

Why the Vulture is Bald ~ A Traditional Folktale from Burma

The vulture was originally a humble old bird and rather stupid. His plumage was not exceptionally beautiful but quite passable. One day, however, the vulture noticed that his feathers were falling off. He consulted other birds, who told him that he was merely molting and new feathers would grow later. But the vulture was pessimistic and soon became thin and sickly with worry about his plumage. At last the other birds took pity on him, and each gave him a feather to stick on his body. When all the birds had given him their feathers, the vulture looked like a wonderful bird with plumage of all colors.

The vulture now became conceited. He strutted about in his borrowed feathers and declared that he was the most beautiful of all the birds. He became more and more proud until he asked the birds to recognize him as their king. At this insolence, the birds pecked off not only the feathers that they had given the vulture but also the vulture's own feathers. So when the birds had finished with him, the vulture looked old and ugly and bald. That is why even to the present day, the vulture is a sour and ugly old bird.

---

21. How are these two stories alike? R1-I

    A. Both of the stories try to explain something.

    B. Both stories are American folktales.

    C. Both stories are about animals.

    D. Both stories are about warriors.

22. What does the first story explain? R1-D

    A. how the sky became dark

    B. how the stars were made

    C. how the moon was made

    D. how the sun and moon were made

23. How are these two stories different? R1-I

    A. The first story has a moral lesson.

    B. The second story has a moral lesson.

    C. One is true, and the other is fiction.

    D. The first is a folktale; the second is a legend.

24. In the second story, the other birds are angry at the vulture because he is R1-B

    A. prettier than they are.

    B. selfish and unkind.

    C. proud and arrogant.

    D. smarter than they are.

25. What is the theme of "Why the Vulture is Bald"? R1-D

    A. Offering help to others will always pay off in the end.

    B. Being proud and conceited will always get you into trouble.

    C. Beauty is always admired by others.

    D. Never ask someone to do something you can do yourself.

Dangerous Predators?

Think sharks are dangerous? Although they are the ocean's most feared and fascinating predators, most sharks, such as the whale shark and the megamouth, are gentle giants. These sharks prefer to dine on algae and small fish rather than large prey and pose no threat to people.

There are, however, a few sharks that prefer larger prey and can be very dangerous to people. The most dangerous sharks include the great white, the hammerhead, the tiger shark, and the bull shark. These sharks have been known to attack humans. However, according to some scientists, shark attacks occur only about 100 times a year and, out of those, only 10 are mortalities.

In contrast, people kill thousands more sharks each year for food and sport than sharks kill people. Shark fin soup and steaks are popular delicacies in many countries. In America, mako is one of the most popular items on the menu. Up until the 1950s, shark liver was used to create vitamin A supplements. Today, sharks are hunted for their fins and their cartilage. Certain shark populations have decreased so dramatically over the last decade, their names have been added to the endangered species list.

From a shark's point of view, people pose a serious threat to shark survival. So, who's the dangerous predator?

26. What is the author's argument in this passage? R1-D

A. Sharks are incredibly deadly and dangerous creatures.

B. More people are killed by sharks than any other animal.

C. Sharks are not as dangerous to people as people are to sharks.

D. Sharks have never attacked people.

27. What kind of evidence does the author use to support his/her argument? R1-E

A. Data about how few shark attacks occur each year.

B. Humans kill thousands of sharks for food and sport each year.

C. Certain shark populations have been added to the endangered species list due to human hunting.

D. all of the above

28. What is the concluding sentence of the second paragraph? R1-A

A. There are, however, a few sharks that prefer larger prey and can be very dangerous to people.

B. So, who's the dangerous predator?

C. Up until the 1950s, shark liver was used to create vitamin A supplements.

D. However, according to scientists, shark attacks occur only about 100 times a year and out of those only 10 are mortalities.

29. What is the author's MAIN reason   RC2-E
for writing "Dangerous Predators"?

   A. to persuade readers that sharks are a dangerous threat to all of us

   B. to entertain readers with interesting stories about sharks

   C. to convince readers that sharks are not as dangerous as we think

   D. to convince readers to swim with sharks

30. How many shark attacks occur   R1-E
each year?

   A. around 100

   B. 10

   C. 50

   D. too many to count

31. A word that has a similar meaning   RC3-A
to *decreased* is

   A. lessened.   C. grew.

   B. risen.   D. reclined.

32. What is the BEST way to describe   R1-C
how this passage is organized?

   A. chronological order

   B. logical order

   C. compare and contrast

   D. there is no order

33. According to the passage, what was   R1-E
shark liver used to make?

   A. soup   C. supplements

   B. steaks   D. cartilage

34. Who or what are the "gentle giants"   R2-C
described in the passage?

   A. the whale shark and megamouth shark

   B. the great white shark and the bull shark

   C. fishing boats

   D. tiger sharks

The Moon

Through space exploration, scientists have constructed a history of the moon dating back to its infancy. Rocks collected from the lunar highlands date about 4.0 to 4.3 billion years old. It's believed that the solar system formed about 4.6 billion years ago. The first few million years of the moon's existence were so violent that few traces of this period remain. As a molten outer layer gradually cooled and solidified into different kinds of rock, the moon was bombarded by huge asteroids and smaller objects. Some of the asteroids were the size of small states like Rhode Island or Delaware, and their collisions with the moon created huge basins hundreds of kilometers across.

The catastrophic bombardment died away about 4 billion years ago, leaving the lunar highlands covered with huge overlapping craters and a deep layer of shattered and broken rock. Heat produced by the decay of radioactive elements began to melt the inside of the moon at depths of about 200 kilometers (124 miles) below its surface. Then, from about 3.8 to 3.1 billion years ago, great floods of lava rose from inside the moon and poured over its surface, filling in the large impact basins to form the dark parts of the moon called maria or seas. Explorations show that there has been no significant volcanic activity on the moon for more than 3 billion years.

35. Which organizational structure does   R1-C
this passage use?

A.   persuasive

B.   comparison and contrast

C.   cause and effect

D.   transitions

36. Which of the following is the topic   R1-A
sentence of this passage?

A.   "The first few million years of the moon's existence were so violent that few traces of this period remain."

B.   "Rocks collected from the lunar highlands date about 4.0 to 4.3 billion years ago."

C.   "Through space exploration, scientists have constructed a history of the moon dating back to its infancy."

D.   "Explorations show there has been no significant volcanic activity on the moon for more than 3 billion years."

37. Based on context clues what does RC4-C the word *constructed* mean in this passage?

    A. put together   C. imagined

    B. guessed   D. broken

38. How do we know this passage is RC2-F nonfiction?

    A. Because it is based on facts and not on imagination.

    B. Because it describes a real planet.

    C. Because it is based on imagination rather than facts.

    D. Because it has only two paragraphs.

39. You want to create a Web site that LSV2-A contains information about the moon that would be useful for students working on science reports. Which of the following would be LEAST relevant to have on your Web site?

    A. photographs of the moon

    B. links to information about other planets

    C. links to scientific reports about the moon

    D. a page of basic facts about the moon

Everyone knows how the teachers feel about vending machines in the hallways. They think they're distracting and make us late to class. I know that teachers don't want their students to be tardy, but I think most of us do a good job of making it to our classes. And the people that are late almost every day are not late because they're trying to get a snack. They're late because they're talking to friends and taking their sweet time. I don't see why we have to punish all the students because of the tardiness of a few. Although there are some negative sides to this issue, it is important to have vending machines available to us between classes. I always eat breakfast in the morning before school, but I am still starving by lunch time. It makes my math class, which is right before lunch, very hard to get through. Then, I'm so hungry that I eat too much at lunch, and I get sleepy in the afternoon. There have been many reports in the news about the importance of eating snacks throughout the day to keep up energy and concentration. In the end, I think the vending machines help our students do better in class!

40. Which of the following sentences   R1-D
    BEST establishes the author's opin-
    ion about the issue of vending machines in
    school?

    A.   "I always eat breakfast in the
         morning before school, but I am still
         starving by lunch time."

    B.   "Everyone knows how the teachers
         feel about vending machines in the
         hallways."

    C.   "Although there are some negative
         sides to this issue, it is important to
         have vending machines available to
         us between classes."

    D.   "And the people that are late almost
         every day are not late because
         they're trying to get a snack."

The following set of instructions explains how to program a coffee maker to start brewing coffee at a set time.

Manually Programming a Preset Brewing Time

1. Press and hold Program for two seconds. The TIME display will flash.

2. Press Hour and Min to advance to the desired time.

3. When the desired time appears, press Program to save your automatic brewing time.

To Activate Automatic Brewing

    A.   Press Program to briefly display the time for preset brewing to begin.
          TIMER will appear in the display.

    B.   To activate automatic brewing, press Select.
          TIMER READY will appear in the display.

The Coffee Maker will begin brewing at the programmed time.

    C.   When the coffee is ready, ON READY will appear in the display. The Coffee Maker will stay on for one hour and then automatically shut itself off. You may turn the Coffee Maker off manually at any time by pressing On/Off.

---

41. What appears in the display after you press Program for two seconds?   R1-F

    A.   TIME
    B.   TIMER
    C.   TIMER READY
    D.   ON READY

42. How do you save your automatic brewing time?   R1-F

    A.   press Program
    B.   press Select
    C.   press On
    D.   press TIME

The Mystery of Easter Island

There are few places on the earth more mysterious and intriguing than Easter Island. It is one of the most isolated islands in the world, with the nearest country over 2,300 miles away. About 1200 years ago, seafarers from a distant culture managed to land upon its remote shores. Over the centuries that followed, a remarkable society developed in isolation on the island.

For reasons still unknown, they began carving giant statues out of volcanic rock. These monuments, known as "moai," are some of the most incredible ancient relics ever discovered. Hundreds of these statues cover the island. Each statue, some over 40 feet tall, has the same appearance: Their stony expressions have no eyes. The statues weigh many tons each, and some wonder how the islanders moved the statues. One legend even claims that the statues "walked" by themselves to their site.

Why an ancient people carved these amazing statues is still a mystery. Some scientists claim that they carved them for protection. Others claim they were made to honor ancestors. Whatever the reason, the statues of Easter Island continue to fascinate scientists and tourists.

43. What kind of graphic accompanies this passage? R1-B

  A. a chart

  B. a map

  C. a diagram

  D. a photo

44. Based on the passage, what can we conclude about the people who built the statues? R1-B

  A. Very little is known about their culture.

  B. They were not a very advanced culture.

  C. They did not know how to write.

  D. They carved the statues as gifts for one another.

45. Which quote from the passage does the photograph BEST support? RC2-F

  A. "About 1200 years ago, seafarers from a distant culture managed to land upon its remote shores."

  B. "It is one of the most isolated islands in the world, with the nearest country over 2,300 miles away."

  C. "Each statue, some over 40 feet tall, has the same appearance: Their stony expressions have no eyes."

  D. "One legend even claims that the statues 'walked' by themselves to their site."

46. Who or what are the "moia"? RC3-C

    A. the ancient people of Easter Island

    B. the massive statues on Easter Island

    C. the area where the massive statues stand

    D. the people who discovered the statues

47. What is the main idea of this passage? RC2-A

    A. Easter Island is a mysterious and fascinating place.

    B. The people who carved the statues on Easter Island were technologically advanced.

    C. Easter Island is a dangerous place for tourists to visit.

    D. Scientists are uncovering new evidence about Easter Island.

48. What does the word *isolation* mean in this passage? R2-D

    A. emptiness

    B. distance

    C. confinement

    D. desertion

49. What is the author's main reason for writing "The Mystery of Easter Island"? RC2-E

    A. To frighten readers so they will not visit Easter Island.

    B. To convince readers to visit Easter Island.

    C. To inform readers about the mysterious statues on Easter Island.

    D. To teach readers about the ancient people who live on Easter Island.

50. How is the meaning of the passage enhanced by the graphic? LSV2-A

    A. It helps readers understand the size and impressiveness of the statues.

    B. It gives readers a better idea of where Easter Island is located.

    C. It helps readers understand the culture of the people of Easter Island.

    D. It gives a better idea of the shape of Easter Island.

Passing the Georgia 7th Grade CRCT in Reading Practice Test 2

The purpose of this practice test is to measure your knowledge in reading comprehension. This practice test is based on the GPS-based CRCT standards for reading and adheres to the sample question format provided by the Georgia Department of Education.

General Directions:

1. Read all directions carefully.

2. Read each question or sample. Then choose the best answer.

3. Choose only one answer for each question. If you change an answer, be sure to erase your original answer completely.

GO ON

Poor Fool's Gold

1 "Ow! Ow! That hurt—confounded egg!" Farmer Hash hopped around holding his injured foot, fussing and complaining at the egg which now lay quiet and still on the grass. After a few minutes, Farmer Hash reached down to pick up the egg, very carefully, so he would not drop it again on his other foot. The egg was heavy and cold to the touch even though the mother goose had just been sitting on it.

2 "Hmm, there's something different about this egg. Maybe it's rotten," he thought to himself, as he carried the egg out from under the dim shade of the weeping willow tree. The farmer had not been happy when the mother goose had chosen this overgrown patch of marshy land to make her nest, but she had laid many eggs in the cozy but squishy spot. Walking into the bright sunshine, the farmer almost tripped over the mother goose.

3 "Get out of my way!" he snarled, aiming an impatient kick at her for good measure. Farmer Hash carefully laid the egg on the hay wagon to see it better. Now, Farmer Hash was very nearsighted and color-blind. But even he could see the bright glow glinting off of the egg's shell.

4 "Must be bad . . ." he grumbled to himself, since he had never seen an egg shine like this before.

5 "Papa!" a voice called him. The cheerful voice belonged to his daughter, Felicity. She had come to tell him that Mrs. Hash had his lunch ready: wheat grass soup again. Felicity, however, forgot to give him the message when she saw the egg lighting the hay with a golden glowing radiance.

6 "Oh!" she breathed in admiration. "It's lovely, Papa. Where ever did you find an egg of gold?"

7 "Huh?" Farmer Hash answered her. "An egg of gold?"

8 Felicity began to name the good things and the happiness they could now have with the treasure that lay before them. Before she could finish her thoughts, Farmer Hash was in the wagon headed to town to sell the egg. He came back with a new wagon and horses but no more money.

9 First thing every morning, Farmer Hash would run to the goose's nest to look for another golden egg. The farmer was furious when he realized that the goose laid an egg only once a week, on Fridays, and his family was saddened to realize that the egg money was gone by Saturday night.

10 After three months of this unexplained but mixed blessing, Farmer Hash stood watching Felicity feeding the goose from a bag of marigold and mustard seeds. He hated to think of the cost of such fine food for a goose which would lay her golden eggs only once a week. The words of Felicity came back to him about the fortune they would have and their guaranteed happiness.

11   "Of course," the farmer yelled aloud, "we need all the eggs at once to be truly happy! I will cut open the goose, and we shall have many eggs to sell for our good fortune."

12   "Oh no! Please, no, Papa!" Felicity begged, weeping bitterly. "The goose has been a faithful creature to us and deserves our care, not our greed . . ."

13   The farmer paid no heed to the words of his daughter, setting the day for butchering the goose. That day dawned with a blood-red sky. It was a Sunday, after the money from the last egg was spent on Saturday night. Farmer Hash carried his sharpest ax out to the bank of the pond, near the weeping willow tree. He had never really looked at the geese he owned and could not tell which was the goose that laid the golden eggs. The farmer simply waded into the flock of geese and slaughtered every one of them, looking in vain for the glint of gold among white feathers.

14   At the end of the day, Farmer Hash dropped his dulled ax with a muffled thud into the quiet of the barnyard. As the sun set with rays of golden light wickedly beaming through breaks in purple clouds, he shuffled slowly towards the house listening to the soft sound of his wife and child weeping for lost golden promises.

1. Which of the following phrases is   R1-E
the best example of foreshadowing?

    A.   "… farmer Hash carefully laid the egg on the hay wagon."

    B.   "…and the family realized that the money from each egg was gone."

    C.   "…farmer Hash stood watching Felicity feeding all the geese."

    D.   " 'Must be bad,'" he grumbled to himself, since he had never seen an egg like this before."

2. Which of the following is the best   R1-E
example of a flashback in the passage?

    A.   "Walking into the bright sunshine, the farmer almost tripped over the mother goose."

    B.   "Now, Farmer Hash was very near-sighted and color-blind."

    C.   "The words of Felicity came back to him about the fortune they would have and their guaranteed happiness."

    D.   The farmer simply waded into the flock of geese and slaughtered every one of them, looking in vain for gold among the white feathers."

3. Which of the following statements   R1-D
    best describes the theme of the   R1-A
    passage?

    A. Generosity is something fathers can teach to daughters.

    B. Geese are fickle, silly creatures with big appetites.

    C. Greed is destructive to families and can cloud good judgment.

    D. Family closeness and money can be difficult to manage in hard times.

4. Based on the author's description,   R1-F
    we can conclude Farmer Hash is

    A. a patient, gentle man.

    B. a greedy and somewhat cruel man.

    C. a thoughtful and kind man.

    D. a hardworking and generous man.

5. At the end of the story, we can pre-   R1-F
    dict Farmer Hash feels

    A. satisfied.   C. excited.

    B. triumphant.   D. guilty.

Read the following sentence from the passage:

> *"That day dawned with a blood-red sky"*

6. This sentence foreshadows which   R1-E
    event from the story?

    A. the goose laying the golden egg

    B. Farmer Hash kicking the goose

    C. Farmer Hash slaughtering all the geese

    D. Farmer Hash going to town to sell the egg

The Magic Paint Brush
A Chinese Folktale

Once there was a young man named Ma Liang who was very poor and helped tend the cattle of a rich man in his village. Although he had nothing, he was very kind. His favorite activity was drawing, and the villagers often saw Ma Liang drawing pictures everywhere.

One night, he dreamed that an old man gave him a magic paintbrush, which he could use to help poor people. In the morning, he woke up and saw the paintbrush sitting on his desk! From then on, he helped people by using his magic paintbrush. When people needed water for their crops, he drew rivers that came to life. When he saw people toiling in the fields, he drew cows that came alive and helped the people plow the land. It went in this way for a long time. Whenever Ma Liang saw people in need, he would draw something with his paintbrush to help them.

Eventually, everyone knew about the magic paintbrush. The rich man who Ma Liang used to help heard about it too. Sadly, the rich man was very greedy and wanted to steal the paintbrush from Ma Liang, so he had some people arrest Ma Liang and send him to prison. Then, the rich man had the magic paintbrush all to himself. To his dismay, the paintbrush didn't work! He became very angry and realized he needed Ma Liang's help.

The rich man went to Ma Liang and said, "If you draw things for me and make them come to life, I will free you." Ma Liang was troubled, because he knew the man was up to no good. But he had an idea. Ma Liang replied, "I will help you, but remember your words."

The rich man said, "Excellent. I want a golden mountain, so I can go there and harvest gold." Ma Liang drew a sea. The rich man was angry. "Why did you do that? Draw me a mountain immediately!" Ma Liang drew a golden mountain that was on the other side of the sea. The rich man was relieved and said, "Draw a ship, so that I may travel to the mountain and get the gold."

Ma Liang smiled and drew a big ship. The rich man quickly jumped into the ship, with his friends and family following behind him. When the ship sailed to the middle of the sea, Ma Liang drew a huge wave that destroyed the ship, leaving the rich man and his friends swimming in the ocean, never to return to the village of Ma Liang.

After that, Ma Liang lived happily with his family and continued to help the poor people of his village. Everyone knew about the magic paintbrush, but they were wise not to abuse its power.

Questions 7–9 are related to "Poor Fool's Gold" AND "The Magic Paintbrush."

7. How are "Poor Fool's Gold" and   R1-I
   "The Magic Paintbrush" similar?

   A.   Both have a young girl character.

   B.   Both take place in the same village.

   C.   Both stories are about greed.

   D.   Both are very funny.

8. What material represents great   R1-I
   wealth in both stories?

   A.   gold

   B.   crops

   C.   geese

   D.   money

9. Which positive characteristic below   R1-I
   is NOT presented in either story ?

   A.   helping the poor

   B.   being thankful for what you have

   C.   being kind to others

   D.   giving gold to everyone

10. What is the setting of "The Magic   R1-C
    Paintbrush"?

    A.   a farm

    B.   a small village

    C.   a mansion

    D.   a shack

Aron Ralston: Extreme Climber and Survivor

The adventure began on a seemingly ordinary day in April of 2003. Aron Ralston, a 27-year-old experienced climber and <u>avid</u> outdoorsman, departed for Canyonlands National Park in Utah to climb the remote Bluejohn Canyon. Intending to make the hike in less than a day, and considering the trek a fairly easy one, Ralston told no one where he was going, leaving only a note reading "Utah" for friends.

Less than seven miles into the hike, disaster struck when a one-thousand-pound boulder suddenly shifted and came tumbling toward Ralston. When the boulder finally came to a stop, it landed on Ralston's hand, crushing it. Trapped between the canyon wall and the massive boulder, Ralston fought against mind-numbing waves of pain and thought of ways he could survive. He had made a fatal mistake by not notifying anyone about where he was going; he also knew the chances of another hiker finding him in this remote area were slim.

With little food and only enough water for a couple days, Ralston knew the only hope he had of surviving was to free his hand himself. The only tools he had with him were a rope, a first-aid kit, and a pocketknife. With this limited equipment, Ralston had three ways to try to survive: the first was to slowly chip away at the boulder with his knife; the second, to devise a pulley system with the rope to lift the boulder off his hand; and the third, if all else failed, was to amputate his own arm.

After discovering the boulder was too heavy to lift with rope and the rock too hard to chip away, Ralston fell into despair. It had been three days since the boulder had pinned him to the canyon. The two burritos and water he had brought for the hike were gone. At night, the temperatures in the desert were brutally cold, and Ralston fought against <u>hypothermia</u>. Overwhelmed with fatigue, dehydration, and the increasing possibility of his own death, Ralston engraved his own epitaph on the face of the boulder, "RIP[1] April 2003."

On the sixth day of his entrapment under the boulder, Ralston took his pocketknife and pierced the skin on his injured arm. He was amazed to find he had no sensation—no feeling at all—in the crushed hand. What alarmed him, however, was the hissing sound his skin had made when he'd punctured it. He realized his arm was decaying and his blood was beginning to be poisoned. In desperation, Ralston decided to do the unthinkable, his final survival option, and cut off his own arm. In a kind of trance, Ralston carried out the task of amputation methodically: Breaking the bones of his wrist, cutting through tissue and muscle, cauterizing[2] major arteries to prevent blood loss, and finally fashioning a first-aid tourniquet[3] out of his bicycle shorts. Although he was now finally free from the boulder, Ralston had to crawl through the canyon, rappel down a cliff, and walk several miles before he finally encountered hikers.

---

[1]RIP: Rest in Peace

[2]cauterizing: to burn, sear, or put pressure on a wound to prevent bleeding and infection

[3]tourniquet: a tight bandage to stop bleeding and slow blood flow

Rescuers were called, and Ralston was taken to the nearest hospital. The hand was retrieved from under the boulder but could not be reattached. Witnesses at the site of the accident reported the hand looked like a withered black leather glove. After undergoing several operations and having a high-tech plastic limb fashioned for his missing hand, Ralston lived on to tell others of his trying ordeal.

Ralston's ordeal at the Bluejohn Canyon has made him an international sensation. Although the incident has changed Ralston's life, it has not stopped him from climbing; he still enjoys scaling impossible heights, but he is more careful now and always tells someone where he is going. Ralston's passion for life and his courage and determination are stronger than ever. Ralston now tours the country as a motivational speaker, telling others his incredible story.

11. What mistake did Ralston make   R1-C
    when he left for his hike?

    A. He packed too much gear for such a short hike.

    B. He forgot water.

    C. He didn't tell anyone where he was going.

    D. He didn't make any mistakes.

12. Based on the author's description,   R1-A
    what kind of person was Ralston before the accident?

    A. cautious and careful

    B. witty and charming

    C. depressed, angry, and lonely

    D. reckless, brave, and adventurous

13. Ralston's three survival options   R1-A
    included all of the following EXCEPT

    A. chipping away at the boulder.

    B. building a signal fire.

    C. devising a pulley system with rope.

    D. cutting off his arm.

14. As it is used in the passage, *avid*   R2-A
    most nearly means

    A. knowledgeable.

    B. inexperienced.

    C. uninterested.

    D. poor.

15. Suppose you decide to create a   LSV2-A
    Web site about Aron Ralston's story. Which of the following would be LEAST relevant for the site?

    A. a video of Ralston giving a speech about his ordeal

    B. safety advice for people interested in going to Bluejohn Canyon

    C. advice on where to find a good pocketknife

    D. a picture of the canyon where Ralston was trapped

16. In which class are you MOST   RC2-C
    likely to learn more about the physical hardship (hypothermia, dehydration) that Ralston suffered?

    A. art   C. social studies

    B. language arts D. science

17. Which of the following statements   RC2-F
from the passage BEST expresses
the main idea of this passage?

   A.   "Aron Ralston, a 27-year-old
        experienced climber and avid
        outdoorsman, departed for
        Canyonlands National Park in Utah
        to climb the remote Bluejohn
        Canyon."

   B.   "The adventure began on a seem-
        ingly ordinary day in April of 2003"

   C.   "Although the incident has changed
        Ralston's life, it has not stopped him
        from climbing; he still enjoys scal-
        ing impossible heights, but he is
        more careful now and always tells
        someone where he is going."

   D.   "Ralston now tours the country as a
        motivational speaker, telling others
        his incredible story."

18. Based on context clues, what does   R2-D
hypothermia most likely mean?

   A.   freezing to death

   B.   starving to death

   C.   parched and dry

   D.   dazed and confused

19. The organizational pattern of this   R1-C
passage is best described as

   A.   comparison and contrast

   B.   cause and effect

   C.   chronological

   D.   logical

20. What is the author's purpose in   RC2-E
writing this story?

   A.   to warn people not to venture into
        the outdoors

   B.   to tell an inspiring story of one
        person's survival

   C.   to warn people not to travel in parks
        alone

   D.   to persuade someone to pursue a
        career as a rescuer

---

excerpt from "The Enchanted Bluff"

by Willa Cather

We had our swim before sundown, and while we were cooking our supper the oblique rays of light made a dazzling glare on the white sand about us. The translucent red ball itself sank behind the brown stretches of cornfield as we sat down to eat, and the warm layer of air that had rested over the water and our clean sand bar grew fresher and smelled of the rank ironweed and sunflowers growing on the flatter shore. The river was brown and sluggish, like any other of the half-dozen streams that water the Nebraska corn lands. On one shore was an irregular line of bald clay bluffs where a few scrub oaks with thick trunks and flat, twisted tops threw light shadows on the long grass. The western shore was low and level, with cornfields that stretched to the skyline, and all along the water's edge were little sandy coves and beaches where slim cottonwoods and willow saplings flickered.

21. What is the setting of this passage? R1-C

   A. a cotton field

   B. a farm by the ocean

   C. a beach by a river

   D. a small stream in the woods

22. What type of figurative language is R1-G
used in the phrase "cornfields that
stretched to the skyline…"

   A. alliteration

   B. hyperbole

   C. simile

   D. onomatopoeia

23. Which of the following words R1-H
BEST describes the tone of the passage?

   A. violent

   B. lonely

   C. fearful

   D. peaceful

Read the following from the passage:

> *"The translucent red ball itself sank behind the brown stretches of cornfield as we sat down to eat…"*

24. What is the "translucent red ball"? R2-C

   A. the sun   C. sunflowers

   B. the moon   D. moonlight

Dear Editor:

Every year, the U.S. military sends shoppers to Europe. These shoppers are looking for a very special product: well-bred, intelligent German shepherds or other dogs, suitable for use by U.S. armed forces. These government shoppers have a lot of money to spend: money that comes from the taxes each American citizen pays. They need a lot of money. They have to spend at least $3,000 for each dog. And they buy more than 300 dogs. These canine prizes are shipped back to the United States and trained in military camps for 100 days. After they graduate, they take on some of the most dangerous and risky work any soldier can do. Often they are in the line of fire, along with their

trainers. Many dogs suffer terribly and die. In Vietnam alone, hundreds of dogs were killed in battle. Most military dogs brought to Vietnam never returned. Here at home, you would not want your pet to be put in harm's way on purpose. We have animal protection laws to prevent that; however, these laws don't seem to apply to all dogs.

Yours truly,

a concerned taxpayer and dog lover

25. Which of the following best describes the author's argument in this passage?   R1-D

A. Recruiting dogs for military service is cruel and inhumane.

B. Recruiting dogs for military service is too expensive.

C. Training dogs for military service is hard work.

D. Military dogs are brave and courageous.

26. Which of the following sentences from the passage BEST supports the author's argument?   R1-E

A. "They have to spend at least $3,000 for each dog."

B. "Every year, the U.S. military sends shoppers to Europe."

C. "And they buy more than 300 dogs."

D. "In Vietnam alone, hundreds of dogs were killed in battle."

27. Which of the following is NOT an example of supporting evidence? R1-E

    A. "Most military dogs brought to Vietnam never returned."

    B. "Here at home, you would not want your pet to be put in harm's way on purpose."

    C. "These canine prizes are shipped back to the United States and trained in military camps for 100 days."

    D. "These government shoppers have a lot of money to spend: money that comes from the taxes each American citizen pays."

28. What is the author's main purpose for writing this passage? RC2-E

    A. To inform readers about the work military dogs are involved in.

    B. To convince readers dogs are unable to perform military service.

    C. To persuade readers that using dogs for military service should be stopped.

    D. To inform readers of the training practices dogs have to go through before they are ready for military service.

29. Which of the following graphic features would best emphasize the author's argument? RC2-F

    A. a bar graph showing the number of military dog fatalities over the years

    B. a diagram showing how much money is spent training military dogs

    C. an illustration of a military dog in action

    D. an illustration of military dogs being trained and cared for

The following is excerpted from "The Red-Headed League," a story by Sir Author Conan Doyle. Dr. Watson, friend of Sherlock Holmes, is the narrator of this story. Watson has arrived at Holmes' apartment while Holmes is meeting with a client.

The portly client puffed out his chest with an appearance of some little pride and pulled a dirty and wrinkled newspaper from the inside pocket of his coat. As he glanced down the advertisement column... , I took a good look at the man and endeavored, after the fashion of my companion, to read the indications which might be presented by his dress or appearance.

I did not gain very much, however, by my inspection. Our visitor bore every mark of being an average British tradesman, obese, pompous, and slow. He wore rather baggy gray trousers, a not very clean black coat, unbuttoned in the front, and a drab waistcoat with a heavy brassy chain and a square bit of metal dangling down as an ornament. A frayed top-hat and a faded brown overcoat with a wrinkled velvet collar lay upon a chair beside him. Altogether, look as I would, there was nothing remarkable about the man save his blazing red head, and the expression of extreme chagrin and discontent upon his features.

Sherlock Holmes's quick eye took in my occupation, and he shook his head with a smile as he noticed my questioning glances. "Beyond the obvious facts that he has at some time done manual labour, that he takes snuff, that he is a Freemason, that he has been in China and that he has done a considerable amount of writing lately, I can <u>deduce</u> nothing else."

Mr. Jabez Wilson started up in his chair, with his forefinger upon the paper, but his eyes upon my companion.

"How, in the name of good-fortune, did you know all that, Mr. Holmes?" he asked. "How did you know, for example, that I did manual labour. It's as true as gospel, for I began as a ship's carpenter."

"Your hands, my dear sir. Your right hand is quite a size larger than your left. You have worked with it, and the muscles are more developed."

"Well, the snuff, then, and the Freemasonry?"

"I won't insult your intelligence by telling you how I read that, especially as, rather against the strict rules of your order, you use an arc-and-compass breastpin."

"Ah, of course, I forgot that. But the writing?"

"What else can be indicated by that right cuff so very shiny for five inches, and the left one with the smooth patch near the elbow where you rest it upon the desk?"

"Well, but China?"

"The fish that you have tattooed immediately above your right wrist could only have been done in China. I have made a small study of tattoo marks and have even contributed to the literature of the subject. That trick of staining the fishes' scales a delicate pink is quite <u>peculiar</u> to China. When, in addition, I see a Chinese coin hanging from your watch-chain, the matter becomes even more simple."

Mr. Jabez Wilson laughed heavily. "Well, I never!" said he. "I thought at first that you had done something clever, but I see that there was nothing in it, after all."

"I begin to think, Watson," said Holmes, "that I make a mistake in explaining… My poor little reputation, such as it is, will suffer shipwreck if I am so candid."

Read the following sentences from the passage:

> "I have made a small study of tattoo marks and have even contributed to the literature of the subject. That trick of staining the fishes' scales a delicate pink is quite <u>peculiar</u> to China."

30. What does the word "peculiar"   RC4-C
most likely mean in this passage?

   A.   ordinary

   B.   common or particular to that area

   C.   cloudy and uncertain

   D.   malformed or disfigured

Read the following quote from the passage:

> *Mr. Jabez Wilson started up in his chair, with his forfinger upon the paper, but his eyes upon my companion.*
>
> *"How, in the name of good-fortune, did you know all that, Mr. Holmes?" he asked.*

31. What is the mood of this excerpt?   R1-H

   A.   humorous   C.   angry

   B.   scornful   D.   surprised

In the passage, Holmes says:

> *"I have made a small study of tattoo marks and have even contributed to the literature of the subject."*

32. What does he mean by "contributed   R2-C
to the literature of the subject?"

   A.   He has written articles or books about tattoos.

   B.   He has given money to tattoo artists in China.

   C.   He has bought pictures of Chinese artwork.

   D.   He is a tattoo artist.

33. Which of the following BEST describes the topic of this passage?   R1-D

    A. You can discover a lot by looking at a person.

    B. Sherlock Holmes insults the intelligence of his client.

    C. Sherlock Holmes makes accurate observations about his client.

    D. Watson finds that his observations about the client are correct.

Read the following from the passage:

> *"Our visitor bore every mark of being an average British tradesman, obese, pompous and slow. He wore rather baggy gray trousers, a not very clean black coat, unbuttoned in the front, and a drab waistcoat with a heavy brassy chain, and a square bit of metal dangling down as an ornament."*

34. Based on this description, what does Watson most likely think of Wilson?   R1-B

    A. He thinks he is very clean and tidy in his appearance.

    B. He thinks he is a criminal.

    C. He thinks he is very intelligent and clever.

    D. He thinks he looks like the typical British working class.

35. At the very end of the passage, Holmes is slightly concerned because   R1-B

    A. he thinks that Watson and Mr. Wilson don't understand his explanations.

    B. he thinks that Watson is better at observing people than he is.

    C. he is worried that his predictions about his clients will be wrong.

    D. he is worried that he is giving away the secrets to his observations too freely.

Read the following sentence from the passage:

> *"'Beyond the obvious facts that he has at some time done manual labour, that he takes snuff, that he is a Freemason, that he has been in China, and that he has done a considerable amount of writing lately, I can deduce nothing else.'"*

36. As it is used in the passage, what does the word *deduce* mean?   R2-D

    A. believe

    B. figure out

    C. put up with

    D. common sense

The following question does not pertain to the passage.

37. Fundamental and often universal ideas explored in a literary work, which are usually implied rather than explicitly stated, are called   R1-D

    A. tone and mood.

    B. main ideas.

    C. topics.

    D. themes.

TSURU NO ONGAESHI (The Grateful Crane or The Crane Wife)

A traditional Japanese folktale

Long, long ago in a far off land, there lived a young man. One day, while working on his farm, a brilliant white crane came swooping down and crashed to the ground at his feet. The man noticed an arrow pierced through one of its wings. Taking pity on the crane, he pulled out the arrow and cleaned the wound. Thanks to his care, the bird was soon able to fly again. The young man sent the crane back to the sky, saying, "Be careful to avoid hunters." The crane circled three times over his head, let out a cry as if in thanks, and then flew away.

As the day grew dark, the young man made his way home. When he arrived, he was surprised by the sight of a beautiful woman whom he had never seen before standing at the doorway. "Welcome home. I am your wife," said the woman. The young man was surprised and said, "I am very poor, and cannot support you." The woman answered, pointing to a small sack, "Don't worry, I have plenty of rice," and began preparing dinner. The young man was puzzled, but the two began a happy life together. And the rice sack, mysteriously, remained full always.

One day the wife asked the young man to build her a weaving room. When it was completed, she said, "You must promise never to peek inside." With that, she shut herself up in the room. The young man waited patiently for her to come out. Finally, after seven days, the sound of the loom stopped and his wife, who had become very thin, stepped out of the room holding the most beautiful cloth he had ever seen. "Take this cloth to the marketplace, and it will sell for a high price," said the wife. The next day the young man brought it to town and, just as she said, it sold for many coins. Happy, he returned home.

The wife then returned to the room and resumed weaving. Curiosity began to overtake the man, who wondered, "How can she weave such beautiful cloth with no thread?" Soon he could stand it no longer and, desperate to know his wife's secret, peeked into the room. To his great shock, his wife was gone. Instead, a crane sat intently at the loom weaving a cloth, plucking out its own feathers for thread.

The bird then noticed the young man peeking in and said, "I am the crane that you saved. I wanted to repay you so I became your wife, but now that you have seen my true form I can stay here no longer." Then, handing the man the finished cloth, it said, "I leave you this to remember me by." The crane then abruptly flew off into the sky and disappeared forever.

38. Which of the following statements   R1-A
    BEST describes the theme of this
    passage?

    A.   Acts of kindness will be repaid, but
         don't make promises you can't keep.

    B.   Cranes are magical creatures.

    C.   Making beautiful cloth is hard work,
         but it pays off in the end.

    D.   Helping others can create problems.

39. The author wants to insert a caption   R1-B
    under the crane photograph with a
    quote from the story. Which of the follow-
    ing would be the BEST choice?

    A.   "Taking pity on the crane, he pulled
         out the arrow and cleaned the
         wound."

    B.   "Thanks to his care, the bird was
         soon able to fly again."

    C.   "The man noticed an arrow pierced
         through one of its wings."

    D.   "When he arrived, he was surprised
         by the sight of a beautiful woman
         whom he had never seen before
         standing at the doorway."

40. The author wants to add an illustra-   R1-B
    tion to the end of the story. Which of
    the following ideas would be LEAST
    appropriate?

    A.   the crane flying into the sky from the
         man's house

    B.   the crane sitting at the loom and
         looking at the man

    C.   the man holding the finished cloth

    D.   the crane with an arrow through its
         wing

The following instructions explain how to connect a printer to a computer.

---

1. Shut down the computer, but leave it plugged into the surge suppressor

2. Compare the connectors at the opposite ends of the cable. Attach the 25-pin end of the cable to the parallel, or printer, port on the computer. (The plug will go in only one way.) Tighten the hand screws securely. Connect the other end of the cable into the printer's socket. Latch the retaining clips (on most printer ports).

3. Plug the power cord into the printer and into the surge suppressor. Turn on the printer.

4. Install cartridges according to the printer manufacturer's instructions. Turn on the computer.

5. Install printer driver software according to the manufacturer's instructions.

6. Add the printer to the list of printers your computer recognizes.

---

41. When do you turn the printer on?　　R1-F

    A.   immediately after shutting down the computer

    B.   after installing the printer cartridges according to the manufacturer's instructions

    C.   after plugging the power cord into the printer and surge suppressor

    D.   right before shutting down the computer

42. What is the next step after turning　　R1-F on the computer?

    A.   Plug the power cord into the printer.

    B.   Turn the printer on.

    C.   Install the printer cartridges.

    D.   Install the printer driver software.

FDA Issues Warning on Decorative Contact Lenses

Responsible and appropriate use is very important when it comes to contact lenses. That means getting an eye exam and a valid prescription, and buying contact lenses from an eye care professional licensed to sell them. It's also important to follow directions for cleaning and wearing contact lenses and to have follow-up eye exams.

These precautions apply to all contact lenses, including contact lenses that only change the appearance of the eye in a decorative fashion, such as to turn brown eyes blue.

Fortunately, most decorative contact lenses have been approved by the Food and Drug Administration (FDA) for marketing. FDA approved brands of decorative contact lenses are safe when used responsibly. But the FDA has learned that some firms are not seeking FDA approval before marketing decorative lenses. Places such as malls, video stores, and arcades are selling decorative contact lenses that have not been approved by the FDA.

The FDA has received reports of eye problems, such as damage to the cornea and eye infections, connected with decorative contact lenses. Most of the reports involve teenagers. One doctor reported a case of a 16-year-old girl who bought contact lenses at a flea market. "She wore them for a couple of days and ended up in the emergency room with burning, itching, redness, and sensitivity to sunlight," the doctor says. The main problem was poor lens fit. The doctor treated her with antibiotic drops for five to six days, and she recovered.

Others haven't been as lucky. In September 2001, a 14-year-old girl needed treatment after wearing decorative contact lenses she bought for $20 at a video store. "She wanted to turn her brown eyes green to match an outfit," her doctor said. "The result was a lot of pain and suffering."

She had an aggressive infection caused by *pseudomonas* bacterium in one eye. "You can not only lose vision from this infection, but you can lose the eye," the doctor stated. The teenager had to be hospitalized and treated every half hour with drops for four days. The girl was blind in the infected eye for two months. In June 2002, the doctor performed a corneal transplant, which involved removing her diseased cornea and replacing it with a donor cornea. Recovery from this operation takes about a year, and the teenager has still not fully recovered her vision.

Along with informing consumers about the potential dangers of decorative contact lenses, the FDA is seizing decorative contact lenses on the market that violate federal law.

The FDA encourages people to discontinue use of decorative contact lenses that were bought without a prescription and a proper fitting. They also recommend contacting your ophthalmologist if you experience any eye problems.

43. What organizational pattern does   R1-C
this passage MOSTLY use?

    A.   narrative

    B.   comparison and contrast

    C.   cause and effect relationships

    D.   chronological order

44. Based on this passage, you can tell   R1-D
that the author's argument is that

    A.   people should keep buying and wearing decorative contact lenses.

    B.   people should be careful and mindful of the dangers of buying decorative contacts.

    C.   decorative contact lenses are safer than corrective contact lenses.

    D.   people should avoid wearing contact lenses and should wear glasses instead.

45. A student wants to place this story   LSV2-A
on a Web site about eye health for contact lens wearers. Which of the following would be the BEST addition to this passage?

    A.   a link to a company that sells decorative contacts

    B.   a link to the FDA reports mentioned in the passage

    C.   a link to an ophthalmologist's office

    D.   a picture of a person wearing decorative contacts

46. After reading this article, where do   RC2-A
you think it's safe to buy decorative contact lenses?

    A.   a beauty salon

    B.   a friend

    C.   an eye care professional

    D.   none of the above

47. Based on the passage, an ophthal-   RC3-C
mologist is MOST likely

    A.   an eye doctor.

    B.   a doctor who studies light.

    C.   a doctor who studies animals.

    D.   a doctor who is optimistic.

48. What subject area does this   RC2-C
passage mainly deal with?

    A.   history

    B.   fitness and diet

    C.   beauty and fashion

    D.   medicine and health

49. What is the main idea of this   RC2-A
passage?

    A.   Wearing decorative contact lenses without a prescription can cause damage to the eye.

    B.   The FDA has to approve all contacts before they go on sale.

    C.   Teenagers like to change the color of their eyes.

    D.   Decorative contact lenses are safe and easy to use.

50. Which of the following words   R2-B
contains a prefix that means "to stop or take away"?

    A.   reverse

    B.   interrupt

    C.   discontinue

    D.   unable